Developing Organisational Cons

Many organisational consultants find the pressure of work leaves them little time to study the theory and methods of their profession. They tend to be motivated to learn only when a particular consulting problem presents itself.

In *Developing Organisational Consultancy* experienced consultants from the UK and the USA present case studies from many different sectors and discuss the theoretical perspectives and methodological approaches they have found beneficial in dealing with a particular problem. The authors demonstrate how their outlined approach can have a general application and make suggestions for further reading.

The book concentrates on three key areas: evolving a professional stance, considering psychodynamic approaches and applying organisational theory. Each chapter presents a snapshot of important development within the organisational consulting field and addresses an issue which consultants are likely to face in the course of their work. For experienced and newly practising consultants this book constitutes an accessible and affordable opportunity for professional development, and an essential guide to developing successful consultancy practice.

Jean E. Neumann, from The Tavistock Institute, is Co-ordinator of the Organisational Change and Technological Innovation programme and Core Faculty of the Advanced Organisational Consultation programme, **Kamil Kellner** is Senior Lecturer at South Bank University Business School and **Andraea Dawson-Shepherd** is a Director of Hedron Consulting Ltd, all in London.

Contributors: Howard Atkins; John Bazalgette; Raphe Berenbaum; Petruska Clarkson; Bill Critchley; Thomas North Gilmore; Richard Holti; Jean Hutton; Kamil Kellner; Jane Linklater; C. Paul Lynch; Helena Memory; Eric Miller; Enid Mumford; Jean E. Neumann; Bruce Reed; William E. Schneider; David Wasdell; Jon White.

Developing Organisational Consultancy

Edited by Jean E. Neumann,
Kamil Kellner and
Andraea Dawson-Shepherd

Brunner-Routledge
Taylor & Francis Group

HOVE AND NEW YORK

First published 1997
by Routledge
11 New Fetter Lane, London EC4P 4EE

Simultaneously published in the USA and Canada
by Routledge
29 West 35th Street, New York, NY 10001

Reprinted 2002
by Brunner-Routledge
27 Church Road, Hove, East Sussex, BN3 2FA
29 West 35th Street, New York, NY10001

Brunner-Routledge is an imprint of the Taylor & Francis Group

Typeset in Times by Keystroke, Jacaranda Lodge, Wolverhampton
Printed and bound in Great Britain by TJ International Ltd, Padstow
Cornwall

British Library Cataloguing in Publication Data
A catalogue record for this book is available from the British Library

Library of Congress Cataloging in Publication Data
Developing organisational consultancy / edited by Jean E. Neumann,
    Kamil Kellner, and Andraea Dawson-Shepherd.
        p.   cm.
    Includes bibliographical references and index.
    1. Business consultants. 2. Organisation. I. Neumann, Jean E.
II. Kellner, Kamil III. Dawson-Shepherd, Andraea
HD69. C6D437 1997
001—dc21   96–50308

ISBN 0–415–15702–1 (hbk)
    0–415–15703–X (pbk)

Contents

Figures

Tables

Contributors

Howard Atkins works as a consultant and lecturer in organisational development and change management. He has taught on a variety of Masters courses at Sheffield Business School and his consulting work spans clients in the private, public and voluntary sectors. He has recently completed doctoral research looking into institutional pressures and organisation change in health care.

John Bazalgette joined The Grubb Institute in 1969 from a background in teaching. Working within a systemic and psychodynamic frame of reference, he consults widely to senior managers and their teams, designs and directs action research projects and group relations conferences, and undertakes organisational role analysis. His special interests include the place of teaching in the learning organisation.

Raphe Berenbaum has many years experience as a manager covering most business functions, followed by twelve years with overall responsibility for internal consultancy and client consulting for IBM UK. He is now an independent consultant, mainly concerned with achieving business change and process re-engineering.

Petruska Clarkson is a consultant, a chartered clinical and counselling psychologist, psychotherapist, and supervisor of supervisors. She has been an independent OD consultant in the public and private sectors for more than two decades. She has designed or co-designed several national and internationally accredited courses on these subjects and is founder or has been chair of many organisations in these fields, including Metanoia. She works internationally and independently under the name of Physis, is a visiting lecturer at several universities and has published more than 70 professional papers and 8 books.

Bill Critchley MBA, is a Business Director of Ashridge Consulting Group, and an independent organisation change agent and counsellor. His recent research has been an approach which integrates classical OD practice with phenomenologically based psychodynamic theory. He has written several books and articles.

Andraea Dawson-Shepherd B.Sc., MBA, is a Director of Hedron Consulting, the Communication and Change Consultancy which she co-founded in 1993. She consults in a wide range of leading predominantly private sector organisations and in several cases has helped develop and commercialise internal consultancy functions.

Thomas North Gilmore is Vice President of the Center for Applied Research. He has written extensively on psychodynamic issues and is a founding member of the International Society for Psychoanalytic Study of Organisations and the programme on organisational consultation at the William Alanson White Institute in New York City. He has written *Making a Leadership Change: How Organisations and Leaders Can Handle Leadership Transitions Successfully.*

Richard Holti has a degree in physics and philosophy of science from Cambridge University and a doctorate in industrial sociology from Imperial College London. He is based at The Tavistock Institute, engaged on research and consultancy projects on the process of designing and introducing both organisational and technical change, looking at the implications for organisations and society as a whole. He is Assistant Editor of *Human Relations*, and a member of the Core Faculty of the Institute's Advanced Organisational Consultation Programme.

Jean Hutton joined The Grubb Institute in 1969 from a background in management and administration. Working within a systemic and psychodynamic frame of reference, she is a consultant to senior managers in a wide range of organisations, directs group relations conferences and action research projects, and undertakes organisational role analysis. Her special interests include the development of 'organisation-in-the-mind' as a working tool for managers.

Kamil Kellner M.Sc., FIPD is an organisational consultant and a lecturer in organisational development. He has developed an M.Sc. in Human Resource Development, a professional development programme for senior managers and HR professionals at South Bank Business School, and a Masters programme in Organisational Consulting with Ashridge Consulting. His consulting integrates a systemic approach with a psychodynamic perspective on organisations. He also provides consultation and training for organisational consultants.

Jane Linklater has been a consultant in organisation development since 1990 working in the public, private and voluntary sector. Her main focus is on working with organisations to manage effective change. She has a particular interest in working with groups and teams where conflict and difficulty are to the fore. Her group work is underpinned by a group analytic framework and is supervised by an analyst from the IGA (Institute of Group Analysis). Prior to her entry into organisation development Jane was a senior manager for local government, working with children and families. She has a Masters Degree in Organisation Development and a CQSW (Certificate of Qualification in Social Work). She trained as a family therapist at the Tavistock Clinic where she also attended power and authority workshops.

C. Paul Lynch CA, FIMC, CMC, is a general management consultant with thirty years experience working for a wide variety of large and small, public and private, manufacturing and service companies. He has worked for P-E International and for Price Waterhouse, and for the last ten years has operated his own consultancy specialising in strategy and training. He has written and broadcast on management consultancy ethics and will take up the office of President of the UK Institute of Management Consultants in June 1997.

Helena Memory is a consultant with Hedron Consulting Ltd, with twenty years experience working with organisational communication issues both as a line manager and in a consulting role.

Eric Miller MA, Ph.D., was an anthropologist in India and Thailand and an internal consultant to companies in the USA and India before joining The Tavistock Institute in 1958. His main field is organisational research and consultancy, combining systemic and psychodynamic perspectives. He works internationally. He has authored numerous papers and six books, the most recent being *From Dependency to Autonomy: Studies in Organisatonal Change* (1993).

Enid Mumford is an Emeritus Professor of Manchester University, a visiting senior fellow at the Manchester Business School, a companion of the Institute of Personnel and Development, a fellow of the British Computer Society and a council member of The Tavistock Institute. She is the author of many books and papers and an adviser to CSG, a Dutch consultancy that specialises in the management of change.

Jean E. Neumann BA, MA, Ph.D., works at The Tavistock Institute where she co-ordinates the Programme for Organisational Change and Technological Innovation, serves as Core Faculty on the Advanced Organisational Consultation Programme and as an editor for *Human Relations*. During the last 22 years, Dr Neumann has undertaken over four hundred consultancy projects.

Bruce Reed has specialised in the study of organisational behaviour since the 1960s when he founded The Grubb Institute of Behavioural Studies. Working within a systemic and psychodynamic frame of reference, he is a consultant to chief executives and their teams in national and international companies, using organisational role analysis. His special interests include the interaction between task and identity.

William (Bill) Schneider, president of the Corporate Development Group, Inc. (USA) has a Ph.D. in Clinical Psychology from Saint Louis University. He practises as a consulting psychologist and specialises in organisational development, culture and change. A member of the American Psychological Association and Society for Industrial and Organisational Psychology, he is author of *The Reengineering Alternative: a Plan for Making Your Current Culture Work*.

David Wasdell is the founding director of the Unit for Research into Changing Institutions (URCHIN). He consults, trains, facilitates and lectures internationally, focusing on OD, advanced learning systems and the psychodynamics of large systems change. As well as pioneering the application of matrix design to advanced human relations training, he is the author of many articles and papers, including *Learning Systems and the Management of Change*.

Jon White consults in management and organisational development. He is a visiting professor in public affairs at City University Business School and formerly a member of faculty at Cranfield School of Management.

Acknowledgements

This book was made possible by the nearly 600 organisational consultants – both experienced and novice – who participated in two weeks of Organisational Consultancy MasterClasses that took place during a hot July in London, 1995. The international consultants who accepted the challenge of 'being a Master' in the diverse field that is organisational consultancy further inspired the idea for this book: indeed, several contribute chapters. We appreciate their willingness to take an educational stance with colleagues in an occupation known generally for being counter-dependent. Finally we acknowledge our organisations for providing the resources for both the MasterClasses and this book. Without support from The Tavistock Institute, South Bank University and Hedron Consulting Ltd our time and energy would have been directed elsewhere.

The Editors, London, December 1996

Introduction

SYNOPSIS

With this book, the editors aim to provide practising consultants with an opportunity to continue their professional development by learning about those theoretical perspectives and methodological approaches other consultants have found beneficial. The book is intended to provide snapshots of some developments within the organisational consulting field which the editors think worthwhile in terms of quality, depth and integrity. Three areas have been selected for special attention:

- evolving a professional stance through consultancy competence;
- considering psychodynamic approaches to working with social-psychological processes; and,
- applying organisational theories to complex, inter-connected change initiatives.

Developing Organisational Consultancy is comprised of 14 chapters that have been written by well established organisational consultants from the UK or the USA. Each chapter describes a consulting problem or organisational problem, along with the author's theoretical perspective or methodological approach for dealing with it. At least one case study, and in some chapters more, demonstrate application of the theory or method, including offering guidelines for more general application. Each chapter includes references and suggestions for further reading.

RATIONALE

Many practising consultants are too busy making a living to take much time out from their schedules to study. They tend to be motivated to learn when a particular organisational or consulting problem presents itself. This book takes this into consideration by presenting contemporary problems alongside theory and methods to address them. Lively case studies, from many different sectors, communicate actual details from the accumulated practice of experienced consultants.

Organisational consultants are notoriously isolated and often under-prepared for the work they do. While North America and Europe both have some university-based diploma and degree programmes, opportunities for systematic professional development that consultants can fit into their working lives are practically non-existent. Many consultants barely have basic training in consulting competence. Few have sufficient academic links to libraries in order to stay abreast of their fields. Further, they often feel compelled to present themselves as competent to potential and current clients in order to make a livelihood.

This can lead to concealment of learning needs, especially about the theory and practice of consulting to organisations. Thus, organisational consultants tend to need private, affordable and convenient mechanisms for pursuing their professional development. The editors intend that this book will make such a contribution.

AUDIENCE

The book is aimed at organisational consultants who are experiencing the practice of consultation. While such people often have academic backgrounds of some kind, they usually identify as educated practitioners, rather than academics. Therefore, this book has been conceptualised as a source of help about issues consultants are likely to encounter in practice. It has been designed to be of use to opportunistic learners, those who might dip into different chapters and sections as needed.

People holding a formal role as an organisational consultant would find this book useful, as would those who are engaged in particular types of organisational change and development without the title of 'consultant'. Both external and internal consultants will find it relevant to the challenges facing them. University departments might find it of interest as a supplementary text for courses related to consulting.

Authors come from several different disciplinary backgrounds and work in many different sectors. About a third of the authors are practising psychologists as well as being organisational consultants. Another third have their advanced degrees from business schools having first studied a social science. The remaining authors have unique credentials ranging from social anthropology to public affairs and architecture.

The majority of the authors have around 20 years experience in their particular domain of consulting. Three have over 30 years and two have just over 10 years. Cases have been selected from services (e.g. hospitals, insurance, telecommunications, social work, consultancy), from manufacturing (e.g. continuous process chemicals, batch filtration systems, automobiles) and from the public sector (e.g. post office, water, local government).

CONCEPTUALISATION

This book grew out of a highly successful professional development event held in July 1995 in London. The event took the form of 32 1-day organisational development 'MasterClasses' scheduled for 8 consecutive days, with 4 'MasterClasses' on each day. Consultants could attend one or more as their resources and interest allowed. Nearly 600 consultants from Europe, North America, Australia and Israel participated. For each 'MasterClass', an experienced consultant designed and led a day on a topic of his or her choice. All the authors in this book also presented a 'MasterClass' on the topic that they have written up as a chapter.

The 'MasterClasses', and this subsequent book, were authorised by the London-based organisations with which the editors are associated. These are: South Bank University (an institution of higher education that offers post-graduate degree courses in consulting); The Tavistock Institute (a registered charity with an international reputation in action research that offers a certificate programme in 'advanced organisational consultation', known as AOC); and Hedron Consulting (a small, private firm offering communication and organisational consultancy). These organisations came together, in the form of the three editors, because they shared a concern about the lack of high quality, professional development opportunities for organisational consultants.

The considerable response to the 'MasterClasses' clearly indicated a thirst for more opportunities for consultants to develop themselves. A book had the attraction of being able to bring the practical and theoretical knowledge of many of the experienced consultants who had led 'Master-Classes' to the attention of a wider audience. That event had been conceived as a means of bringing together into one place learning from different approaches to organisational consultancy. An overview of the field suggested that approaches primarily based in psychology, sociology and experiential learning had to be included somehow.

Working to the same overall themes, the editors commissioned a broad spectrum of chapters from the 'MasterClass' presenters. These have been clustered into three sections for *Developing Organisational Consultancy*: evolving a professional stance, considering psychodynamic approaches and applying organisational theory. The logic for developing consultants seems clear in the light of experience.

Evolving a professional stance requires the consultant to recognise that there is a body of accumulated knowledge, skills, attitudes and values that comprise the overall field of organisational consulting. Certainly, the field is broad and lacks sufficient consensus that would result in societal recognition and requirement for state-approved qualifications. But this lack of consensus does not mean that there is not much to learn from others who have gone before. Organisational consulting, as a field of applied social science, can be traced to the late 1930s (depending on which aspect of the field one identifies with it goes back even before that). Evolving a professional stance means taking responsibility for engaging with the existing knowledge in the profession and for continuing to develop one's own consulting competence.

Considering psychodynamic approaches becomes necessary the more one consults to organisations. Working in the field automatically places the consultant in relationship to a complex social system with multiple political and psychological dynamics. Whether one wants to or not, a practising consultant cannot escape interpersonal dynamics with his or her immediate client and others in the target client system. Further, even the most structural and technical of consulting domains presents the consultant with groups and larger sub-sections of an organisation. These social phenomena cannot be separated from their dynamics. Considering psychodynamic approaches means taking responsibility for gaining competence at dealing with social and psychological issues sufficient to the type of organisational consulting one offers.

Applying organisational theory is inherent in any organisational consulting that one might do. The challenge is to become more aware and intentional in the application of that theory. *All* consultants have an implicit theory about how organisations do and should function. They have beliefs about what causes what and what needs to be done in order to change particular aspects of organisation. Sometimes this theory is called, 'common sense'; other times, the theory-in-use is held unawarely; just as often the theory is one that has been handled down from a mentor. Applying organisational theory means taking responsibility for studying how effectively one's organisational theory-in-use assists clients in addressing the problems and opportunities facing them, and making adjustments in theory and practice in light of experience and reflection.

A further discussion of these three themes appears in the introductory comments at the beginning of each section (see table of contents). An abstract of each chapter also appears in those section introductions. With this classification and conceptualisation, it should be apparent that the book does not intend to be an exhaustive review of organisational consultancy. Rather it is a selection of subjects which the editors, as both academics and consultants, feel are worthy of exploration and believe would be of interest to fellow practitioners.

Part I

Evolving a professional stance

Evolving a professional stance: Introduction

The editors have brought together five chapters for this first section of *Developing Organisational Consultancy*. Each chapter concerns an essential part of the consultant evolving a professional stance towards his or her practice. What we are advocating as editors, through the vehicle of our authors, is a standpoint that engages us all in an intentional application of applied social science and advanced self-directed learning. We believe that such a stance leads gradually by a natural process to greater professionalism in the practice of consultancy.

The authors are experienced consultants who have taken the time and energy to make explicit an aspect of their tacit knowledge. Through this process of articulating accumulated competence, it becomes possible for the organisational consulting profession to build a body of knowledge, skills, attitudes and values that can be passed on to the next generation of practitioners. More importantly, once written down, the craft of our profession can be subjected to debate and, thus, further development.

Although they are writing on different features of consultancy development, the authors of this section share a certain attitude of mind. They are asserting their opinions about what a professional practice of organisational consulting actually means. These assertions combine an element of craft, rules of engagement and reflection on experience in order to learn. In some regard, they focus on considerations to be made before, and in some cases after, a consultant embarks on an intervention with a client.

This section opens with 'Negotiating entry and contracting', which for many consultants is the toughest part of the consulting process. Author Jean Neumann provides a comprehensive discussion of the difficulties experienced during this crucial phase. It is during this phase that the consultant–client boundaries are set and mores established which then dictate the ongoing nature of the consulting relationship and the quality and value of the consulting intervention. The chapter covers: getting to the right level of authority to agree the remit of the intervention; how and when to discuss the fee and how to decide when the 'meter' starts running; how to ensure that the proposal which gets accepted allows the consultant to carry out a thorough job; fully paid for, without having to cut corners, particularly on the diagnosis and follow-up; and how to set up the relationship such that the objectivity and integrity of the consultant is not compromised. Powerful, yet commonplace case examples are used to illustrate these points. A set of guidelines provides practical advice on optimising the outcome of this step for both consultant and client.

With entry satisfactorily negotiated and the contract agreed, the next step in many situations is to consider how the intervention will commence, and in particular how any required interventions with groups will be structured. Tom Gilmore's chapter, 'The social architecture of group interventions', looks at the issues of optimising the participation by individuals in large and small groups in order to maximise the outcome of any event. Focusing on the requirement of the group as created by the intervention's objectives, Gilmore provides an overall design process as well as a range of specific tools to deliver successful group events. Detailed case examples show specifically how the process and tools can be used. Particular emphasis is given to the design of the highly popular 'retreat' for senior managers. The author is clear, however, that the guidelines he offers apply equally well to other types of group interventions.

The issue of consultant learning is addressed through the third chapter by David Wasdell. 'The consulting organisation as an advanced learning system' uses an evocative case study to guide the reader through the development of a learning process for a consulting organisation. The chapter explains the concepts of single, double and triple loop learning, and uses the chapter itself to demonstrate learning. Guidelines are provided on how consultants and their consulting organisation can learn to learn through their work and to continue to refresh their ways of learning over time and changed circumstance.

The fourth chapter by Raphe Berenbaum focuses on the particularities of being an 'Internal consultant', a topic of interest to internal change agents as well as to external consultants eager to collaborate across organisational boundaries. A suggestion on the merits for the client of using internal consultants as compared to external consultants is offered before discussing the special considerations internal consultants have to factor into their work. These additional considerations both aid and hinder the work of the internal consultant. In the latter category, the author covers three major issues: structure, perception and politics. The use of an explicit case study enables the reader to understand the issues faced and what factors will be key in making the choices on how to position and structure the intervention for a successful outcome.

Last in this section is a chapter entitled, 'Ethics in management consultancy'. This is a subject which is not widely written about, but here author Paul Lynch discusses the major ethical issues facing consultants operating in a fast growing, increasingly competitive and yet unregulated market. Everyday examples are used to illustrate the potential dilemmas consultants face. Lynch puts forward the UK Institute of Management Consultants' Code of Professional Conduct as a good set of guiding principles to ensure that consultants offer an ethical as well as professional stance to all their consulting work.

This opening section does not claim to be a comprehensive review of all aspects of developing a professional stance. The five chapters have been selected because they appear to the editors to be of interest to a wide range of consultants. Each chapter provides a list of references and further reading, enabling the reader to enrich their knowledge and explore issues raised in greater depth.

Chapter 1

Negotiating entry and contracting

Jean E. Neumann

THE PROBLEM

In order to be able to consult with an organisational client, practising consultants must successfully enter the organisation and come to an agreement. This agreement is with those people with whom they will be consulting, and is often called a 'contract'. Negotiating entry and contracting requires consultants to undertake two tasks at about the same time. Consultants need to cross those geographical and social boundaries relevant to the immediate purpose of the consulting agreement; and they need to develop a mutual understanding with an authorised representative of the organisation. This understanding includes, at minimum, agreements about: the purpose of the consultancy; the general activities that will comprise the consulting work during a specified phase; the individuals or groups of people who will be involved and the relevant financial arrangements.

These seemingly straightforward tasks of entry and contracting often prove challenging to practising organisational consultants. Problems emerge almost at the first contact with a potential client; problems that fall on a point between two extremes. On the one hand, consultants become aware that they cannot enter in order to clarify the unique nature of the organisation until a detailed agreement is reached through telephone and written correspondence with a client representative. On the other hand, consultants find themselves spending vast amounts of time inside the organisation clearly having entered and often having started diagnosis. But, despite repeated efforts, they cannot manage to make a contract with an appropriately authorised individual.

An illustration of the contract-before-entry challenge is a situation in which the client system requires a tender. Here, the client requests a written proposal from the consultants for how they would work on a particular issue. The client representative expects the consultants to accept proffered information as valid fact and to propose an intervention based solely on a telephone call or a brief letter. The opportunity to enter properly is withheld until after the written proposal has been vetted. Consultants are faced with the challenge of presenting their consulting practice as if the unique qualities of the organisational client were irrelevant.

An illustration of the entry-without-contract challenge is a situation in which a middle manager, without authorisation, decides to initiate exploratory conversations with consultants. Here, consultants are invited into the organisation for an initial conversation with the manager. The generally positive chat ends with the manager encouraging the consultants to write a letter summarising the ideas explored. After more delays, the manager invites the consultants to come back into the organisation to meet the senior managers. After this meeting, time passes and the consultants or client suggests that the consultants meet others in the organisation to help clarify the way forward. This process can drag on for months. The consultants do not have a contract, but spend more and more (usually unpaid) time trying to get one. In fact, the consultants are doing the work of organisational consulting without the authorisation represented by a contract negotiated with a sufficiently senior manager.

These two challenges to successful entry and contracting grow out of a broader problem. It is not unusual for both consultant and client to be uninformed about the basic underlying cycles of activity that constitute professional organisational development. They naïvely imagine that entry and contracting is a short, straightforward business deal and not the more complex social–political interaction that it is.

Disregard for the importance of a proper diagnosis tends to be the most common casualty of this mutual ignorance. In the contract-before-entry version, the client assumes that standard interventions used by any and all organisational consultants will suit their needs. Consultants who refuse to offer tenders are assumed to be insufficiently skilled at selling and providing suitable products. More insidiously, the client hopes to decide which approach to purchase by comparing tenders from different consulting firms. It is not unusual for a client system to take the ideas of consultants in order to implement them without hiring any firm. It can be very difficult to convince such a client that interventions should be planned based on a competent, customised diagnosis of the unique, organisational problem.

In the entry-without-contract version, consultants assume that they need to diagnose the problem before an initial phase of work can be proposed. However, consultants also feel that the need for organisational diagnosis is their personal problem and therefore they should not be paid by the client. Or, perhaps, the consultants feel that they cannot convince the client to pay for diagnosis and, in the interests of not losing the entire contract, agree to undertake diagnosis for free.

This sense that diagnosis is illegitimate can be traced to both 'super-consultant' and 'super-client' fantasies. A 'super-consultant' can assess an organisation in a matter of minutes over the telephone and determine the appropriate intervention immediately. Therefore, consultants should be able to propose detailed organisational development interventions without even entering the site, as in the contract-before-entry example. A consultant who lacks this 'super-consultant' power should feel humble and not expect the client to pay for the consultant to learn about their organisation.

When it comes to diagnosis of their organisation's needs for consulting, a 'super-client' has all the expertise of a professional organisational consultant. They already know everything there is to know about their organisation and have used this wisdom to come up with a request for proposals. They are able to avoid the bias or blind-spots to which lesser clients fall prey in their assessment of the organisation. They do not need to pay for an outsiders' view of the situation; all they need is a pair-of-hands to implement the intervention they have already planned.

Unfortunately, this caricature captures an all too common attitude towards entry and contracting enacted between consultants and clients. The results are that clients often pay for improperly conceptualised interventions, and actions taken to resolve a particular organisational problem simply do not do so. Furthermore, consultants often feel exploited by their clients. Instead of insisting on their need to engage in a professional practice of the craft of organisational consulting, they accept whatever they can get from the client.

NEGOTIATING WITH THE WHOLE IN MIND

Negotiating entry and agreeing a contract are the first two steps in a larger set of activities that comprise organisational development. Consultants need to undertake entry and contracting with this in mind. For short-term working agreements, the larger set of activities includes those necessary for effectively completing one entire cycle of organisational development.

For medium to long-term working agreements, the picture is slightly more complicated. Consultants need to consider activities necessary for completing one complete cycle of organisational development which constitutes a first contract or initial phase of work with the client. They also need to conceptualise the possible directions that the organisational development might take. That is, consultants need to be aware of how multiple cycles of organisational development might unfold.

The organisational development cycle

The practical literature on organisational development offers widely accepted definitions of the consulting cycle, in general, and the early stages in that cycle, in particular. For nearly 25 years, few authors have improved on Kolb and Frohman's (1970) formulation of six basic stages. These are: scouting, entry and contracting, diagnosis, negotiating and planning intervention, taking action, and evaluating that action. The result of the evaluation is either to start another round of organisational development or to terminate the consultant–client relationship. Successful entry and contracting requires keeping the whole cycle in mind while completing the tasks unique to entry and contracting. Each stage is described in more detail below, with reference to how the work of the latter stages can be kept in mind during the early stages. Figure 1.1 illustrates Kolb and Frohman's six basic stages, with the addition of either ending the contract or going onto another iteration of work as a result of evaluation.

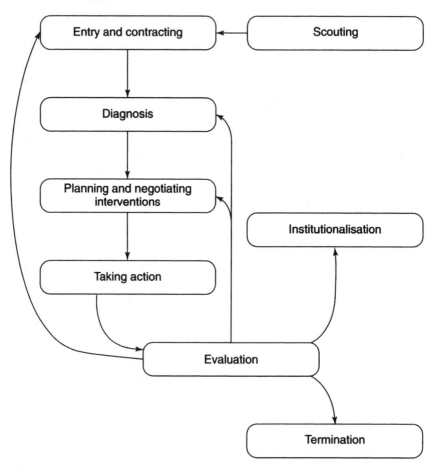

Figure 1.1 The cycle of planned change in organisational development
Source: Kolb and Frohman 1970; Neumann 1989

Crossing boundaries and building relationships within a client system involves consultants in the first two stages – scouting as well as actual entry and contracting – and in negotiating some elements of the third stage, diagnosis. But, in order to be effective – literally and metaphorically – in stepping across the geographical and social boundaries that constitute the organisation, consultants need to be aware of the work that should be reserved for later stages of the cycle. Each stage in the cycle has a set of activities that need to be undertaken by the client and consultant. Information and commitment are generated during the activities that make up each stage, thus building towards an effective intervention that will be genuinely developmental for the organisation. Skipping or rushing stages of the cycle endangers the quality of the organisational development.

Stage one: scouting

The overall task during the scouting stage is to decide whether to proceed with entry and contracting. In order to take this decision, the consultant needs to: define the presenting problem or opportunity; identify the type of consultation being requested; determine whether or not there is a 'good enough' fit; assess the degree of openness and potential for confidentiality; judge the source of authorisation of the client representative; and clarify the time schedule, logistics and finances for the next step.

'Scouting' is where, before either consultant or potential client invests resources, both sides attempt to assess what is on offer and how closely it matches conscious and unconscious needs. Cherniss (1984) labels this 'pre-entry' during which the consultant ought to ask 'should one provide consultation in this situation?', 'whose interests will the consultant serve?' and 'what will be the primary focus of the consultation?'. Call it scouting or pre-entry, this is the first point at which both parties take an initial decision to proceed or not.

Typically, the telephone or a brief meeting at a conference or other unexpected venue will be the vehicle for scouting. Issues for consultants include hearing the presenting problem, understanding the type of consultancy being requested, and judging the degree of fit between themselves and this client system. Should the 'yes or no' decision of this stage be positive on both sides, an agreement needs to be reached on the next step – almost always some sort of meeting – and the financial arrangements and logistics for this activity.

Two other issues need to be kept on the consultant's mind as *relevant to entry and contracting*. The consultant begins to ascertain the status of the client representative(s) to determine whether or not the appropriate people, with the corresponding decision-making authority for the type of problem and consultancy being proposed, will be present at the next step. Also, certain intuitive feelings about psychological compatibility are experienced. Menzies Lyth (1988: 168) describes the initial contacts as enabling 'the clients' organisation and the consultant to explore each other as personalities, with their own particular orientations to the problems of social organisations'.

Stage two: entry and contracting

The overall task during the entry and contracting stage is to decide whether to work with the client or not. In order to take this decision, the consultant needs to: clarify who is the main client and their objectives and motives; agree objectives and overall scope for the consulting work; plan the general sequence and duration of a specific phase of work; agree how the work will be communicated to others; consider who might be in steering roles in relation to diagnosis and mutual planning of an intervention; assess access to people and sections of organisation for stages three and four; agree finances, logistics, frequency of contact, confidentiality; and clarify roles of consultant and client in relation to specified phases of work.

If exploration of orientation barely gets started during scouting, it rushes ahead at full speed during entry and contracting. This second stage has the dual task of negotiating a formal agreement to work together – to let the consultants into the organisation or to keep them out – and of negotiating an informal psychological contract (Sherwood and Glidewell 1971) of mutual needs and expectations. Schein (1969) adds to the tasks of formal and informal contracting that of defining the support and involvement the consultant needs from the client, including commitment from senior managers to proceed.

In addition to re-visiting several issues discussed only briefly during scouting, a clearer definition of the problem needs to be discovered and the client needs to be identified. Schatzman and Strauss (1973) extend the scouting metaphor further by using the idea of 'casing the joint', for the purposes of assessing suitability, feasibility and suitable entry tactics into other parts of the organisation.

Elements of beginning to understand the client system get mixed in with establishing objectives for the consultancy and clarifying the overall scope of the organisational development. Many questions must be asked on both sides to discover, and then to decide, elements of both the formal contract – e.g. objectives, timing, fee and confidentiality – and of the informal contract. The latter tends to include negotiating the role of both consultant and client, as well as exploring the concepts being used by both parties to explain and make sense of the situation.

Agreeing a few overall issues about the initial phase of diagnosis tends to be necessary during entry and contracting. This involves both sides in gathering data about how the other works. Block (1981: 46) summarises these issues as 'the boundaries of your analysis', 'the kind of information you will seek', 'the product you will deliver', and identification of the people to whom a feedback will be presented. Another concern requiring attention, although not necessarily as a part of entry and contracting, includes access to significant stakeholders, and records and documents of relevance to the problem for which the consultancy has been requested.

As this consideration raises questions about how broadly across and deeply into the organisation the consultant will be allowed, examination of assumptions about the definition of the problem, possible solutions, and identification of the client tend to re-emerge. The representatives of the client system authorised to engage in this examination tend to be those people who attend the contracting meeting, set the objectives for the project, approve any action to be taken, and receive the report on the results of the initial diagnosis (*ibid.*: 56).

Frequently, these people are known as 'the client'. However, several other aspects of the client system will need to be considered at this stage. Lippitt and Lippitt (1984) point out that in addition to this body with whom the initial contract is agreed, there are target clients (those who are supposed to change in some way), leverage clients (those who can make or break a change effort), and beneficiary clients (those who will benefit from the efforts of others).

The beginning stages of the organisational development cycle are over when a formal and informal contract is understood to exist by both parties. At a minimum, such a contract includes timing, sequence and duration of the initial consultancy activities as well as financial and logistical arrangements. Frequently, issues of internal and external confidentiality and publicity need to be resolved in order to establish sufficient trust to begin. And finally, a first attempt at determining who will be included and who will be excluded from 'steering' roles has been made.

Stage three: diagnosis

The overall tasks during the diagnosis stage of the organisational development cycle are to develop working hypotheses about the organisational client system and to consider recommendations for action that will address the problem or opportunity for which the consulting work has been undertaken. In order to carry out this study and thinking, the consultant needs to: finalise decisions about the type of information to collect, from which people in which roles located where in the organisation; schedule time and engage in data collection, data analysis and working hypothesis generation; ensure that the client has arranged for the release of employees to be interviewed and for other relevant information to be available; establish objectivity and trustworthiness with informants, including maintaining confidentiality; ensure that the client has established 'steering' mechanisms by which results can be reported, including agreement for feedback mechanisms; and prepare information collected, analyse it, and produce a written or verbal report.

In practice, the depth or superficiality of an organisational diagnosis depends on the scope and duration of the intervention being used. The shorter the duration of the consulting work, the smaller the diagnosis required. The longer and more extensive the involvement with more aspects of the organisation's life, the more in-depth and comprehensive is the diagnosis required.

The shortest diagnosis sensible is one for short-duration skills training workshops. In this instance, a lengthy conversation with the training officer and a review of any existing training needs assessments, supplemented by early data collection with participants during the workshop, may offer sufficient information to provide a good workshop. However, even a one day 'away-day' requires direct data collection from as many participants or their representatives as possible.

All other organisational development interventions require that a proper diagnosis be designed and undertaken prior to implementation. Talking with people directly or asking them to complete written surveys, reading archival records and observing the organisation in action are the basic techniques of data collection. As this chapter is not about diagnosis *per se*, but about keeping diagnosis in mind during negotiation of entry and contracting, additional information about diagnosis will not be offered.

The consultant needs to keep diagnosis in mind *during entry and contracting* because only enough data is gained during the early stages of interaction with the client to complete the work of scouting, entry and contracting. The temptation to be avoided is engaging in diagnosis during entry and contracting. This temptation is great in short-term contracts because the client may not allow an opportunity for a proper diagnosis. It is also great in medium to longer-term contracts because the consultant feels that she needs more and more information to propose an intervention. In this instance, a data feedback intervention can be proposed as a phase one of work.

Stage four: planning and negotiating intervention

The tasks during the planning and negotiating intervention stage are to engage organisational actors in developing a common understanding of their organisational situation and to agree the general direction for an intervention into that situation. In order to accomplish these tasks, the consultant needs to: ensure that at least those in steering roles meet to consider the results of the diagnosis and to decide how to proceed; plan with those in steering roles how the results of the diagnosis are to be disseminated; help organisational clients to work through reactions to the results and plan for intervention; clarify purpose, target and scope for intervention; offer options for how to intervene, and ensure that plans are agreed for next steps, who will be involved, resources, schedule and leadership from within the client system.

Planning and negotiating the intervention – as opposed to simply just mounting an intervention without adequate mutual planning – is a stage intended to build commitment before action. By making sure that significant organisational actors are involved in receiving the results of the diagnosis, working through their reactions and planning the action to be taken, the likelihood of resistance emerging during the intervention decreases. This benefit will be increased by the extent of other organisational members also having the opportunity to receive the results of the diagnosis, work through their reactions and be informed thoroughly about the planned intervention. If other organisational members who are likely to be affected by the intervention can be involved in some aspect of the decision-making – for example, selecting representatives or voting on particular options – then their commitment to the outcome of the intervention will also increase.

The important principle related to mutual planning of an intervention that needs to be kept in mind *during entry and contracting*, is that of appropriate involvement. Regardless of the intervention, the client and consultant need to establish early in their relationship how to include those people most likely to have a stake in the outcome of a particular intervention. Generally, this means starting with a smaller number of authorised people and working outwards to include more and more members of the organisation in subsequent phases of organisational development.

The client needs to understand the principle of appropriate involvement during entry and contracting. Once the results of the diagnosis are reported, a client who has not agreed in advance to this principle may refuse to release the results to other organisational members who have a legitimate stake in the outcome and from whom the consultant gathered information. Resentment and suspicion can be stirred up unnecessarily by refusing to communicate the results of diagnosis. An opportunity to develop trust and commitment in the organisation – one of the primary assumptions of organisational development consultancy – will be lost.

Stage five: taking action

The main task during the taking action or intervening stage of the organisational development cycle is to implement the planned intervention in such a way as to maximise realisation of the agreed objectives for the consulting work. In order to accomplish this task, the consultant needs to: co-operate with those in steering roles as they co-ordinate the overall effort throughout the relevant parts of the organisation; assist those in steering roles and other organisational members in making time, releasing people and allocating space for participation in the intervention; adjust the pace and other elements of the intervention, keeping crucial similarities and allowing for appropriate differences; maintain one's own competence in implementing the rules of practice for a particular intervention; consult with those in steering roles and other organisational members as they compare action with expectations, including dealing with unintended consequences; assist those in steering roles in helping previously excluded groups to work through reactions; and consider implications for next steps in the light of the evolving intervention.

This amount of work during the intervention stage of organisational development is unlikely to be necessary for short, one-off consultancy. But even weekend 'retreats' and 'away days' need to be placed in the context of the relevant socio-technical system. Larger, longer-term interventions will have an obvious action stage that follows on from diagnosis and negotiating the intervention.

During entry and contracting, it is important for the consultant to be aware of those interventions offered as a part of the consultant domain. Each intervention has rules of practice that have been evolved over time by other consultants. Being competent in an intervention means being knowledgeable about these rules of practice and skilful in implementing these rules with a client. Organisational consultants typically specialise in one of four categories of interventions: human process issues, human resources issues, structural and systems issues, or business and strategic issues. A summary, adapted from Cummings and Huse (1989), appears in Table 1.1.

Stage six: evaluating action

The main tasks of evaluation are to assess what worked well during the organisational development intervention, what needs further development and what next steps, in terms of further diagnosis or intervention, are required, if any. Especially for longer-term consultancies, setting up an evaluation mechanism during an initial round of work will be crucial for ongoing review. In order to undertake this task, the consultant needs to: co-operate with the client in developing a mechanism for evaluation of the intervention; consult with those in steering roles as they generate and/or review evaluation material; assist the client in recognising various stakeholders' perspectives; determine one's own evaluation of the intervention and suggestions for next steps; and prepare self and clients for another phase of entry and contracting with those implicated in the next round of appropriate involvement or for terminating the relationship.

Technically, evaluation is the end of a single cycle of organisational development with termination of the relationship between consultant and client taken as a matter of fact. Practically, evaluation functions as either a termination process or another round of entry and contracting. Evaluations

Table 1.1   Four categories of organisational development interventions

Human process interventions
- *Focus*: improving comunication, interaction and leadership for the way forward.
- *Examples*: role consultation, process consulting, team building, and data feedback.

Human resources interventions
- *Focus*: developing processes and procedures for the attraction, development and reward of people.
- *Examples*: management development, skill training, appraisal and reward systems, career planning and development.

Structural and systems interventions
- *Focus*: how to divide labour, cluster activities, plan, control and co-ordinate.
- *Examples*: organisational design, job design, IT systems design, and lateral relations between departments and organisations.

Business and strategic interventions
- *Focus*: which functions, products, services and markets an organisation will operate and how it will relate to its environment.
- *Examples*: strategic planning, total quality management, strategic culture change and IT strategy.

are usually informal, short-term and with limited involvement: a meeting with those in steering roles for a few hours is typical of short and medium-term interventions. However, medium and long-term consultancies – especially those with multiple simultaneous interventions – might require a more formal evaluation with broad involvement. Such an evaluation becomes another round of organisational development, similar to diagnosis, and must be treated as such.

During entry and contracting, it is important for the consultant to give thought to what sort of evaluation might make sense for the particular consulting work under negotiation. Adding an extra day for review can be difficult if it has not been negotiated up front. Just as clients and consultants tend to neglect diagnosis, evaluation is often considered a luxury that can be foregone.

It is also useful for the consultant to consider how they would like the relationship with the client to end. Very little has been written in the practical literature about terminating a contract with a client. Indeed, many consultants feel that they have no control over ending; that the client decides when to end the working relationship. But, in practice, a consultant often has a sense during the early stages of working the client whether the relationship is likely to be of short or longer-term duration. During entry and contracting, the consultant can raise the issue of how to end and build a general principle into the contract right from the start. For example, a written contract might contain a clause placing conditions on both parties for how they end the relationship.

Conceptualising multiple cycles

The practice of organisational development tends to flow more smoothly and with greater chance of success when consultants have a working model in their minds about the stages or steps through which they're working with the client. The model described above is one well established, professionally recognised way of conceptualising a single cycle of organisational development from the first contact with the client to the end. The actual duration of a single cycle can be as short as few weeks and as long as 6 to 10 months.

However, there are very few interventions of organisational development that can be achieved in one single cycle. Short-term interventions, by definition, are constituted by fairly rapid movement through the stages. Probably the most typical examples would be one-off management development and skill training sessions lasting for one-half day upwards to over a week. Another intervention amenable to a single cycle would be one round of data feedback in a small to medium-sized system, combined with an action planning or problem-solving session. Of course, time-bounded human process interventions using role consultation, executive coaching, team building and process consulting can be negotiated as a single cycle or multiple, repeating cycles separated by evaluation.

Most organisational development requires multiple, repeating cycles. In addition to keeping the tasks unique to each stage of the cycle in mind during entry and contracting, the practising consultant needs to develop the capacity to conceptualise multiple cycles that follow on from each other in developmental logic. This capacity comes from two sources: keeping up-to-date with theoretical and practical progress being made within the domains in which one specialises by reading and attending professional conferences; and, reflecting on previous experiences with current and past clients (with or without a supervising consultant).

Some consultants offer 'packages' of interventions which they sell during entry and contracting to their clients. These standardised packages are made up of a series of activities that follow on from each other in multiple, repeating cycles. Whether a consultant offers such standardised 'packages' or customises an overall intervention for each client, it is useful during entry and contracting to offer some idea of the various possible, follow-on directions that might emerge. Such ideas can be understood as the consultant's working hypothesis about which intervention strategy will address the client's concerns.

It is often possible to conceptualise a minimum of three cycles as a part of an initial entry and contracting process. For medium and long-term interventions, keeping the whole in mind includes being aware of how interventions might flow or, in other words, how the organisational development process might be extended or expanded depending on likely outcomes. To a great extent, consultants' ideas about such extension or expansion will be consistent with their notions of how organisations change and develop. Consultants without some theory or belief in this regard will find it difficult to predict, or guess, likely outcomes of their interventions, and subsequent developments.

Here is an illustration of how a consultant who specialises in resistance to change might conceptualise a three-cycle organisational development intervention. The first cycle or phase of work with a client might include limited participation of a selected group of significant actors, in a short-term single intervention addressing their thoughts, feelings, attitudes and beliefs about the change and why people are resisting it. The second cycle or phase of work might begin to broaden participation with a somewhat wider diagnosis and longer intervention with a few more activities than during the first cycle. The third phase or cycle spreads involvement even further in the organisation and uses multiple, simultaneous activities which address actual decision-making related to the change being resisted.

In summary, successful entry and contracting requires the consultant to keep the whole in mind. There are two 'wholes' which are relevant. The primary consideration is keeping the whole organisational development cycle in mind. The consultant needs to ensure that the work of scouting, entry and contracting and a few aspects of diagnosis are completed as a part of the early stages with the client. By the time a formal contract has been agreed, this work needs to have been done.

The second consideration is keeping the whole intervention strategy in mind during entry and contracting. Consultants need to ensure that they have laid the groundwork formally and informally for subsequent cycles of organisational development that are likely to follow on from this first cycle. While the outcomes of the first cycle of organisational development cannot be predicted precisely, the types of outcomes that are likely can be. For example, one type of outcome is that of failure and termination of the contract with the client seeking assistance elsewhere. Another is success of the intervention. Both the consultant and client can imagine, based on the objectives and motives behind the requested consultancy, what each possibility might be. Contingencies can be imagined for follow-on cycles of organisational development without locking either party into rigidity. The evaluation stage of the organisational development cycle, which needs to take place between subsequent cycles, can protect the client and consultant from too much advanced planning and from refusal to learn from preceding interventions.

CASE STUDIES

The following cases illustrate two different types of consulting contracts with corresponding challenges for entry and contracting. Information about the client and their requirements, and the consultant's response to those requirements, is provided during the presentation of case. Details of the complete organisational development cycle are not provided, as the purpose of this chapter is to focus on the early stages of contact with the client – specifically, entry and contracting. Characteristics which might identify the client have been changed to protect confidentiality.

A case of negotiating a single cycle intervention

This case illustrates negotiating entry and contracting while keeping in mind the whole of a single organisational development cycle. The case also illustrates a mild version of the contract-before-entry challenge. The type of consultancy work required by the client was 'facilitation' of a single, 'away day'.

Scouting

The consultant was working abroad at the point of initial contact with the client. The consultant's administrator sent a facsimile to the consultant recording a telephone call she had had with the client's representative. The facsimile read,

> On Thursday, a woman rang from 'a social services organisation'. She said she wanted a trainer to come into her company for one day, to focus on two groups of six managers each, who due to changes within her organisation were going to have to work together as a single management group of twelve. She wanted someone to come to the company and help them to work together. She also wanted someone here to produce a side of A4 paper briefly describing what they would do to achieve this. She said she already had a date in mind which is in five weeks time. I explained that you were out of the office at the moment. I suggested she write to us, and I received the attached letter from her this morning. As you can see from the letter, even though I said I could not confirm the date she had in mind and that you had a busy diary, the letter indicates that she is keen on that date. She also tried to get me to tell her how much we would charge.

The attached letter, unsigned and with no indication of name or roles, was addressed to the consultant's administrator who had noted a name, Maria Eden, and telephone number in handwriting. The client's representative reiterated the request for 'a brief outline of a proposed programme for the day' that would reach her in five working days. The letter included two short paragraphs describing the situation. Two groups had been managing separate departments for the previous four years and were being amalgamated. The letter explained, 'The two groups differ in culture, history and ways of operating. People have a variety of feelings about the amalgamation. These have been acknowledged, but not identified or explored.' The purpose of the away day was 'to develop more comfortable working relationships and to begin to resolve underlying difficulties'.

Before ringing Maria Eden, the consultant thought about the request. He did have the particular date free, and also had several days available in the weeks leading up to it. What seemed required was an inter-group event that might also have some elements of conflict resolution or team building in it. The stated purpose seemed ambitious for a one day event, although twelve people was not too large and something useful could be done with proper diagnosis, planning and negotiating a suitable intervention. The use of titles like 'trainer' and 'facilitator' suggested an inexperienced client. Depending on the larger organisational context and the complexity of the social system, it might not make sense to encourage their planned intervention. Given the request for a written proposal in advance, this potential client appeared to be naïve about the need for careful diagnosis and planning of such a potentially emotionally fraught away day.

The consultant rang the telephone number and asked for the client representative by name. When Maria came on the line, she did not recognise the consultant's name and seemed embarrassed. At the consultant's invitation, she repeated the request for assistance, described the organisation and answered a few specific questions. What was the context for the away day, what was her role, what process was being used to select a consultant, why had she contacted the consultant's organisation and how many managers would be involved?

Maria was one of thirteen people who would be participating in the away day: the twelve managers and their boss, the manager of the division which included the two departments. The change was being mandated by larger governmental reorganisation and most of the managers were against it. She worked in one of the departments, had been a significant force behind the argument to bring in a consultant and had known one of the consultant's colleagues. She was one of two other managers who were gathering information about potential consultants. The entire group was meeting in five days time and would take a decision about which consultant to invite at that time.

The consultant expressed his initial thought that probably expectations were too high for what could be accomplished at a one-day event. He also described the need for adequate diagnosis and mutual planning of the intervention. Maria did not think this would be possible as there was very little money to be spent. Further, the twelve managers worked at offices scattered throughout a very large county. They only came together for two days each month.

The consultant stated that he would only do the work if arrangements could be made for some sort of diagnosis and mutual planning. He considered the time and financial constraints, the size of the group involved and the fact that it would be fairly easy to travel to the client's site. He suggested that the diagnosis could take one day made up of an individual interview with the divisional manager and two group interviews – one with each of the former departmental management teams. This meant that, if the client wished to work with the consultant, money would need to be authorised for three days work: one day for diagnosis, one half day for data analysis and customised design of the away day, one day for the away day itself, and one half day for a follow-up and review visit.

The consultant also suggested that the next telephone contact should be with someone authorised to negotiate the contract. He declined to send a proposed programme for the day, as he did not design such days without a diagnosis. Maria Eden stated that she had sufficient information to present at the managers' meeting. She wondered if the consultant would reduce his fee given that the client system was a social services organisation. The consultant, aware that social services organisations often paid consultant fees higher than his own, said that a reduction would not be possible. This scouting conversation lasted about twenty minutes.

Entry and contracting

Five days later, the consultant received a message *via* his administrator from Maria Eden, 'We want you to work with us for the date originally mentioned.' An appointment had been scheduled for a longer conversation the following week. During this telephone contracting session, Maria stated that she had been authorised by the management group to negotiate with the consultant. Also that she had spoken with the divisional manager and gained his approval for the requested fee. There were, however, difficulties with scheduling all three interviews on the same day. The complicated meeting schedule that they usually operated meant that the two groups only met on the same day once each month: that meeting had happened already and the next one was not until the scheduled away day. That meant that one of the two groups would be inconvenienced.

Could the consultant come on different days? The consultant refused for two reasons, one stated and the other not: the stated reason was because the double travel would mean spending more than the allocated one day on diagnosis; the unstated reason was because the consultant felt that the client was attempting to export their internal conflict onto the consultant. Other possible dates, times and locations were explored for both the diagnostic interviews and the away day. Maria agreed to resolve the issue and inform the consultant accordingly. The consultant requested a letter of agreement from the divisional manager confirming the contract.

It was now four weeks to the away day. In the next two weeks, Maria or the divisional manager's secretary rang three more times trying to change the date for the diagnostic interviews. Each time the consultant or his administrator dealt with the request by simply indicating whether the consultant was available or not on the date in question. The contract letter arrived two weeks before the away day and, shortly thereafter, the diagnostic interviews were confirmed for the next week. The consultant considered that the entry and contracting stage was complete.

A case of negotiating a multiple cycle intervention

This case illustrates negotiating entry and contracting while keeping in mind the whole of a single organisational development cycle *and* possible multiple, repeating cycles of organisational development. The case also illustrates the challenge of entry-without-contract. The type of consultancy work required by client, in the first instance, was a third party intervention between the Executive Vice President in charge of general management located at USA headquarters and the Managing Director (MD) of English operations.

Scouting

The consultant was working from home at the point of initial contact with the client. The consultant's administrator rang with a telephone message that she had taken at 12.50 p.m. UK time: 'The Executive Vice President of a USA company, called Ron Meadows, is trying to get in touch with you about some project work. You were recommended to him by one of your previous clients and he would like to talk with you urgently.' The urgency of the call seemed confirmed by the fact that the potential client had made the telephone call at 7.50 a.m. USA time.

When the consultant rang back, Ron Meadows offered to return the call so that he would be paying for it. The consultant refused the offer and invited Ron to indicate what sort of project he had in mind. Ron spoke quickly and at length. First, he explained that the consultant came highly recommended through his son, who was working as a corporate intern with a former client of the consultant. Then, Ron spoke of his own work background leading to his current position. A crucial part of that background was his relationship with 'a dear friend who was an expert on the human side of enterprise'. This colleague, a Human Resources Manager, had died unexpectedly and suddenly just as Ron was investing in the expansion of an English operation. The Human Resources Manager had an important developmental role with the English senior managers. Without him, there was a vacuum that Ron was looking to fill.

Ron needed little prompting from the consultant. As he told his story relevant details about the company were disclosed as well. 'Our headquarters is located in the Midwest USA. We are a highly successful engineering firm; so much so that we have gone international in the last three years. There are about a dozen people at the English site. About a year ago, we started to expand, sending the son of our owner to work in senior management. Yesterday, the English Managing Director resigned. He doesn't feel like he has any control. He lacks supervisory and leadership skills. He complains about interference from the owner and others at headquarters.' Ron wanted an immediate meeting with the consultant to think through how to proceed; he wanted her to fly to the USA site as soon as possible or, if that was not possible, he would fly to London as soon as tickets could be reserved.

While listening to Ron, the consultant had noticed that he was disclosing sensitive information about himself and his company. He seemed to have already decided to work with the consultant based on the recommendation of someone else, whom he barely knew. Given references to his 'dear friend', the 'son of our owner', the recommendation coming through Ron's son and the idiosyncratic details of the English expansion, she was forming a working hypothesis that this was a very family-oriented company, inexperienced in international management. The consultant felt it was important to have a clear business relationship and not to presume compatibility without additional data.

Formally, Ron was asking for immediate assistance that would, as a first round of organisational development, probably take the form of a third party consultation. Informally, he was looking for someone to replace the deceased Human Resources Manager and to help with development of the senior managers at the English operation. The initial social system involved in an urgent intervention would, of course, include Ron plus the English Managing Director. The likely site for follow-on cycles of organisational development would be the European one. Further, the MD felt like he had no control. To meet only with Ron would be to exclude the MD from decision-making that affected him directly in the short term, and that would influence the shape of an intervention into his site, in the medium or longer term. In order to build trust and to start in a way that would lay the groundwork for a future working relationship, it made sense to enter and contract simultaneously with representatives of both the USA headquarters and the English site.

Thus, the consultant proposed to Ron that she meet with both him and his English Managing Director as a first step. This would address the urgency of the situation while laying the groundwork for thinking through how to proceed more broadly with the English site. The consultant suggested a meeting at the London airport, which would be a neutral site and convenient to both parties. She would design the meeting in such a way that data would be collected from both Ron and the Managing Director, followed by a facilitated discussion between the two of them about how to proceed with both the MD's resignation and with the problematic context that had led him to take such drastic action. The consultant would charge Ron for this day. Should a decision to move forward together be made on that day, she would like a signed formal agreement. Ron agreed to this, suggested a date in the next week and agreed to ensure that the MD was informed and present for the meeting. He also stated that he was sure they would move forward together: 'I like the way you are talking. You seem to have a soft, easy approach like my friend had.' The scouting telephone conversation had taken forty-five minutes.

Entry and contracting

Between that first telephone call and the day-long meeting, confirmed for one week later, Ron rang the consultant twice to offer updates on the situation and think out loud about ideas. The consultant kept the length of these calls to a minimum in order to minimise being pulled into the 'backstage' dynamic which she had indicated to Ron she wanted to avoid. Ron flew in from the USA the night before the scheduled meeting and ate dinner with Thomas Jones, the English MD. The next morning, Ron said that they 'had not talked about all this other stuff'.

The meeting began with the consultant reviewing the planned agenda for the day. Both men spoke briefly and seriously about the context of the meeting and what they hoped to get out of it. Then, each one listened while the consultant interviewed the other about the context for the current, urgent situation. The consultant offered her understanding of the situation and both Ron and Thomas responded to her and then to each other.

This simple data collection and analysis led fairly naturally into a broader discussion about numerous difficulties at the English site and challenges facing the operation. The solving of the immediate issue of Thomas's resignation was handled. Thomas felt that he wanted to be freed up from the organisational building required for the expansion to focus on sales and marketing. Ron was keen to bring in a Vice President from the USA who could handle the organisational building and related expansion issues. They agreed that Thomas would retain his Managing Director title and the new person would be brought in on equal status.

While the search process was going on for the Vice President, both Ron and Thomas were keen to 'get an objective opinion on the human issues coming up in the business'. The consultant suggested a data feedback and action planning intervention that would involve data collection with all employees on the English site and relevant actors from the USA head-quarters. Data would be presented to the English senior managers who would plan a first cycle of intervention within the English site. This would be reported to all English employees as well as to the USA people who had been interviewed. This first phase of organisational development would end with an evaluation meeting with Ron and Thomas. Ron would pay for this initial work from his general management budget, with the expectation that the English site would pay for subsequent developments. This contract was agreed and the consultant sent a formal agreement to Ron, with a copy to Thomas.

GUIDELINES FOR ENTRY AND CONTRACTING

As the above two cases illustrate, negotiating entry and contracting takes place in the real world of the organisation into which the consultant is being invited. The initial scouting contact always brings with it rich data about the organisation in which any developmental work might occur as well as the particular situation that motivated the client to seek out a consultant. The process of entry and contracting, itself, reflects those issues that are likely to be significant and/or relevant during the organisational developmental cycle. Guidelines for negotiating entry and contracting need to honour this complexity while completing the business of the initial stages of work.

Guideline One: Negotiate entry and contracting by keeping in mind the whole of the organisational development cycle as well as possible multiple cycles that might follow on.

For most short-term and even some medium-term organisational development projects, the client has an idea of the type of intervention they would like to commission. While the consultant may broaden that notion considerably through negotiation, many entry and contracting interactions proceed with the assumption that the client's initial judgements are to be taken seriously. In such cases, experienced consultants usually have a pattern of working through the organisational development cycle that they can – and probably should – communicate to the client.

While details will become clearer through diagnosis and during negotiating and planning an intervention, consultants need to be sure that any agreements that might be controversial are made during entry and contracting. In the social services case, for example, the client expected to pay for one day of consulting and did not expect to engage in diagnosis. The consultant needed these issues resolved during scouting in order to determine whether to pursue entry and contracting. The consultant also felt concerned about the status and authorisation of his client representative and insisted on that being clarified before going forward. In the engineering firm case, the client seemed to prefer an informal style that neglected open consideration of differences in power and status, while excluding those who needed to be involved appropriately. The consultant strongly recommended appropriate involvement of the Managing Director from the start. She also insisted on payment from the first meeting as recognition of an authorisation to consult.

For many medium and longer-term projects, appropriate involvement and scope of the project need to be discussed and agreed, at least informally, before the first contract is signed. In the engineering firm, entry and contracting exclusively with the USA Vice President would have neglected the fact that subsequent cycles of organisational development required the co-operation of senior managers and their employees in England. An opportunity to lay the groundwork for trust and co-operation between the consultant and the English client would have been delayed and, possibly, lost. Additionally, the sheer volume of potential difficulties demanded that an in-depth diagnosis be undertaken sooner in the consulting relationship instead of later. Involving both the USA headquarters and the UK site in evaluation recognised the stake held by the USA owners.

Guideline Two: Ensure that the conditions necessary for the consultant to undertake professional organisational consultancy are agreed at the point of entry and contracting.

Many consultants consider that meeting the needs and constraints expressed by their potential client is the same thing as entry and contracting. Consultants often agree to undertake work for which they and the organisation do not feel properly prepared, for which they do not feel adequately compensated and about which they do not feel sufficiently influential. Such conditions make it difficult for an organisational consultant to undertake professional work. Professional consulting is guided by theories and rules of practice designed to bring about effective development of individuals, groups and organisations.

Both the consultant and the quality of work suffers when significant issues like preparation, compensation and influence are inadequately addressed during entry and contracting. In the social services case, the consultant felt unable to design and deliver a professional away day without adequate diagnosis and compensation. The consultant made these conditions mandatory to doing the work. In the engineering firm case, the consultant judged that it would not be possible to engage in entry and contracting without feeling compelled to offer consultation to the Vice President and that there existed a danger of becoming too closely identified with the client's representative. Therefore, the consultant proposed that payment began immediately upon the next contact and strongly advised in favour of involving the Managing Director.

Guideline Three: Craft an entry and contracting process that honours the unique characteristics of the organisational client while completing the overall tasks of this initial stage of work.

The model of a consulting cycle that appears in this chapter is based on accumulated assumptions about how to work with organisational clients in a way that maximises their development. It is one model that consultants might carry in their heads to guide professional work with an organisation. Models matter because they contain the theoretical and practical ideas of how people and organisations change and develop that shape what a consultant does with a client. That said, each client presents the consultant with unique challenges in applying theoretical and practical ideas. The client also has a model, sometimes conscious and sometimes not, of how their organisation might be or should be developed.

The challenge during scouting and entry and contracting, therefore, is to customise the work of these initial stages. Customisation is complete when the consultant succeeds in crossing the unique, idiosyncratic geographic and social boundaries of the organisation and begins to build (or is in position to begin to build) relationships appropriate to the objectives of the consultancy. In the social services case, the dispersed geography of the social groups constituting the client system demanded that the organisation create one geographic location into which the consultant could step to meet all social groups. The alternative of the consultant going to three separate locations was not possible due to limited funds. The technique of using group diagnostic interviews, rather than individual interviews, was selected as appropriate given the inter-group quality of the request and the limited time, space and money available.

In the engineering firm's case, the geographical distance between the client's representative and the targeted client characterised an essential problem of international management, suggesting the necessity of a 'both-and' approach to entry and contracting. Data apparent during multiple telephone conversations with Ron Meadows suggested that the immediately pressing problem of handling the Managing Director's resignation was more a starting point for conversation, and less a need for conflict resolution between two entrenched positions. Agreeing to plan a meeting for the two men, without further diagnosis, addressed the Vice President's need for urgent assistance, and – conceptualising the day as paid entry and contracting for an initial organisational development cycle – made it possible to take the time to complete the overall tasks of this stage.

Guideline Four: Avoid engaging in diagnosis and intervention during entry and contracting.

In order to propose a cycle of organisational development to a client, the consultant needs to gather relevant information. The challenge is to gather enough information to negotiate entry and to contract without actually engaging in diagnosis and its subsequent stage of mutual planning. This is difficult in both the contract-before-entry and entry-without-contract situations for slightly different reasons.

In the contract-before-entry situation, the consultant needs to gather enough information from the client's representative in order to propose a plan of work. This leaves the consultant vulnerable to the particular position and biases of the representative or of the tender documents. In the social services case, Maria Eden had thoughts and feelings about what was required for the away day. As luck would have it, she happened to wield sufficient weight at the joint meeting of the two groups of managers and with the divisional boss to influence the outcome. In a case where the consultant is one of several who make a sales pitch to a scheduled meeting of a decision-making body, the vulnerability is heightened. Consultants tend to be judged based on whose approach and personality most closely fits the dominant coalition's views.

In the entry-without-contract situation, the consultant gets pulled more and more across the geographical and social boundaries of the client system. The consultant collects more and more data, tries a number of possible entry points but is never encouraged by a person in sufficient authority to agree a contract. In the engineering firm's case, the consultant was able to avoid this problem by charging for the first meeting and by negotiating entry and contracting with both major stakeholders. But many consultants would have gone ahead with a meeting at no charge; perhaps meeting first with Ron Meadows, then separately with Thomas Jones and then back to Ron with a suggestion etc. If the consultant had travelled far for these meetings, it might have been possible to take advantage of being on site to meet with other relevant actors. In other words, the consultant would be engaging in diagnosis and planning an intervention without a contract.

Guideline Five: Avoid beginning work as a consultant without a contract and fee agreed.

A consultant who has begun work *without* a contract or fee agreed is usually a consultant who has neglected to follow one or more of the above guidelines. Work has started on tasks relevant to latter stages of a project cycle without clarifying issues relevant to the earlier stages (guideline one). One of the basic conditions for professional organisational development consultancy – an agreement authorising the consultant to undertake work on behalf of recognised members of the client system – has been allowed to move out of focus in conversations with the client representative (guideline two). The consultant has responded to the unique qualities of the potential client but ignored the tasks requiring attention in the early stages of crossing boundaries and building relationships (guideline three). And, diagnosis and planning of an intervention has begun without fully entering and contracting (guideline four).

In the engineering firm's case, the consultant started to be paid before there was technically a contract. This decision was taken because it was apparent that there was no way the consultant could meet with the client without also engaging in consultancy work with him. In the social services case, the consultant did no work until a written letter of agreement from the divisional manager had been received. Thus, the contract indicated that sufficient authorisation for the diagnosis, design and delivery of an away day had been achieved. The process of working through this commitment within the client system was handled by the client's representative and their colleagues – not the consultant.

SUMMARY

Successful entry and contracting requires the consultant to cross the geographic and social boundaries relevant to the immediate purpose of the potential consulting agreement. Inherent in this crossing is the need to develop a mutual understanding with an authorised person. The organisational development cycle provides a useful model for thinking about specific items that should be addressed in that mutual understanding. For a single cycle project, the model also can serve as a check-list of what implications latter stages of the cycle might have for what takes place in the earlier stages. For multiple cycle projects, the consultant needs an awareness of how different interventions might follow on from each other in order to maximise development. Keeping the whole organisational development cycle in mind during entry and contracting will help consultants avoid typical problems like consulting without a contract or payment, with inadequate preparation and with insufficient influence.

REFERENCES AND FURTHER READING

Alderfer, C. P. and Brown L. D. (1975) *Learning from Changing Organizational Diagnosis and Development*, Beverly Hills: Sage Publications.

Argyris, C. (1970) *Intervention Theory and Method: a Behavioural Science View*, Reading, MA: Addison-Wesley.

Block, P. (1981) *Flawless Consulting: a Guide to Getting Your Expertise used*, Austin, Texas: Learning Concepts.

Cherniss, Cary. (1984) 'Pre-entry issues in consultation', in R. J. Lee and A. M.

Freedman (eds) *Consultation Skills Reading*, Arlington, Virginia: NTL Institute, 47–52.

Cummings, T. G. and Huse, E. T. (1989) *Organization Development and Change*, St Paul, MN: West.

Glidewell, J. C. (1984) 'The entry problem in consultation', in R. J. Lee, and A. M. Freedman (eds) *Consultation Skills Reading*, Arlington, Virginia: NTL Institute, 47–52.

Hirschhorn, L. (1985) 'The psychodynamics of taking the role', in A. D. Colman and M. H. Geller (eds) *Group Relations Readers 2*, Washington DC: A. K. Rice Institute, 335–52.

Kolb, D. and Frohman, A. (1970) 'An organizational development approach to consulting', *Sloan Management Review*, 12: 51–65.

Lippitt, R. and Lippitt, G. (1984) 'Consulting roles', in R. J. Lee and A. M. Freedman (eds) *Consultation Skills Reading*, Arlington, Virginia: NTL Institute, 35–6.

Menzies Lyth, I. (1988) *Containing Anxiety in Institutions, Selected Essays*, Volume 1, London: Free Association.

Neilsen, E. (1984) *Becoming an OD practitioner*, New Jersey: Prentice-Hall.

Neumann, J.E. (1989) 'Why people don't participate in organizational change,' in W. A. Pasmore and R. W. Woodman (eds) *Research in Organization Change and Development*, Volume 3, Greenwich CT: JAI Press 181–212.

—— (1994) 'Difficult beginnings: confrontation between consultant and client', in R. Casemore, G. Dyos, A. Eden, K. Kellner, J. McAuley and S. Moss (eds) *What Makes Consultancy Work – Understanding the Dynamics*, London: South Bank University Press, 13–47.

Ruma, S. (1984) 'A four-phase developmental model', in R. J. Lee and A. M. Freedman (eds) *Consultation Skills Reading*, Arlington, Virginia: NTL Institute, 45–7.

Schatzman, L. and Strauss, A. L. (1973) *Field Research: Strategies for a Natural Sociology*, New Jersey: Prentice-Hall.

Schein, E. (1969) *Process Consultation: Its Role in Organization Development*, Reading, MA: Addison-Wesley.

Sherwood, J. J. and Glidewell, J. C. (1971) 'Planned re-negotiation: a norm-setting OD intervention', in Jones and Pfeiffer (eds) *The 1973 Annual Handbook for Group Facilitators*, LaJolla, California: University Associates Publishers, Inc. 195–202.

Steele, F. (1975) *Consulting for Organizational Change*, Amherst: University of Massachusetts Press.

Weisbord, M. R. (1984) 'Client contact: entry and contract', in R. J. Lee and A. M. Freedman (eds) *Consultation Skills Reading*, Arlington, Virginia: NTL Institute, 63–6.

Chapter 2

The social architecture of group interventions

Thomas North Gilmore

THE PROBLEM

Never before have the pressures on organisations been so great. Competition is relentless and has created an imperative for 'strategic speed' (Eisenhardt 1990). Product life cycles are shortening. New technologies create new opportunities. The power of smart, demanding customers creates pressure for more value for less cost. Organisations face the challenge of being innovative in their products and services as well as in their ways of operating and structuring.

However, just as we need more ability from our organisations to support fast, innovative thinking among the appropriate stakeholders, we find ourselves trapped in old structures and concepts. Leaders such as Jack Welch of GE or Ray Smith of Bell Atlantic are more articulate in attacking and deauthorising the old paradigm than they are in inventing and implementing new ways of doing business. As Figure 2.1 suggests, we are in transition: moving from one way of conducting our affairs to a new way that is being shaped in real time. What a leader intends as 'empowering' can easily be experienced by others as 'dumping responsibilities', especially in the context of pervasive downsizing. We are at a particular moment of vulnerability in our organisations in this period of reduced organisational competence when the rate of change creates tremendous pressures for fast, high-quality decision-making.

In a sense, this transition is from tightly coupled, hierarchical forms to loosely coupled organisations (Weick 1982) in which the relationships among the parts are more negotiated than predetermined. Loosely coupled systems have various properties. Actions in one part of the system can have little or no effect in another or can trigger unpredictable responses out of proportion to the stimulus. Linkages among elements are often unpredictable, ill-understood or uneven. The forces for integration – worrying about the whole, its identity, its integrity and its future – are often weak compared to the forces for specialisation. And, central authority is derived as much from the members, as from the member elements receiving delegated authority from above.

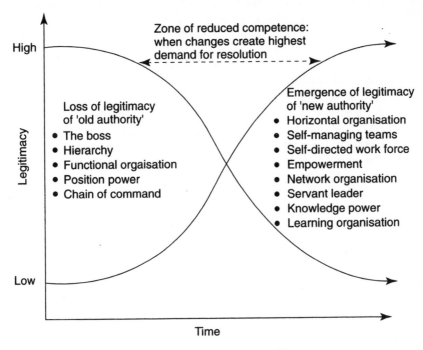

Figure 2.1 Dilemmas of realigning authority from old to new

Examples of loosely coupled organisations would be universities, associations, and professionally dominated organisations such as global consulting firms. In such settings the challenge is creating a 'good enough' (Winnicott 1971) authority structure to channel and contain the diversity of thinking that is present in individuals and groups in order to create and implement some common strategic thrust.

As many corporations have unleashed total quality or re-engineering initiatives, their leaders have created a parallel structure that cuts across levels and functions to focus on core processes or aspects of a cultural transformation (Gilmore *et al.* 1997). The relationships among the many elements of a complex change initiative are often loosely coupled among themselves and in relationship to the standing authority structure (Bushe and Shani 1991). The premier example would be GE's workout process or Bell Atlantic's Bell Atlantic Way – a series of workshops, special assignments and quality teams that stand to the side of the existing authority structure.

Not only are single organisations becoming more loosely coupled, but outsourcing, joint ventures and federated structures are creating new dilemmas for reaching the necessary collective actions (Handy 1994). In addition, more of our societal challenges are not going to be resolved by working within the single organisation's boundaries, whether loosely or tightly coupled. When intervening in organisational ecologies (Trist 1976; Gray 1989), often a critical initial step in the work is creating the structure and authority for the work to proceed.

In such a setting the issues of leadership, risk taking, thinking divergently and reaching closure are problematic and make critical the competencies that this chapter suggests can be encompassed in the term 'social architecture' (Gilmore and Barnett 1992; Perlmutter 1967; Nadler et al. 1995). This chapter focuses on the social architecture of participation in engagements with loosely coupled systems. Loosely coupled systems are linked to the dynamics of large groups when it comes to identifying the challenges in getting effective work done.

Social architecture includes the processes and structures that bring people together from temporary scaffolding to semi-permanent arrangements that channel how people think and relate to one another. A social architecture thinks of a gathering as a live, dynamic, interacting whole. It looks to amplify the communication linkages among the stakeholders within the membership that most need to interrelate with one another as well as their links to groups not in attendance. It looks to contain effectively the anxiety that surrounds difficult work enabling every ounce of energy to be focused on the existential uncertainties in the task. Effective design can create the conditions of safety for people to explore, think the unthinkable, have the conversation with somebody that they might not have back home, and can help them at the end of such a gathering carry back important insights to their own work roles. As the architect of the Vietnam Memorial, Maya Lin said, 'I create places in which to think, without trying to dictate what to think.'

Frequently, the ways in which we bring people together for the purposes of thinking, planning and acting collectively often have the paradoxical results of frustrating people and making them feel that the collective is less smart than the sum of individuals or units. Individuals are disempowered rather than empowered. One of the significant indicators of this effect is the shift in vitality and spontaneity from the formal or official forums into the hallways or bars. The following examples illustrate this.

Case one

A national association of some of the smartest people in science finds that working with its governing board is stultifying. They do not feel the talent that comes to their various meetings gets applied to the critical issues facing their field. Different stakeholders who have important differences among themselves fall silent during the board meeting only to work these same issues vigorously when in homogeneous caucuses or in informal gatherings outside of the meeting.

Case two

A large convention of a trade association finds sporadic attendance at the key substantive meetings and a widespread belief that the real value of these meetings is only contained in the spaces between the formal programme: the deals over the bar, the intelligence one gets from talking to colleagues and competitors, and the opportunity of scheduling personal meetings just because key people are all at the same event.

Case three

A telecommunications company conference is addressing the issue of empowerment and critical changes from deregulation. Paradoxically, the convention itself is structured in ways that are highly paternalistic, allows very little individual autonomy, entrepreneurship and creativity, and in essence treats participants bureaucratically.

In all three of these cases it is as if we are trying to play a symphony but only have three notes on our instruments.

First, the plenary/presentation: This has the assumption that someone on a podium can sustain the title of expert and that the members of the audience in that same time period are not experts, they are to be filled up with wisdom from above.

Second, the panel: Four or five distinguished people are brought together under the rubric of some common topic. Most of the time each member prepares his or her own short talk disconnected from the other members of the panel. Many unassertive moderators fail to regulate the talks sufficiently so that they end with an apology that there was no time for the rich interplay of questions between the audience and the panellists that was envisaged.

Third, the breakout or buzz group: This is a subgroup of the participants often with a designated chair or facilitator who is assigned a topic. Its dilemmas often have to do with the variability in the local leadership of such sessions and a lack of clarity about the relationship between what goes on in those sessions and how it connects to either the broad conference themes or to the work that is going on in other groups.

LARGE GROUP DYNAMICS

In addition to the challenges of loosely coupled organisations, many more of the situations that require large system change inevitability involve both a great number and considerable heterogeneity of stakeholders. As Weisbord (1987) has suggested, the field of organisational development has moved from *experts* in small-group problem solving, to *participative small-group* problem solving, to *experts* doing large systems change, finally to *participative* large-system change. This means we face working increasingly with large groups (Bunker and Albans 1992) whose dynamics are considerably different from the small, face-to-face workgroup for which we have developed many well tested techniques.

Workgroups (as contrasted with audiences) are termed 'large' when it becomes impossible for each member to maintain eye-to-eye contact with everyone else (Turquet 1975) and face-to-face interaction among members is impossible (Alford 1989). The authors discussed below have studied large groups predominantly in therapeutic or short-term, self-study conferences. Clearly, bureaucracy and structure, both in the formal organisation and in any particular meeting, suppress these dynamics. However, they do so often at the cost of learning and development. Large group dynamics are beneath the surface and have to be acknowledged in clinically coming up with enough structure to prevent regression, but not so much as to foreclose real learning from the experience of the individuals in the room.

Large group dynamics begin somewhere when the numbers exceed 15 to 20. In large groups, participants increasingly make sense of their relationship to the full group *via* identifications that can shift rapidly among different subgroupings. The risks of finding one's voice in a large group increase because one does not have the informal correction processes in interpersonal encounters; hence the links to reality are more tenuous among large groups as misperceptions can go unchallenged. Turquet (1995) suggests two opposite defences on the part of individuals: they either withdraw deeply into isolated alienation or submerge their individuality with others. In both cases the climate works against coherent development of ideas, with people building on one anothers' remarks. Alford (1989) suggests the thought experiment of imagining the sequence of comments in a large group as coming from a single individual, trying to come to know his or her own mind. He suggests it would be characterised by 'fragmentation, disjointedness, one assertion [one speaker] not responding to another, topics rapidly changing with only the loosest association between them, obviously false assertions going unchecked' (Alford 1989: 70).

Another feature of large groups is the envy that members can feel for anyone who stands out as an individual, other than the leader. As Freud (1959) noted, often followers will identify intensely with the leader whom they idealise as a way of escaping their anxiety. Kernberg (1985: 225) describes how the intolerance for individual creativity can play out covertly as members of different subgroups fight one another, often being subtly encouraged by 'innocent bystanders.'

As Main (1975) writes, 'Members will sit in long, uneasy silences with even the most resourceful apparently lacking the capacity for contributing usefully. They have denied, split off and projected much of their mental vigour outside themselves . . . [T]hey will actually feel stupid, helpless and afraid of what it may do to them if they speak or move incautiously.'

In summary, the key features of large group dynamics that are particularly antithetical to the adaptation to complex, fast changing situations are that extreme stereotyping occurs, with differences often exaggerated and similarities ignored for example, characterising all physicians or the central office in ways that capture a complex group of individuals in a single untested generalisation. Ownership of one's ideas decreases. Participation is weak and *via* identification with parts of what others have said or by expressing one's ideas *via* silent alliances with others instead of honestly stating one's own views. This manifests itself linguistically with more abstract terms, e.g., group, speaker, administration, the nursing staff, versus personal identifications. Risk taking and the ability to usefully discriminate is decreased; and there is fear of being 'original or unique in thought or capacity' (Main 1975: 78).

In light of these dynamics surrounding large groups, we unconsciously react by overstructuring the time, filling it with presentations and 'running out of time for questions'. A speaker asks for comments, yet only allows eight to ten seconds to elapse before moving on when no one speaks out. Turning a group into an audience is comfortable for both the speaker and the participants.

INTERVENTION DESIGN PRINCIPLES AND STRATEGIES

The design challenge in working with large groups is to steer between too much anxiety that will stimulate the maladaptive responses of dependency, fight/flight, or an unrealistic hope for salvation from a key pair in the group (Bion 1961). Irving Janis (1958) talked about the 'work of worry' in connection with coping with the stress of being a patient. How can leaders design a structure and process for a large group that allocates 'worry' in appropriate amounts among the group so that real learning can occur? Traditionally, the leaders have to worry and the participants sit and take in a few ideas and judge the event. A measure of how asymmetric the work of worry is in most organisations is to ask who feels the risk of the meeting not going well. When it is in a single person or perhaps a few, it suggests that all the others are being allowed to be spectators.

The challenge in large group design is to create an environment in which individuals are encouraged to come to know their own minds. E. M. Forster once asked, 'How do I know what I think until I hear what I say?' suggesting that thinking is a social process. Particularly in light of the anxiety of finding one's voice in a large group, many of the techniques we have used afford opportunities to collect one's thoughts privately and to talk informally in pairs or small groups to sharpen ideas and begin to connect them to others.

A second challenge is to take the under-the-table dynamics of stereotyping by group identifications (for example, privately thinking that a command is 'typical of headquarters') and provide occasions in which people are allowed to caucus by these groupings. Two results follow. First, within the small groups, people explore both similarities and difference – for example, the whole of headquarters is not of one mind on the issue. Second, in the reporting, people can build more sophisticated theories about the effects of one's identity or organisational unit on the issue under discussion.

One of the values of getting 'the system in the room' as Weisbord (1987) has stated it, is the opportunity to use live dynamics to study and learn about key dynamics that also exist in the ongoing organisation. For example, an issue might surface in which one group knows much more than another. This affords a here-and-now opportunity to study the communication links, including the informal ones that grow up to compensate for underdeveloped channels.

Four design principles for effective social architecture of large groups have evolved. First, create opportunities for people to safely explore similarities and differences in their thinking. Second, take risks to put real, controversial, not yet completely resolved issues into play. Third, purposefully use different logics for subgroups – random, intact, organisational units and identity groups – to match the task. Fourth, pay careful attention to transitions both into and out of the overall event as well as between different stages of the work.

CASE STUDY: AN ACADEMIC MEDICAL CENTRE FACES A FAST-CHANGING ENVIRONMENT

In the context of significant transformations in American health care, an urban hospital, its medical school and the governing board realised the need for a significant change in culture to adapt to major external changes. The faculty needed to be much more marketplace-oriented, much better able to change their clinical practices rapidly and to join with the hospital in significant cost cutting. The leadership for the retreat, as is often the case, came from the CEO of the hospital, the element that was experiencing the change pressures most acutely. The hospital had recently been spun out from under the university trustees and had its own board but with significant overlap with the university board. The CEO explored with the dean of the medical school jointly sponsoring this event, but the dean was hesitant, fearing reactions among his faculty. However, he did agree to come.

This is a common situation in which one or more key stakeholders wish to stay in a customer-type role versus actively collaborating with the leadership group. As consumers, they can gingerly explore getting more involved but keep their options open. In this case three stakeholder groups were present: the board (including some key university leaders such as the provost), the dean of the medical school and the heads of the major clinical departments, and the CEO of the hospital and his top staff, making a total group of about thirty-five. The CEO accepted the leadership and worked with a team of process and subject expert consultants to design and facilitate the sessions. The preparation was asymmetric as the CEO and his staff did a considerable amount of analytical work on the marketplace and cost challenges, while the faculty and trustees simply showed up.

To get everyone into the work, the consultants used interview design. In this process the leadership sets six to ten questions on significant issues and randomly distributes one to each of the participants. Participants interview one another in pairs and then switch partners several times such that each person collects information on his or her question from others, and in turn, is interviewed by others on different questions. Next, all those with the same question get together pooling all the responses (usually about one-third of the total group). They post the major themes and interesting outliers on flipcharts. Finally, all participants review all the sheets and prioritise the most important themes balloting with a scarce resource (three to six) of red dots. They have about an hour and a half.

The effects of interview design are several. All group members are forced to be active in both inquiry and contributing modes. In large groups, people often feel anonymous and do not feel their contribution really matters. Usually people are more open and candid in pairs and also get a chance to gauge reactions to ideas before the anxiety of putting them into play in a large group. People see the full group's thinking being constructively structured into major themes. A written record is left for informing subsequent work and to support next steps. And finally, many people meet one another over important substantive questions, mixing both horizontally and vertically.

By beginning the retreat in this way, the participants pooled their intelligence and surfaced in a safe way similarities and differences. Out of a large-group discussion of key themes, the group settled on six issues and formed mixed teams (trustees, faculty and administrators) and were charged with preparing an initial report on their assigned issue. Note that despite the advanced preparation of the hospital leadership, the central themes for the retreat were settled on in real time with all three groups equally participating in both surfacing the issues *via* the interviewing and analysis and ranking the top issues *via* each balloting on his or her top six issues.

A noteworthy issue was the growing tensions between the dean and the CEO. The consultants were perceived to be working for the CEO and, hence, found it difficult to consult to the growing tension directly. However, there was plenty of evidence of the dean's anxiety growing as he saw his chairs of key clinical departments distributed across six different groups, addressing potentially significant issues that he had not had the opportunity to review. Realising the legitimacy of his concerns, the consultants proposed a 45-minute caucus in the middle of the afternoon's small group work in which each of the three stakeholder groups – board, hospital, medical school – would convene to take stock on how their different issue groups were going and get fresh instructions prior to entering the final round of issue work.

The intervention was successful. The dean had the chance to meet with his chairs, hear what was going on, give counsel on the school's stakes as he saw them and suggest how the interests of the medical school could be furthered. In each of the other groups a similar process took place.

The next round of work was far more effective as each individual had a revitalised sense of their home-base perspective to contribute as well as new ideas that flowed from the cross-fertilisation. This is a good example of how often in social design one needs to think paradoxically. To transcend stakeholder interests and achieve an integrative solution, one needs to honour people's home group identifications.

As noted above, this event was sponsored asymmetrically with the hospital in the lead, but needed to go forward with broader involvement in the overall steering group. The consultants suggested that the groups report to a standing group that met weekly called the 'small clinical executive group' which would sit in a fishbowl and listen as each group reported. This group was chosen because it had good representation from both the hospital and faculty side. The first learning came when this group was asked to come to the front to sit as a panel because there was widespread confusion as to who was on the group and who was not. This is not at all uncommon in loosely coupled systems where representation is significantly underlegitimised. Simply to see the group that would be holding the thinking from the six issue groups increases its legitimacy and in return makes it more publicly accountable for follow-up.

Prior to letting the group hear the reports, the consultants invited its members to converse among themselves (in a 'fishbowl') about what their regular, ongoing meetings were like. This was revealing because they were both enacting their dynamics in the here and now as well as talking about them. Asking a group to work publicly is powerful in loosely coupled systems because there is considerable curiosity, even paranoia, about what leadership groups do. In this instance, participants could see the gingerliness between the dean and the CEO over leadership. Different members spoke to their strengths and weaknesses as a team, ending up with considerable consensus that their weakest trait was follow-through even when they had a good substantive discussion of a topic. This obviously was an important fact as they faced the thirty or so participants with the understanding that they would take accountability for overseeing follow-through from the retreat.

Then each of the issue groups reported to this panel, in front of the other participants. Others could watch the panel react, make comments, and challenge the findings of the workgroups. The panellists had to react spontaneously without the chance to know how their fellow panel members might react. Participants have the chance to audit the thoughtfulness of their leadership group by noticing what they did and did not say. Often at the end of this type of process, the participants can be invited to give the group in the 'fishbowl' some feedback.

Because they were presenting to a real standing group, the participants pushed during their presentations in terms of what the specific plans would be. Because the accountability was being publicly enacted by this group, it triggered a spontaneous process of first the provost and then the chair of the board, each speaking to the full group about the accountabilities they were carrying out of the session.

The above is an example of how a retreat moved from being initially asymmetrically sponsored by the CEO to being a fledgling intergroup becoming more publicly authorised to take up its leadership on the many issues that genuinely arose on the seams between the medical school and the hospital. At the end of this session, a 'good enough' scaffolding was in place, collaboratively created and authorised to sustain and contain the necessary follow-through work on the emerging issues that did not fit neatly inside any one of the participating organisations.

GUIDELINES FOR PRACTICE

The conceptual framework for thinking about the issues involved in social architecture as a life cycle has five stages:

1 Before the beginning;
2 Authorising;
3 Overall design;
4 Design of specific events;
5 Managing endings, transitions.

1 Before the beginning

This phase is complex because it is often clearer with hindsight. Yet the choices that get made about timing, who is involved and the scope are often long-lasting.

Sub-topics here are shadows of previous initiatives that either create hope or cynicism and alternatives about authorising the initial steps (e.g., jointly, unilaterally, from above, from below, etc.). There are critical points concerning how the issue gets framed, how open or closed is the charge, who gets to shape it and how it is positioned in terms of continuity or discontinuity with the past.

If an individual in an organisation experiences the need for some space or place to think either with different partners or in different ways about one's situation, how can they thoughtfully advocate some new, more loosely structured setting for innovation and exploration? Acknowledging a need for help is often associated with people perceiving the person as vulnerable or having a particular problem that needs to be solved. In our present culture, when a leader in a public organisation has a retreat it is often received with snickering by external reviewers. Therefore, in the initial seeking of help there are issues of both one's self-perception, feeling depleted, or not up to certain parts of one's responsibilities, and external views that may be demeaning. We have not yet created widespread support for leaders and organisations spending time in reflective retreats.

Often someone in a formal leadership position can offer to support a retreat or to begin an *ad hoc* process on an issue but cannot successfully command participation on the part of the key stakeholders. Often one needs to work with a 'pull' versus 'push' strategy.

2 Authority/host

Paradoxically, the issues of authority – who is the host or who is the sponsor – often do not come up right at the beginning. This is in part because it is only after one has moved quite far down the road that somebody often steps into the leadership role. Frequently out of that discussion emerges some steering group and a dynamic in which the group has to cycle through both the issues and who is going to be asked to participate. These interact in that new issues require rethinking about participants. When new stakeholders are legitimated they will bring a richer, broader or different slant on issues than the earlier group. In a sense, these have to be considered iteratively. A process has to start somewhere. Some people will feel more included and legitimated and others will have to work through feelings of being asked in after the beginning.

A simple process strategy can be effective at the launch of some steering group. Each participant is asked to think of some of the most sceptical questions that a colleague might ask upon learning of the launch of this effort. Then members of the group can ask each other these questions and practice responding improvisationally. Many times there is a switch from talking about the effort as if one is not a part of it to owning one's membership on the steering group. Some of the questions often challenge scope, membership or timing so that participants can revisit these issues in light of potential stakeholder reactions. Getting some of the cynicism out *via* the device of imagining sceptical questions can help the members work through their own ambivalence and become more fully ready to 'champion' the initiative.

Often there can be a productive cycle of authorising in which a person or group takes a risk to initiate an event or process. Then, during the next cycle, there is openness to renegotiating and challenging the authority. Finally, at the closure, there is a reconsolidation such that there is 'good enough' authority to oversee next steps.

One of the more complex issues is the triangle between the authorising individual or group, the consultants and the participants. Especially in loosely coupled systems or with large-group dynamics there is a risk of the outside consultant overfunctioning as the leader. Often the true leader will want to be on the sidelines. Given the central importance of building 'good enough' authority within the emerging system, high consultant control is often not effective in the long run.

3 Overall design, rhythms of the work and preparation

Frequently these processes are too event driven and not sufficiently connected to the real, ongoing organisational work. Many organisations, particularly technical or international organisations such as the UN, have a tradition of retreats or high-level seminars that are incredibly rich in content but are almost totally cut off from any operational consequences. Over time this leads to a jadedness about such events. They are regarded as treats or perks rather than seen as difficult thinking work that needs to be connected to the operational apparatus. This may parallel the recent tendencies to split leadership and management in a dysfunctional way (Gilmore and Krantz 1990).

Three things help prevent this. First, is beginning the work before the beginning. This means always having some form of active preparation for people prior to coming. This might be a written document, interviews, a meeting conducted with key others who will not be attending, reading and reaction to some report, etc. Second, is to think in a series of events rather than a single one. For example, it can often be powerful prior to an offsite retreat to schedule a half-day, follow-up meeting at the regular work site to ensure some carry back into the ongoing organisation. Finally, there needs to be careful attention to the ending and transitions in each stage of the work to ensure that people know what the accountabilities are for follow-up. For example, it can often be effective to have a steering group reauthorised and even its membership changed as a process unfolds across time, winning the involvement of new relevant stakeholders, as was illustrated in the case.

4 The design of a particular event or episode

In considering both the overall flow and the design of any one element, we have found it is useful to think in four phases:

- *Phase one – joining*: getting people to arrive, to care about the issue, to feel heard.
- *Phase two – divergent*: embracing diversity, brainstorming, thinking outside of the box, generating options; everyone's thinking should feel welcomed.
- *Phase three – convergent*: searching for 'yesable' packages, common ground, coming to hard choices or limiting the options and managing the process of losing.
- *Phase four – signing up*: testing people's commitments to the choice made by challenging them to stay involved.

The beginnings then are critical because they have both the psychological task of 'hooking' participants as well as the substantive task of communicating the scope and dimensions of the issues. The opening session is tone setting in terms of whether participants will be talked at or actively pulled in. It sends a powerful message to get people working actively immediately on substantive issues. Too often people see introductory exercises as 'ice breakers' rather than going at important issues. The interview design described in the case above can be a strong start.

One of the most deadening openings can be the 'keynote' speaker implying the issues can be resolved by some expert rather than through honest collaboration among the ongoing stakeholders. A 'motivational speaker' often creates a 'not me' experience by talking rapidly and manically about other organisations in ways that paradoxically deplete rather than energise the group. Such presenters often come into the retreat and leave in ways that make it very difficult to discuss the lack of connection between their content and the rest of the session. Alternatively, they get used by participants who ask seemingly innocent questions and let the prestigious outside speaker take up a stand that is oppositional to the leadership of the organisation. For example, at one corporate event an outside speaker responded to a question about matrix organisations and went on at length about their complexity and the difficulty of making them work while the organisation (and the aim of the retreat) was moving to a matrix structure!

There needs to be a thoughtful sequence of different groupings such as small groups, intergroups, plenaries, individual work, etc. Often there is a flow across time that begins with configurations that support divergent thinking. For example, people are in maximally heterogeneous groups, perhaps jointly exploring the wider environment or developing some scenarios. Then, as the event gets closer to next steps, it is useful to meet in groupings that have the most alignment with the ongoing structure because that is the form that can best follow through on the commitments that have been made at the session.

Think about the degree of structure that is necessary. If one mistakenly overstructures, important things will not be allowed in. If one under-structures, it may be too loose and vague, so people will not be able to focus and get something done that is tangible. The degree of structure may be a function of whether the organisation itself is suffering from being over-bounded or under-bounded (Alderfer 1980). Process technologies should fit with one another and the methods used should fit with the culture of the organisation.

5 Managing endings

One of the defences against innovation is to make some *ad hoc* event or retreat special and keep it apart from the real work. Especially when loosely coupled systems have come together to explore an issue complexly shared across many different organisations, holding people and organisations accountable can be a challenge. The steering group should pay a lot of attention to the sanctioning processes and the authorising processes when people go back. For example, people need to be relieved from other obligations if they are to seriously take up new tasks that flow from the retreat. It can be powerful to discuss explicitly what tasks people are going to stop doing to create the time and space to try new behaviours.

A simple process for helping people focus on key learnings is to replace any evaluation with a 'one-minute essay' (Light 1990). Each participant is asked to spend a couple of minutes writing about the one or two important ideas that they are taking away from the session. This helps keep people actively listening and also gives the convening group some feedback in terms of how convergent or divergent the key messages have been from the work.

Often the people who do not get to go to the retreat or participate in the *ad hoc* process have a sense of being left out, which stimulates jealously about the access or new skills that have been given to another set of people. This often leads to a dynamic of holding unrealistic expectations of their new skills such that non-participants become disappointed in how unchanged the participants really are after a retreat.

Assigning members of the workgroups to share back home information with colleagues who are not members or with relevant subgroups not involved at the retreat can build bridges to the ongoing organisational routines. Look for opportunities to assign non-members follow-up tasks that will begin to engage them in the issues that the retreat has provided some leadership on.

Often in the excitement of developing new ideas groups will resist making the transition to the difficult implementation work. As Trist (1989) has noted, imagining that changes are 'ordinary' and do not require any major attention to the change dynamics can serve as a defence against innovation. The steering group needs to ensure that adequate time is put into the implementation and next steps, including anticipating the resistance that may arise.

Retreats often touch on the way too many issues and promise much more than can be delivered, especially in loosely coupled systems, which paradoxically trigger deeper demoralisation and mistrust than might have been the case in the beginning. The lack of follow-through after some initial hopefulness makes people less available for the use of retreat mechanisms in the future.

KEY SKILLS IN LEADING LOOSELY COUPLED LARGE GROUPS

- The ability to tolerate silence after you pose a question without joking, being visibly anxious, with confident body language, calmly gazing over participants, assured that someone will join you in work.
- The ability to join emotionally with the group *via* humour with some apt comment on the here and now situation that connects you to the group. A CEO was interacting with a group of sixty managers and the issue of people not knowing each others' names had come up. In calling on someone, he jokingly failed to recall her name. This enables a beneath the surface anxiety ('I should know everyone's name') to be discharged and for people to connect *via* this common worry.
- The ability to listen unanxiously to a question, criticism or comment and not be filled with your responsibility to answer or immediately react. Asking permission to think it over or to come back to it later are options. Requesting more information from the questioner or pushing the responsibility back onto the questioner to answer or asking for others' comments or testing to see if there are similar concerns among others, are all options that may be more developmental than responding immediately. Tolerating not knowing is critical in light of the regressive pull in large groups for leaders to be omniscient.
- The ability to acknowledge or elicit awareness of differences. For example, if a question arises or one is making a point that is particularly significant to a subgroup (e.g. physicians), one might ask all of that group to identify themselves and then request that they work with you to explore the issue faster *via* commenting or a show of hands in terms of participants' views on an issue. Note that this process probes both similarities (all the MD's) and differences (variety of opinions within that group). Sometimes acknowledging a particular individual (who may have raised an earlier point) can help everyone retain his or her identity in a large group.
- The skill of straw polling during a complex conversation in a large group. The ability to summarise a complex discussion into some broad choices or options and to elicit people's initial thoughts in ways that do not lock them into those positions, but help the group explore its differences. When a participant raises an issue it can be powerful to

invite him or her to poll the group on some aspect of his or her issue directly so that the participant shapes the question.
- The ability to get people to think actively by vividly asking them a question or by accurately guessing thoughts and feelings that are in their minds. For example, a hospital CEO was working with a group of one hundred managers on the dramatic shift in the hospital's environment. He asked people, 'How do you negotiate over your phone bill? What do you do when your utility bill arrives?' After a pause to pressure people to think, he contrasted that with shopping for food where price plays a significant role. He then moved to his key point about the shift from a utility culture (pass any increased costs off to rate payers) to a market-driven culture and invited participants to think about the consequences for their work.
- The ability to speak vividly about one's own experiences in ways that people can connect with.

CONCLUSION

The societal challenges we face are great and increasingly do not fall conveniently into the existing organisational boxes that we have created for them. Therefore, most of the crucial social and business issues we face will need to be addressed within *ad hoc* or emerging structures and processes, often linking across multiple organisations (Bushe and Shani 1991; Jacobs 1994). We need to build the design skills into both leaders and consultants to create these temporary communities where many of the relevant parties can be brought together and take the time to create fresh maps of the new emerging terrain. Far too often we assemble a phenomenal aggregate IQ that goes unharvested because of the thoughtless structure and process of the meeting. By careful attention to how we engage key stakeholders who are loosely coupled to one another, we can tap their intelligence and commitment to the required innovative strategies.

REFERENCES AND FURTHER READING

Alderfer, C. (1980) 'Consulting to underbounded systems', in C. P. Alderfer and C. L. Cooper, (eds) *Advances in Experiential Social Processes 2*, New York: John Wiley.
Alford, C. F. (1989) *Melanie Klein and Social Theory*, New Haven, CT: Yale University Press.
Bion, W. (1961) *Experience in Groups*, New York: Basic Books.
Bunker, B. and Albans, B. (eds) (1992) *Special Issue of Large Groups of Journal of Applied Behavioral Sciences*, 28 (December): 4, NTL Institute.
Bushe, Gervase and Shani, A. B. (1991) *Parallel Learning Structures: Creating Innovations in Bureaucracies*, Reading, MA: Addison-Wesley.
Cohen, M., and March, J. (1974) *Leadership Ambiguity*, Boston: Harvard Business School Press.

Eisenhardt, K. Spring (1990) 'Speed and strategic choice: how managers accelerate decision making', *California Management Review*.

Freud, S. (1959) [1929] *Group Psychology and the Analysis of the Ego*, (J. Strachey, translation), New York: Norton.

Gilmore, T. and Barnett, C. (1992) 'Designing the social architecture of participation in large groups', *Journal of Applied Behavioral Sciences*, 28 (December): 4.

Gilmore, T. and Krantz, J. (1990) 'The splitting of leadership and management as a social defense', *Human Relations*, 43: 2.

Gilmore, T. and Shea, G. and Useem, M. (1997) 'Side effects of corporate transformations', *Journal of Applied Behavioural Science*, June.

Gray, B. (1989) *Collaborating: Finding Common Ground for Multi-Party Problems*, San Francisco: Jossey-Bass.

Handy, C. (1994) *The Age of Paradox*, Boston: Harvard Business School Press.

Jacobs, Robert W. (1994) *Real Time Strategic Change: How to Involve an Entire Organization in Fast and Far Reaching Change*, San Francisco: Berrett-Koehler.

Janis, I. (1958) *Psychological Stress*, New York: Wiley.

Kernberg, O. (1985) *Internal World and External Reality: Object Relations Theory Applied*, Northvale, New Jersey: Jason Aronson.

Light, R. (1990) *The Harvard Assessment Seminars*, Cambridge, MA: Harvard University Press.

Main, T. (1975) 'Some psychodynamics of large groups', in L. Kreeger (ed.) *The Large Group*, London: Constable.

Nadler, D. Shaw, R., Walton, A. and Associates (1995) *Discontinuous Change: Leading Organizational Transformation*, San Francisco: Jossey-Bass.

Perlmutter, H. (1967) *Towards a Theory of Social Architecture*, London: Tavistock Publications.

Trist, E. A. (1976) 'A concept of organizational ecology', presented to three Melbourne Universities.

—— (1989) 'The assumptions of ordinaryness as a denial mechanism: innovation and conflict in a coal mine', *Human Resource Management*, 28: 2.

Turquet, P. (1975) 'Threats to identity in the large group', in L. Kreeger (ed.) *The Large Group: Dynamics and Therapy*, London: Constable.

Weick, K. (1982) 'Management of organizational change among loosely coupled elements', in Paul S. Goodman and Associates *Change in Organizations*, San Francisco: Jossey-Bass.

Weisbord, M. (1987) *Organizing and Managing for Dignity, Meaning and Community*, San Francisco: Jossey-Bass.

Wharton Center for Applied Research, Inc., (1992) *Approach to Panel Discussions*, Philadelphia: Wharton Center.

Winnicott, D. (1971) *Playing and Reality*, New York: Basic Books.

Chapter 3

The consulting organisation as an advanced learning system

David Wasdell

THE PROBLEM

Resistance to change is never more profoundly encountered than in the process of re-learning ways of learning, of changing the way we change. 'Doing' is repetitive. It sustains performance without change. Here non-learning is the order of the day. Learning leads to evolution of performance, to change and development in the cycle of activity. Such a shift often meets with resistance even though the patterns or means of learning remain reassuringly constant. Intervene in the learning system to change those underlying patterns, and anxiety may well escalate. Learning to learn is a fraught activity with powerful built-in reactions tending to restore learning behaviour to previously known processes. This dynamic conservatism is emerging as the critical constraint in the development of advanced learning systems in organisational life. It emerges at every level of the system, from individual to global corporation, and is endemic in every form of organisation.

The consulting organisation is not immune! With attention focused on client systems, it is all too easy to become unaware of the quality and order of learning being modelled by individual consultants or the organisational systems to which they belong. This failure to 'walk the talk' is evidence of lack of integrity in the consulting process, leading eventually to client disillusionment. It encourages the collusion between consultant and client. It dampens the consultant's ability to stay at the leading edge of the profession, limits the ability to sustain competence in a rapidly changing and evolving field and, in the longer term, threatens the ability of the consulting organisation to survive in an increasingly competitive world. In the accelerating complexity of today's world, the capacity of the consulting organisation to survive and thrive is determined by its ability to evolve as an advanced learning system.

The 'case study' used as a framework for this chapter is a composite account, based on real-life events spread over eight years and three continents. It is interspersed with theoretical 'interludes' which anchor the case material firmly in the emerging discipline of organisational learning. '*Inter Alia*' sections invite the reader to use the text as an opportunity for applied double-looped learning in their immediate situation.

CASE STUDY: IMPLICIT ASSUMPTIONS OF THE LEARNING ENVIRONMENT

Come with me into a small conference room in the training suite of a hotel. Screens, whiteboard and flipchart are all arrayed behind the presenter's table, itself bedecked with flowers, glasses, water carafe and crisp white cloth. Projectors stand like sentinels guarding the gap between presenter and workshop participants. They in turn are seated behind three sides of a continuous cloth-covered set of tables arranged as an open rectangle. The missing short side faces the presenter's table. There are a few flowers on the participants' desk, but unlike those on the top table, they are plastic. There is one carafe of water for every three participant places, each of which has a notepad and pencil. No notepad is provided for the presenter.

A video of the entry-dance as the twenty-seven members of a consulting firm took their places, would have revealed some intricate choreography. Power, gender, seniority, aggression and compliance all played their part as the crystal-structure formed and re-formed. Eventually the pattern was complete. The dominant male director of the firm sat in the centre of the short side of the rectangle, opposite the presenter. To his left the men were arranged in descending order of seniority. The co-director, a woman, sat in the central seat of the long side of the rectangle to his right, with the other women grouped around her. The most recent recruit to the team, a young trainee consultant, sat at the end of one long side, nearest the door. The gender split was not complete. One token male sat among the women and one token female sat among the men.

My brief for the day was to introduce the concepts of advanced learning systems and to enable this consulting organisation to apply the material to the dynamics of its own inner life. I was faced with a dilemma. Embedded in the setting was the expectation of a formal lecture, a familiar pattern of learning quite inconsistent with the content or the task of the day's workshop. I felt trapped in a lose/lose position. To collude with the expectations was to provide a role model of saying one thing while doing another. On the other hand, to run a dynamic workshop as I had planned would be a radical transgression of the cultural mores which could well alienate the whole group right at the start of the day. Some creative risk-taking was required.

When the introductions were complete, I moved to one of the long sides of the room and drew attention to the setting. Here was a living example of a learning system, more or less familiar, more or less effective.

Participants were invited to use it as an existential case study and to reflect in pairs on the implicit assumptions about the learning process, the lines of communication and participation, and the dynamics of the consulting team revealed in the seating pattern.

During the next half hour a fascinating 'learning system audit' began to emerge. Issues of power and authority were examined and the subtle signals of status were identified. Communication was expected to be mainly verbal with some illustrations. Notes were to be taken by participants, but the presenter had no need to make notes of his own. Information was directed one way with an assumption of presenter knowledge and participant ignorance. Even if information could be taken in and remembered in this way, there was little hope of its leading to significant change in practice. Dominant eye contact was between presenter and the male director, locked into a potential battle for superiority, while those with least experience sat out of the line of fire. The male power axis was at right angles to the female power line and the two directors crossed each other at almost every point of the process. From the presenter's position, the men sat on his right and related to his dominant verbal side, while the women were grouped on his left. They related more to his sub-dominant visual, intuitive and affective functions. Men were expected to speak while the women remained silent and held the emotions of the team. The basic assumption of the group (Bion 1961) was one of dependency with passing of tradition from active guru to passive disciple without necessarily changing the behaviour of either.

These were institutional patterns of learning. The power dynamics were familial and familiar. The adult–infant transactions were embedded in the formal educational setting. Learning skills were learned in the home and reinforced year after year in school and university (Senge 1992). They remained unexamined, almost unexaminable, since change at this level would involve reworking profoundly entrenched behaviour shot through with deep feelings of dependency and loyalty, fear and guilt. It also raised implications for transformation of dynamically conservative educational institutions at every level of society. Conserving the mores of the learning system sedated the felt anxiety about the unknown and so, paradoxically, reduced the possibility of learning.

By taking this approach the group had started on the path of 'double-loop' learning. The first step was to become aware of the learning processes in operation, to make conscious the implicit assumptions of the learning system. The second step was to change them.

Inter alia I

At this moment you are reading a book. It is a learning process designed to transfer verbal information from author to reader using skills of visual speech-pattern recognition. That is a way of learning which you learned very early in life, possibly at home even before you started school, though it has developed significantly since then. How do you read now? What changes have there been in your reading skills over the last five years? Are there any ways in which your take-up and application of information from the printed page could become more effective? Perhaps you have already tried speed-reading or even photo-reading, increasing the reading rate while improving retention and comprehension. Take a couple of seconds to scan the next page, letting your eyes roam across the text as if it were a picture. Now continue reading and you may well find the material feels somehow familiar. The visual brain centres are already processing the meaning and subsequent input through the verbal centres reinforces the learning. This mode of double-hemisphere reading with a time-lapse between inputs also helps to transfer the material from short to long-term memory (Rose 1985).

The shift from passive to interactive reading opens up a whole new range of possibilities. Use a pencil, pen or high-lighter to mark key points in the text. The neuro-muscular activity reinforces learning and strengthens memory. Engage in critical dialogue with the author, making notes on the page, dictating key quotes and recording your own comments. Open a learning-log folder on computer in which to enter not only important content and your own responses, but also to generate action and application agendas which can be incorporated into work programmes with a planned time-frame and review procedure. Set up a learning contract with a colleague to review recent reading, articulate new understanding, commit to implementation and support each other in action.

Meanwhile, you are still reading a book, except that now you are also becoming more aware of the learning processes being employed and beginning to explore ways of improving them. You have entered the world of double-loop learning.

CASE STUDY CONTINUED: ENCOUNTERING CONSTRAINTS

Back in the conference room there was general agreement that the implicit learning system needed urgent reform if the consulting organisation were to gain the greatest benefit from the day's work. I suggested that the team could re-design the learning system for optimum performance while I left the room and let them get on with it for ten minutes. On my return nothing had apparently changed, yet everything was different. Everyone was still sitting in exactly the same place. No decisions had been reached and no action taken. Each consultant had different ideas about the changes to be made. Consensus about the need for change had fragmented into multiple polarities reflecting the wide variety of preferred learning styles among the members. Attempts by one director to impose a single uniform solution had been blocked by the other director who insisted on a more consultative and systemic form of leadership. The simple battle of the sexes was complicated by conflict between consultants whose dominant learning modes were verbal or visual, activity-based or affect-driven. Another polarity emerged around the preference for content-based learning as opposed to experiential or process-oriented work.

The event had lifted the stone of denial and repression and revealed the seething interpersonal and inter-subgroup dynamics of the team. The outcome was stasis – the preservation of the status quo. At a psychodynamic level the process could be interpreted as collusional maintenance of the defences against anxiety in the face of the fear of the unknown. At another level the conflicting power relations of the team were exposed. The balanced, defensive stalemate effectively aborted creativity and innovation, risk-taking and learning as an organisation. It was a culture which prohibited double-loop learning. It also mirrored the defensive dynamics encountered in client organisations when consultants tried to introduce processes of advanced learning systems. Competence in resolving this impasse within the dynamics of the consultant organisation was essential if the consultants were to have any hope of enabling second-order learning in client systems (Pedler et al., 1991).

Beyond uniformity

The team prided itself on its multi-disciplinary composition with skills ranging from management mentoring and team-building to accountancy, from clinical psychology and group relations training to systems simulation and information technology application. The client portfolio reflected a similar variety from tiny high-tech innovatory enterprises, through business and commerce, multi-national corporations and voluntary organisations, to educational institutions and high level military strategy training. Rich diversity was a team strength, yet, perhaps reinforced by the difficulties in handling complexity, the team was trapped in an oppressive culture of uniformity when it came to the dynamics of organisational learning.

Transforming that culture was an essential priority if the team were to develop as a learning system. The task was to introduce an awareness and celebration of differences and then to build a learning community with high levels of differentiation supported by equally strong processes of integration. As a first step the consultants were invited to build supportive threes which incorporated the highest possible level of difference, taking into account gender, age, experience, social and educational background and field discipline. Within those micro-teams, each person was offered the opportunity to identify some of the most powerful and effective learning experiences of their life, to describe them to their partners and then to collaborate in analysing why those particular processes had been so effective.

SOME THEORETICAL BACKGROUND

Maps and models must never be confused with reality, but they can help to gain an overview and give greater confidence in navigating new territory. An analytic model of the domain of learning systems provides a framework of theoretical understanding. With its roots in differential calculus, it offers a map that begins to make sense of the complexity of real-life experience. It can help us to locate our perspective and to perceive more clearly the kinds of learning processes at work in the organisations and institutions of our everyday life.

In open-systems analysis (Wasdell 1993), an enterprise or organisation is represented as a bounded field set within an environment. As an open system, the enterprise interacts with its environment *via* a series of inputs and outputs, while the boundary itself marks the differentiation between inside and outside. Within the boundary certain processes are applied to the inputs, transforming them before export across the boundary in exchange for rewards of money and other resources which enable the enterprise to survive and continue its task (Figure 3.1). In this basic model the operational system is seen as constant, unchanging and non-adaptive. Performance is repetitive and there are no feedback loops which might generate change. Such a rigid system can only survive in an unchanging environment.

It is extraordinary that this non-learning system is still offered as an ideal goal by some managers and consultants who try to perfect an operating procedure, product, intervention or training programme with a view to its continuance without further modification. One senior Organisational Development (OD) consultant remarked that he had learned everything he needed to know about Organisation Development and was now only concerned to ensure that younger consultants entering the field should 'get up to speed as quickly as possible'. Another director of a consulting firm assured me that 'it would take a traumatic shock' to make him aware of any incompetence in the way he carried out his profession. In a changing world such high-performance, low-learning behaviour is doomed.

Learning, even at its most simple, requires monitoring of system performance within the environment and some feedback procedure linked to an effective performance-modifying mechanism. Monitoring may be uni-dimensional, as in the measurement of room temperature, fed back to a radiator *via* a thermostat. On the other hand it may be highly complex and multi-dimensional with constant measurement of many variables in the environment and in the input, operating and output processes of the system

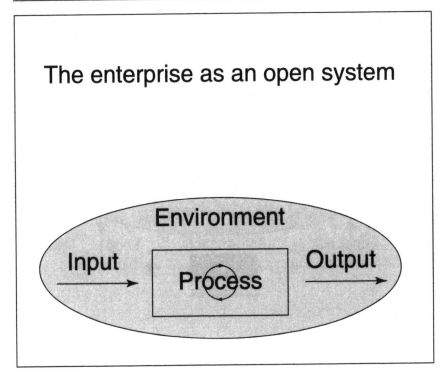

Figure 3.1 The enterprise as an open system

(Figure 3.2). The information, interrelated through a network of sophisticated non-linear linkages, generates a complex set of system-modifying
interventions. The system becomes adaptive, learning from its performance
within a changing environment. This is a 'single loop' learning system in
which, once the learning procedures are in place, they are themselves fixed
and non-adaptive.

The second generation learning system treats this non-adaptive,
single-loop process as the operating system. Monitoring is of the learning
environment, the monitoring procedures, the information-processing and
feedback mechanisms. Interventions are generated which transform the
basic learning skills of the enterprise, the effects of which are in turn fed
back to the first order learning loop. This 'double loop' learning system
(Figure 3.3) is capable of continuous development of its learning
procedures. It is learning to learn better. Its operating procedures are far
more flexible and adaptable and as a result, the enterprise can survive and
thrive in conditions of faster-moving environmental change. However, once
in place the double loop learning system is itself fixed and non-adaptive.

It is of course possible to improve the way the system learns to learn.
Now the double loop processes themselves come under scrutiny and are

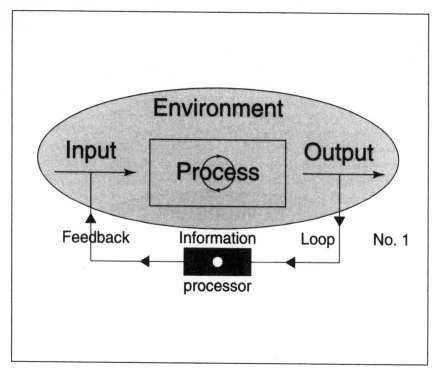

Figure 3.2 Single loop learning

subject to monitoring and transformation. The enterprise has evolved into a 'triple loop' learning system (Figure 3.4). The powerful protocols of this third generation learning system enable the enterprise to out-perform single loop and double loop organisations and to survive in conditions of environmental rapidation which spell catastrophe to less adaptable organisms.

The rapidly evolving field of information technology has made us familiar with the concept of multi-generational development. The products of one generation are used as tools to develop the products of the next. Levels of learning system are now beginning to evolve in similar ways, leading to the emergence of fourth generational, fifth generational, and higher order systems (Figure 3.5). To survive and thrive an enterprise needs to operate with a learning system that is at least one order higher than that of the change processes in the environment. As smooth patterns of environmental change break down into conditions of extreme complexity, unpredictability, turbulence and chaos (Trisoglio 1995), so organisations have to generate the capacity for 'real-time' response requiring an appropriately advanced and sophisticated level of learning system.

The map or model developed so far offers a way of analysing the level of

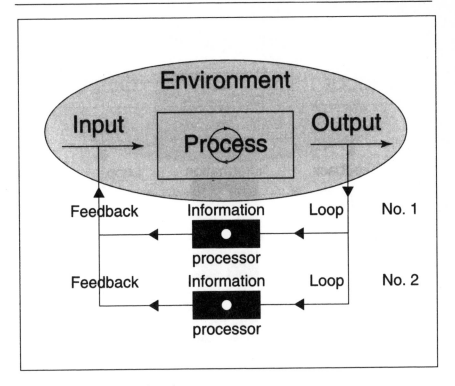

Figure 3.3 Double loop learning

learning system in operation. It also provides a framework in which to examine the processes of shift from one level of learning system to the next. In practice, at any given time different elements of any enterprise or organisation may be operating at different levels of learning. Coincidentally any given element of the enterprise may operate at different levels of learning at different points in time. Management of an advanced learning system requires diagnostic monitoring of the levels and processes of learning throughout the organisation and their evaluation against a backdrop of information about the levels of change in the environments of each element or sub-system. Orchestration and fine tuning of the learning system for optimum performance will also take into account expected future environmental conditions of the organisation. The timing of interventions in the learning system will depend on the dynamics of level-shift. Where resistance and dynamic conservatism are intense the learning curve of the level-shift is flattened and the lead time required for level-change is proportionately longer.

If we consider the client/consultant partnership as a single complex system, then the consultant intervention may be seen as a bought-in resource enabling management to improve the performance of the single loop

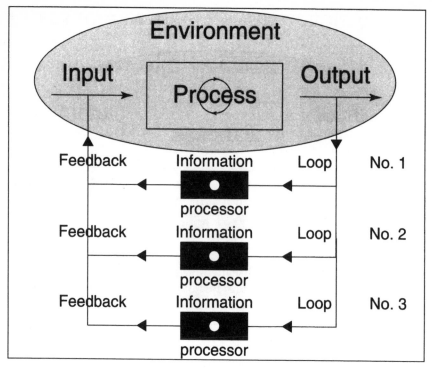

Figure 3.4 Triple loop learning

learning of the organisation. From the client perspective, the intervention is part of their second-order learning system. From the point of view of the consultant organisation, the intervention is an element of their own operating system. First-order learning for the consultant organisation improves the delivery of second-order learning for the client and is therefore equivalent to triple-loop learning for the client system. Where the consultant organisation moves up-level to second, third, fourth or higher orders of learning system, the client enterprise gains access to the resources of equivalently higher learning with respect to its own operational system.

By way of illustration we can now categorise my intervention with the consultant organisation as catalysing change in its learning system from single loop to double loop. As a process-consultant, I was concerned that my client should internalise skills for sustained second-order learning without continuous dependence on external resources. My work represents my own operating level which is in turn subject to review and critical development (my single loop learning). Improving the way in which that review and development is carried out constitutes second-order learning for me, fourth-order learning for the consultant organisation and sixth-order learning with respect to the operating level of their clients.

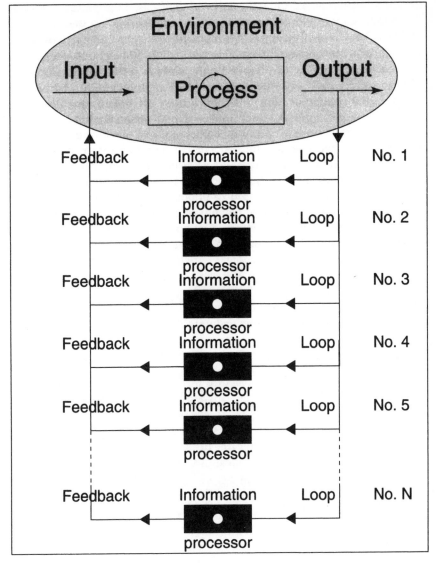

Figure 3.5 Advanced learning system

CASE STUDY CONTINUED: TOWARDS HOLISTIC LEARNING

When the micro-teams of consultants re-convened, two concentric circles of chairs were created in the centre of the room. One person from each triad took a seat in the inner ring with the other members in close support behind them. A rich sharing of a diversity of learning experiences followed. For some, intense learning was always in relationship to one particular individual or in a small group, others learned best while reading in isolation. A few took in and applied information through formal lectures given by an eminent expert, one or two learned only while in action, often alongside a more experienced consultant, in a kind of apprenticeship relationship. While verbal communication, whether written or spoken, was dominant for most, others required visual images if real understanding was to be achieved. Action-learning, group-dynamics and role play were crucial for a couple of the consultants, while one or two others insisted that learning without a high emotional content was without real meaning for them.

As the team reflected on its experience it became clear that any initiative of organisational learning needed to honour the wide spread of learning styles represented in team membership (Rose 1985). A culture that could celebrate diversity began to emerge. Not only were differences in learning style acknowledged, but a few members began to explore the possibility that widening their own palette might enrich their learning competence in a move towards holistic learning. We were reminded of the need to expand the ancient Chinese proverb: 'I hear and I forget, I see and I remember, I do and I understand' to include 'I feel and I make it my own', so adding emotional tone and personal ownership to the dimensions of learning.

Building the learning community

The culture and relationship structure of the consultant organisation had begun to change. It was no longer a fixated group of individuals caught in an aridly polarised power struggle. It was becoming more accepting of differences and supportive of risk-taking. Each member was being recognised as a potential source of learning for all other partners in the team. From uniformity and oppression, the culture was shifting towards differentiation and integration. The rearrangement of the formal furnishing of the lecture room provided a powerful symbol of the overthrow of old cultural norms. The collaborative activity, laughter and emotional release which accompanied the change spoke louder than words, locking the transformation into shared group history.

The application of Kurt Lewin's force-field analysis (Lewin 1951) to the development of double-loop learning gave a creative opportunity for the team to explore different learning modes in practice. The team was invited to monitor what happened to levels of energy, attention and information assimilation as the exercise progressed. First came a verbal presentation of the theory with minimal hand movements. It was entitled 'Force-field analysis and the release of constraints', and went something as follows:

> The dynamic equilibrium of double-loop learning at any given time in the life of an organisation can be seen as the result of the interplay of

those forces driving the development in a positive direction and other constraints resisting it. Positive take-up of second order learning tends to activate an increase in the constraint system so aborting the development and returning the organisation to its original condition of dynamic equilibrium. Significant long-term change in the desired direction cannot be achieved by interventions that are limited to the positive force-field. It is essential to identify the constraint system and intervene to release it. It is also vital to analyse the feedback loops which link positive development with increase in resistance and to uncouple these mechanisms of dynamic conservatism within the learning system.

It was fascinating to watch the rapt attention of a few contrasted with the wide yawns of others. Four consultants gazed out of the window or doodled on their notepads with bored expressions on their faces. There were three aggressive interruptions asking for clarification, criticising a particular point or proclaiming that the material was 'old hat' and not worth repeating. The culture changed from active inter-dependency to passive dependency shot through with aggressive counter-dependency. We were then able to identify the responses with the preferred learning styles of the people concerned.

Next, the same material was presented in visual form with an animated overhead projection cell constructed with cardboard, pins, rubber-bands and string. The combination of visual and verbal modes held the focused attention of all but the action-learners in the group.

Finally we moved out of the lecture room into the foyer of the training centre. A circle of rope some two metres in diameter was provided and each consultant invited to grasp it firmly. The instruction was for each person to try and move the rope ring towards them while making sure it did not move towards anyone else! There was a multi-directional tug-of-war and the circle locked solid in dynamic equilibrium. Stepping into the centre of the circle I announced myself as their new manager and indicated the direction of development in which I planned to take the organisation. Taking hold of the rope I started to push with all my strength. The circle moved a few centimetres, then went into reverse and returned to its original position. There were roars of laughter as consultants recognised, some with wry smiles and painful memories, similar reactions to directive and authoritarian attempts to introduce organisational change in client systems.

Conference centre staff began to get caught up in the psychodrama, so one of them was invited to join me in the centre of the ring. We obviously needed stronger management. Having agreed our strategic direction we both lunged at the rope in concert only to find the dynamic conservatism was overwhelming. The ring was immovable! The assistant manager was fired on the spot for gross incompetence. Two new outsiders were brought in to act as team-building consultants. Most of their interventions had no effect whatsoever, some served to polarise the ring as anti-consultant dynamics built up in opposition. Eventually they too were fired and the organisation faced its despair of ever being able to cope with change.

At this point I left the centre of the ring and came round behind the consultants who were pulling against the direction of development. They represented the constraints in the force-field. Changing the ground-rules of the exercise I encouraged them to ease up and relax the tension on the rope while still urging those on the far side of the ring to keep pulling. The whole system began to move smoothly in the positive developmental direction. It accelerated towards the end of the foyer accompanied by the cheers and applause of the by now not inconsiderable group of intrigued onlookers.

Stimulated by the strenuous physical exercise and bubbling over with insights, comments and applications, team members grouped together in working threes. They were invited to review the process of learning, comparing the effectiveness of the action-based mode with that of the preceding visual and verbal presentations. Then they moved on to reflect on the content communicated and discovered as the modified force-field analysis was applied to the change from single loop to double loop learning. The rope-ring exercise offered a powerful mirror not only to their own experience in the workshop, but also to the dynamics frequently encountered in their engagements with client organisations.

The triads were self-selecting on the grounds of least familiar relation-ship, greatest diversity and differences in preferred learning style. Their final task was to identify and analyse the constraints and resistance to double loop learning whether personally as individuals, or corporately in the team as a whole. Using their own and each others' resources and experience they began searching for reasons why it was so hard to unlearn familiar patterns of learning and to learn to learn in new ways. Time passed almost unconsciously as the exploration went deeper and deeper. Almost without noticing they had begun to build a more effective learning community with high levels of differentiation, though as yet the integrative processes had not started to emerge.

Inter alia II

While the consultant team is busy, it might be worth looking back to *Inter Alia I* to review whether reading about more effective ways of reading made any difference to the way you read the rest of this chapter. If changes did result, are they still in operation, steadily improving, or have you returned to the familiar skills you were using at the beginning? How well does the 'rope-ring simulator' apply to the dynamics of re-learning to read? Can you identify the constraints which tend to return behaviour to old patterns, and, even more importantly, can you find ways of releasing them, so liberating movement into effective second-order learning? If there has been no significant change and you are concerned to enable your own consultant organisation to develop into a more advanced learning system, why are you still reading this chapter! What more effective strategies of learning can you devise in order to achieve your goal?

THEORY OF DESIGN OF LEARNING SYSTEMS

Some characteristic marks of an advanced learning system are already beginning to emerge from the case study, while others need to be introduced. For the sake of theoretical clarity these characteristics, or 'elements of design', can be separated into two fields. The first addresses the set of cultural norms or values which provide an essential milieu if advanced learning is to take root and thrive. The second focuses on the necessary structures and processes involved. Here the learning functions and the organisational framework which supports them begins to take shape.

Cultural norms and values of the advanced learning system

Effective second-order learning needs a culture which sees information, skills and experience of others as a resource for learning rather than as a threat to status. The imposition of uniformity is resisted and diversity is valued. Different learning styles are recognised and used. The culture supports and aims to develop holistic learning, both individually and corporately and welcomes the discovery of incompetence as the starting-point of learning. The climate of the organisation will be one in which creativity, innovation and risk taking are encouraged and the identification and release of constraints takes precedence over the reinforcement of positive drives. The culture will utilise the power of co-operative learning in community, while operating with a high degree of differentiation and integration in the team structure. Within such a culture, the selection of leadership will tend to favour those who are fast-track learners over and above inflexibly defended performers, however competent they may be. The whole system will be permeated by a culture which fosters the continuous improvement of the learning process at every level.

A value set of this nature defines the field parameters which enable delineation and selection of optimal structural elements within the design of an advanced learning system.

Emerging principles: structures and functions of an advanced learning system

The detailed structures and protocols for optimum learning performance of any given consultant organisation will depend on the precise circumstances of that specific system. They will also evolve over time as the circumstances change and as the order of learning systems matures. Certain general principles, modified by the situation-specific variables, can now be described.

For instance, high levels of participation, independent of the number of consultants in the organisation, require the multiplication of parallel-processing of micro-teams as an essential element of design. Furthermore, development of high levels of trust, essential for fostering risk-taking and creativity, sharing and vulnerability, appears to be optimal in groups of three, within which interdependence can be enhanced by role-exhange and the skills of co-consultancy.

Holistic learning harnesses all four dimensions of communication in each micro-team. Spoken and written modes will be accompanied by the use of imaging, art forms and symbolisation. Acting out, psychodrama, role-play and attention to body-language both inner and outer will be encouraged. Feelings and emotional reactions, so often repressed in formal education and training, will be welcomed and supported within certain agreed boundaries of safety. Co-operative exploration and utilisation of all resources for learning will be distributed across the team membership, with the learning inputs shared with the whole team as and when appropriate.

Incorporation of new members and the strengthening of the weakest relationships within the consultant team can be achieved by the dissolution and reconstitution of the micro-teams on a regular basis. Inter-triadic integration can be served by the meeting of representatives. It is even more effectively generated by some variation of a matrix design. The complexity and number of dimensions of the matrix will depend on the size of the consultant organisation. The aim is to establish an optimum set of feedback-loops between all elements of the matrix.

Structural design features are necessary but not sufficient. The learning processes also depend on the quality of feedback attainable within the system. Defensive and repressive filtering of critical signals will abort significant learning just as much as offensive use of criticism as ammunition in an inter-personal or inter-departmental war. As the learning system matures attention will increasingly be paid to the covert and unconscious dynamics of the organisation which constitute some of the most powerful constraints on the evolution of advanced learning systems.

Leadership of an advanced learning system calls for skills and procedures that are significantly different from those employed in the management of the operational level of the team. Competence requires that leaders not only 'walk the talk' by being fast-track learners open to second and higher-order learning in their own life and work, but also have skill in monitoring the learning system of the organisation and ability to facilitate the evolution of the system and to catalyse the learning processes within it (Hitt 1995).

Structures, functions and procedures are necessary but not sufficient parameters. Without the appropriate cultural norms and shared values, learning will be significantly inhibited. Conversely, no matter how benign and supportive the culture, learning will not take place at an optimal level unless it has a skeletal framework or structure and a clear, though evolving, set of functional procedures or protocols. The evolution of an advanced learning system requires the creative and complementary interplay of culture and structure, values and procedures, all of which must be open to examination, assessment and creative transformation.

Holding that theoretical framework in mind we can now return to the workshop to see how some of the principles began to emerge in practice.

CASE STUDY CONTINUED: EVOLVING THE MATRIX DESIGN

Nine parallel-processing triads had been at work seeking to identify and analyse the constraints and resistance to double-loop learning, whether personal or organisational. The first step towards integration of the material was to ask each member of the working triads to meet up with one member from each of the other micro-teams, so creating three parallel-processing small groups of nine members. Each group afforded an opportunity to work not only on the inter-personal dynamics of its members, but also on the integration of the inter-triad dynamics of the whole team. As each member shared the most significant learning of their micro-team, so the similarities and differences began to surface. Creative insight emerging from one individual in one triad became available to every member of the organisation. Problems identified by one triad could now be addressed by all. Every member began to be able to grasp the contribution of the team as a whole.

Returning to their basic triads, members were able to pool insights from all three small groups, representing the total input from the complete set of parallel-processing micro-teams. The triads were no longer comparatively isolated units but found themselves to be handling the inter-group dynamics of the whole organisation in parallel with each of the other threes. With the feedback loops firmly in place (Figure 3.6) the learning began to deepen and accelerate (Wasdell 1992). The information and creativity of all was available to each. Processing was however still being damped by the filtering and defences of individuals and of the subgroups in which they took part. The quality of the feedback loops was being experienced as a limiting factor in the learning of the matrix.

Constraints identified

Next the whole team gathered to share its findings and to review its process. One director identified the way he felt that admitting ignorance or a need to

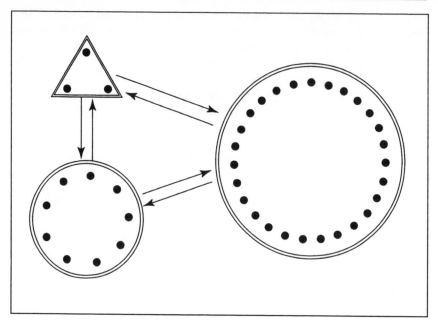

Figure 3.6 The matrix learning design

learn new skills was a threat to his status and undermined his authority in the organisation. His insecurity had not only inhibited his own learning but set a role-model for others and blocked the capacity of the organisation as a whole to gain new competencies. One or two younger members shared how their sense of dependency had made them devalue their own contribution and treat the senior consultants as almost omniscient, so colluding with the director's defences. One, in particular, fresh from a doctoral programme at a leading consultancy-training institute, had been withholding leading edge information from the team because she was aware of her comparative lack of hands-on experience in a client context.

A natural left-hander recalled how parents and teachers had forced the adoption of right-handed behaviour, leading to a whole range of learning difficulties. That opened the floodgates for the identification of experiences from birth and on into school and college which had encouraged learning patterns now identified as handicaps in the field of holistic learning. One dominant concern was the over-emphasis on the skills of verbal, linear, analytic communication together with the under-rating, indeed in some cases positive repression, of intuition, imagination, visualisation and multi-dimensional creativity. The splitting of cognitive functions into two fields with one set idealised and the other denigrated had set up impoverished norms for learning and communication within the organisation. It had also had the effect of down-grading the team's ability for problem solving, lateral thinking and creativity. The gender stereotyping of 'masculine' and 'feminine' functions had contributed to the conflicted projection into the roles of the male and female directors of the team.

With new learning seen as a threat, members had been discouraged from attending workshops and courses. Those who had still persevered had found that new skills or insights brought back to the team were not welcomed. The information technology specialist shared her frustration at the ignorance and resistance to learning of the team in this vital field. She was looking for ways of streamlining the administration and communication, and introducing systems simulation tools which could dramatically enhance the competencies of her colleagues.

The list of constraints continued. Some issues were quite facile, others brought a moment of awed silence as team members recognised the implications of what was being shared. As the constraints were identified and owned, the culture began to change into a more open, learning-oriented stance. The exercise led naturally into a team brainstorm of resources and protocols for learning, (see Table 3.1).

Application and implementation

Two weeks after the learning systems workshop, the group of consultants reconvened for half a day to put in hand the application of their experience. They used the matrix design of parallel-processing triads, small groups and plenary to generate an action programme, the aim of which was to ensure that the consultant organisation optimised its learning procedures including its ability to review and improve those procedures over time. They also decided to hold a second learning systems workshop in one year's time to review the implementation of the action plan, to identify the constraints which they had encountered during the year and to implement some elements of triple loop learning. The goal was to learn ways of improving their procedures for learning to learn both as individuals and as a team.

One outcome was that the organisation as a whole began to operate as a reflexive learning lab, learning from its own experience of trying to implement advanced learning systems. Those lessons and the practical experience gained were of great value in work with client systems, enabling the consultants to avoid mistakes and pitfalls which had already been encountered.

There we will have to take leave of the consultant team with whom we have travelled so far. Not that their process is complete or all the lessons learned, far from it. In a sense they have only just begun to open the door on the potential of advanced learning systems for the life of a consultant organisation. If the experience from other situations is anything to go by, their long-term success will depend on their ability to come to terms with the psychodynamics of transformation and integration – but that is another subject in its own right.

Table 3.1   Brainstormed resources for learning

- Literature search, including new books, field journals, papers, articles and abstracts. Significant material could be circulated round the team and when appropriate, become the focus of a group seminar.
- Improving the information technology of the organisation including the provision of lap-top computers for consultants working at remote client venues. Keeping in touch *via* e-mail and the possibility of referral and team conferencing gave each member access to the expertise of others, rather than feeling isolated and limited to their own knowledge and experience.
- Monitoring of world-wide web sites on the Internet giving access to new research in the field of organisational learning and allied subjects (ENFOLD 1996). Material could be fed into the IT system of the organisation and be used for reference or in the seminar programme.
- Attendance by members of the organisation at outside seminars, workshops, short courses and national and international conferences. This would not only alert the team to new developments in the field, but help to internalise advances in the competence and skill-base of consultancy. It was pointed out that special attention would have to be paid to the processes of sharing the information and applying the learning through the team.
- Release of some members for study leading to higher qualifications, particularly in courses with direct application to the specific consultancy focus of the team. It was also recognised that there would be spin off to the organisation's learning if some members were encouraged to write, lecture, run workshops or conduct consultancy-training events in addition to working with client organisations.
- Introduction of de-briefing groups and shadow-consulting as normal procedures. This would give each consultant resources to review and learn from engagements with the support and creative criticism of colleagues.
- Establishment of a culture in which it was expected that every member of the team would be engaged in a process of life-long learning in pursuit of best practice and professional excellence.
- Putting in place effective feedback loops which would enable continuous improvement of the administrative in-house functions of the team.
- Use of professional supervision from outside the organisation with particular attention to the issues of personal psychodynamic development, and the raising of awareness of unconscious processes in the interpersonal relationships of the team and in the dynamics of the organisation as a whole.
- Holding occasional in-house dynamics workshops which would provide an opportunity not only to become more conscious of the group's own process, but also serve as a learning-lab in which to work on issues of transference and counter-transference between the team and its client organisations.
- Formalisation of a learning-support-and-review matrix structure for the whole organisation with built-in commitment to monitoring and improving its own learning-review procedures.

CONCLUSION

On our first encounter with the consulting organisation, we met a group of highly competent individual performers whose relationships were locked in defensive conflict and whose learning was at a low ebb. As a team they were unconscious of their dynamics and unaware of the blocked and limited nature of their learning procedures. We followed them through a learning system audit, an identification of different learning styles and an uncomfortable exposure of some of the dysfunctional inter-personal dynamics at work. Slowly the organisation developed a new structure of parallel-processing triads, explored new learning styles in practice and began to identify and release the constraints which blocked its capacity to learn new ways of learning. Integration of micro-teams began with a double circle of representatives before evolving into an interactive matrix, its learning supported and accelerated through a network of feedback loops.

Between the lines, we struggle (using 'Inter Alia') with the limitation of learning from the printed word, while its theoretical 'interludes' introduced an analysis of different orders of learning system from the most simple to the more advanced. They also summarised some of the needed values, norms, structures and procedures required for the development of the consulting organisation as an advanced learning system. The case leaves open the worrying possibility that as yet unconscious constraints and defences would emerge with power to block and reverse the progress made by the consultancy. How would the new challenges be met? Could the emergent constraints continue to be identified and released or would the organisation succumb in collusion, leaving further advance to other more open teams who would eventually take their place in a changing world?

As the consultant to the organisation I am left reviewing my own role as a catalyst to the organisation's attempt to move from single-loop to double-loop learning and beyond. I know there are better ways of doing it, and I will never go about it in the same way again! But then, that's learning.[1]

NOTE

1   As part of my commitment to the learning process, I would welcome any comments, reflections or suggestions from readers of this chapter. Please contact me at: URCHIN, Meridian House, 115 Poplar High Street, London E14 0AE, Tele: +44(0)171–987 3600, Fax: +44 (0)171–515 8627, e-mail: 106151.532@compuserve.com.

REFERENCES AND FURTHER READING

Bion, W. R. (1961) *Experiences in Groups*, London: Tavistock Publications. Although dated, this classical analysis of unconscious emotional assumptions in group behaviour is still relevant.

ENFOLD (1996) The newly established European Network for Organisational Learning Development, is already active on the Internet with its own established website, http: //www.orglearn.nl

Hitt, W. D. (1995) 'The learning organisation: some reflections on organisational renewal', *Leadership and Organisational Development Journal*, 16(8): 17–25. This short paper addresses some of the issues of leadership in advanced learning systems.

Lewin, K. (1951) *Field Theory in Social Sciences*, Chicago: University of Chicago Press. Although his analysis has been superseded by our understanding of multidimensional, non-linear complex systems, many of Lewin's powerful insights are still applicable in more simple contexts.

Pedler, M., Burgoyne, J. and Boydell, T. (1991) *The Learning Company*, London: McGraw-Hill. Affords a basic introduction to the development of organisational learning in a variety of client systems.

Rose, C. (1985) *Accelerated Learning*, Aylesbury: Accelerated Learning Systems Ltd. Popular overview with excellent research bibliography. Pages 152ff. introduce the field of preferred learning styles. Up to date access to field literature, training workshops etc. in the area of accelerated learning and reading skills can be obtained from SEAL (Society for Effective Affective Learning), c/o 49 Henley Road, Ipswich, Suffolk, IP1 3SJ.

Senge, P. (1992) *The Fifth Discipline*, London: Century Business. Essential reading for this whole field. In particular he offers some penetrating insight into the dysfunctional effects of formal education.

Tapscott, D. (1995) *The Digital Economy*, New York: McGraw-Hill. Offers a window onto the implications of leading edge developments in information technology for learning systems of the future.

Trisoglio, A. (1995) 'Managing complexity', the Strategy and Complexity Seminar, Working Paper, No. 1., London: LSE. An excellent overview of the contribution of the field of complexity to Peter Senge's world of non-linearity, chaos and adaptive systems.

Wasdell, D. (1992) 'Meridian matrix, experiential learning for tomorrow's world', London: Unit for Research into Changing Institutions. This offers a more detailed description of the application of matrix structures to the task of consultancy training.

—— (1993) 'Learning systems and the management of change', *International Organisation Development Association Journal*, 1(1): 47–73. Gives a more detailed exposition with a wider range of case material.

Chapter 4

Internal consultancy

Raphe Berenbaum

THE PROBLEM

The growth in management consultancy in recent years has been accompanied by a steady increase in the development of consulting capabilities which are internal to organisations. There are obvious advantages in having an effective internal consulting capability, but many organisations have found this difficult to achieve. The use of consultants to tackle problems in organisations is well established. In many ways, however, the very rationales which are put forward in favour of using consultants, would seem to negate the idea of such consultants being themselves members of the organisation.

In particular, one of the principal reasons for calling in consultants is the belief that properly selected consultants will be able to bring in expertise and experience which is *not* available in the organisation (Bloomfield and Daniels 1995: 26) and will provide a fresh view of the issues, uninhibited by assumptions and knowledge about 'the way things work'. Similarly, coming from outside should enable the consultants to give advice without any hidden agenda slanted (or perceived to be slanted) by their own motivation within the organisation. For these reasons the consultants are likely to be listened to as serious contributors to solving problems. While, if any additional reason were needed for paying attention to their views, it is difficult to dismiss proposals which have been as expensive to obtain as is usually the case!

All of these arguments may seem to militate against using internal consultants who, however competent, cannot easily be seen as bringing a fresh, unbiased view and expertise from outside, may well be subject to internal pressures and motivations and will have less inherent credibility with senior management. Despite this, there are clear advantages from the use of an in-house consulting capability which have led many major organisations to establish such groups.

Among the obvious advantages to internal consultants is the cost. The *average* billing expected from a management consultant with a major consultancy is well in excess of £100,000 per year. It should be possible to employ competent in-house consultants for a substantially lower cost.

Then there is continuity. The ongoing availability of the internal consultant to guide implementation of recommendations and to use his or her experience across the organisation cannot be counted upon with external consultants. A recent survey of the effectiveness of management consultants in Government showed that 60 per cent of the projects reviewed were not implemented (HMSO 1994).

From a learning viewpoint, using external consultants makes it harder for skills to be enhanced across the organisation. While they may bring new skills and competencies there is less incentive for these to be shared in a 'learning organisation'. Internal consultants also have an advantage over external consultants during continuous change. Seeing change as an ongoing way of life rather than the older style 'melt, reshape, freeze' approach, once propagated by consultants requires more than intermittent projects directed by outsiders.

Moreover, there are other issues for the external consultant, which may represent undesirable characteristics for the client organisation and which can be more readily avoided by the internal consultant. These issues are inherent in the nature of a professional consultancy which must work within the constraints of achieving and sustaining income and profitability.

A consulting engagement may be performed effectively by external consultants in that the outcome accords with the terms of reference, and yet yield unsatisfactory results for the client organisation. Many Business Process Re-engineering (BPR) projects have fallen into this category; the findings of the studies and the plans for re-engineering have looked sound but the actual implementation process has been slow and ineffective. In many cases this has been traced to the limited involvement of the client management and staff in the studies resulting in little real understanding of what must be done to achieve successful implementation (Hall *et al.* 1995: 37).

All successful consultancies are driven by the need to build on engagements to contract for further work; typically, this is a key measure of the successful project manager. Consultancies rely on such continuation work because the success rate in the expensive business of bidding for contracts with new clients is usually small. This is another factor which inhibits the involvement and training of client staff in ways which will enable them to take over full responsibility for follow-on work and implementation of the findings of the study. Another issue is a willingness to undertake large-scale studies whether or not these are needed.

A well-respected firm of consultants undertook a study to establish and agree the Critical Success Factors (CSFs) for a financial services company. After initial work with the Chief Executive and explanations to the Directors, this involved a series of in-depth interviews with each of the members of the board. Each of these interviews was aimed at eliciting the individual Director's ideas of the CSFs. Repeat interviews were needed where major discrepancies were identified and the process culminated in the production of a report and presentation to the board at which the final list was approved after the opportunity for further discussion. The process took six weeks elapsed time and ten weeks of consultant time.

This may be contrasted with the process described by Hardaker and Ward (1988: 142) which has been extensively used in internal consulting. This also began with discussions with the Chief Executive but continues with a collective briefing to a board meeting and culminates with a one or two day working session by the board, facilitated by two consultants, which reaches agreement on the CSFs. In fact, this latter technique is more likely to achieve real consensus than the interviewing approach – which is often likely to result in the taking of entrenched views before the opportunity for discussion with colleagues can take place.

There is nothing unethical about the external consulting approach; it is simply that it is commercially very unattractive for a consultancy to employ and have available senior consultants, with the necessary skills to facilitate a difficult board meeting, and to use them for only one or two days at a time.

The advantages of coming fresh to the issues are correctly stressed by external consultants. However, a case can also be made for the advantages of the internal consultant's approach which will require less time to gain an in-depth understanding of the organisation – and the particular niche of the industry which it occupies. This will already exist with the internal consultant so that a much smaller lead time will often be needed before serious work can begin. These factors are summarised in Table 4.1.

Table 4.1 Comparing internal and external consultants

Factor	External consultant	Internal consultant
New knowledge and experience	Yes	No
Fresh view of how things work	Yes	No
Personal bias	No	Maybe
Credibility	Yes	Maybe
Cost	High	Low/medium
Continuity	Unlikely	Yes
Share skills	Unlikely	Yes
Minimum effort	No	Yes

THE STRUCTURE OF AN INTERNAL CONSULTANCY

If the decision is taken to set up an internal consultancy, experience shows that its structure and responsibilities must be carefully defined if it is to be effective. This section examines the major issues which must be resolved in order to achieve this. The suggested ideals may not be wholly practicable but, at least, clear decisions must be made about these issues. It will be seen that some of the issues have parallels in independent consultancies, but the concerns and approaches are inevitably different inside the organisation. The five issues, illustrated in Figure 4.1, are: reporting line, confidentiality, recruitment, relationship with external consultancies, and funding.

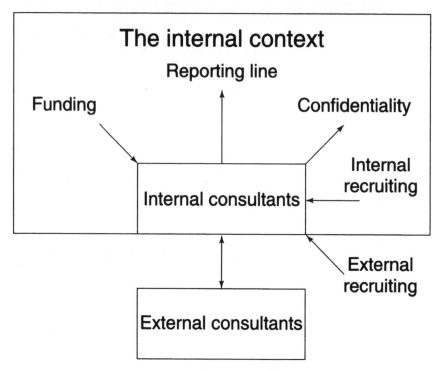

Figure 4.1 Internal and external factors affecting the internal consultancy

Reporting line for internal consultancies

Examination of some of the alternative places and titles of internal consulting groups shows a bewilderingly large range. It includes consultancy services, operation and manpower development, productivity services, organisation and management development, change management, business process improvement, management practice, internal business consulting, efficiency studies, strategy office, business strategy group and internal business O&M consulting.

Similarly, the reporting line and position shows great variation. In a very few cases the head of the unit reports directly to the Chief Executive, but the usual line goes to a departmental head. The most common departments are finance, human resources or information systems. Naturally, each of these carries its own baggage of expectation. The financial emphasis will be perceived to be on cost savings and on controls (the internal consultancy is not infrequently a carry over from an internal audit function, which has its own problems, and the information systems group will be seen as driving computer solutions to all problems. Perhaps the most 'neutral' function is based within human resources and especially when associated with a training function.

A free-standing function which is not part of any of the traditional departments avoids the suspicions described above. This implies a very high level of reporting – probably to a Chief Executive or to an overall Chief Operating Officer. This has the advantages of (1) perceived neutrality – there should be no suspicion that a particular function is empire-building – and (2) immediate visibility with a high level of sponsorship. The level of the reporting line and the related level of the manager of the consulting group is also obviously significant; there will always be some desire on the part of departmental heads to influence or ameliorate the findings of a consulting study. The relative levels of the consulting manager and the departmental head concerned will determine the effectiveness of any pressure exerted.

The Chief Executive of a major UK company established a modestly sized consulting group (ten to twelve people) which reported to him personally, although the level of the manager was substantially lower than that of other reportees to the Chief Executive. This group enjoyed considerable success and a good reputation for several years but when the Chief Executive became the Chairman of the company a new Chief Executive was appointed. He devolved the reporting line of the consultant group (to the Information Systems Director) and the group rapidly lost credibility and, in fact, was disbanded within a year.

Confidentiality

An effective external consultant will always ensure that there is a clear agreement on the confidentiality of both the study findings and of any material which may be disclosed during the study. Normally, the sponsor of the study will expect to have access to all the material and to determine how and what will be made known elsewhere in the organisation. In principle, the same guideline should apply to the internal group. However, there will typically be perceived to be a 'third party' involved in an internal consulting study as is illustrated by the following example.

A major financial institution expanded the activities of its internal audit function to provide a wider range of management consulting, but the activity retained its reporting line and title. Consultants coming into a department were still seen in an audit role – that is, as having a primary mission to find errors or bad practice and to report these to the central financial control function. The relationships with the consultants were largely adversarial and it was extremely difficult to convince operating departments that the consulting role was anything other than that of espionage.

This was an issue of structure as well as confidentiality, but the history of non-confidentiality played a large part in the problems which arose. It is important to the success of an internal consultancy that a departmental or functional head should feel able to call in the consultants secure in the knowledge that he or she will receive their reports and will be as much in control of the dissemination of findings and recommendations as if they had commissioned an external organisation.

Recruitment

There are two important decisions to be made. Should the consultants be hired internally or some or all externally? Should the internal hires, especially, be permanent members of the consulting group or on limited assignments?

If a specific area of business expertise is needed but is not available in the organisation then there will be no alternative to external hiring. However, bringing in experienced consultants to head the group or to play a major part in it requires careful handling.

First, the cultures and attitudes of consultancies are different from most business organisations. There are many examples of consultants being brought in, successfully, to senior line management positions and many unsuccessful examples! A move into an internal consultancy may be more difficult because the changes of behaviour are more subtle. It may be harder for the experienced consultant to appreciate the additional difficulties faced in setting up and completing assignments while lacking the clout and perhaps the prestige which is readily accorded to the external consultant.

A more immediately practical difficulty is the discrepancy in salary scales between typical successful consultants and most non-consulting businesses and organisations. Management consulting is a high reward, high risk activity whose demands in terms of workload, travel and pressure are very high. Recruiting *able* consultants will almost certainly only be possible by paying salaries which are well outside the normal ranges of the organisation for similar levels. The adverse effects on existing staff are obvious.

It may often be possible to find discontented (or unsuccessful) members of consulting practices who will accept lower salaries but such people may be quickly perceived to be of lower calibre than internal hires. The principle advantage of bringing in experienced consultants is the opportunity of inculcating and spreading good consulting methodologies and habits and it is suggested that external hires, if used, should be overtly focused on bringing and sharing consulting skills and methods.

Many internal consultancies have been set up with the intention of working on a temporary assignment basis. That is, managers or specialists will be moved into the consultancy for a specified period – typically one to three years – and will then return to their original function or be re-assigned within the organisation. This is seen to have the advantages of both bringing a constant supply of new skills and expertise to the consultancy and of broadening the capabilities of the individual. These benefits are real but schemes of this kind often fail to materialise.

Unless the organisation has a well established habit of cross-functional movement of managers and specialists, it may be very difficult to find good placements after the consulting assignment. A return to the earlier position or function is often impossible since the position will have been filled and the function moved on and the spell in consultancy may not always be seen by heads of departments as having real developmental benefits. The recommendation is that there be a substantial number of assignees among any permanent consultants, but the difficulties of achieving good outplacements from consulting must be addressed at a high level. Of course, if the outplacements are seen to be unattractive it will quickly become impossible to entice good performers into the group.

A consulting and training function in a large organisation relied on assignments from line functions. It had acquired a bad reputation, was seen as being staffed by 'losers' and consequently functional managers only offered poor quality people for assignment. This vicious circle was stopped by a new manager, who refused to take any staff who did not meet his desired standard and accepted the run down in numbers which this initially implied, even though this meant that he had to cancel courses and projects. He identified some key people, of known high potential, who he wished to recruit and obtained executive management approval to approach them. Once two or three such hires had been achieved, the vicious circle was reversed. The quality of work rapidly improved and good people began to seek entry to the group.

Relationship with external consultants

There will inevitably be a need for external consultants to be used, whatever the size and effectiveness of the internal group. There will always be specific skills or situations which appear to call for additional expertise. The internal consultancy should seek to benefit from this and, indeed, the most effective internal consultancies take advantage of the new capabilities and insights to strengthen their own capacity (Lindon and Rathborn 1991: 269).

However, it is very desirable that the internal group should be formally involved in any such engagements, not least because of the learning opportunity. In the extreme case, some internal consulting groups have control over the budget for external consulting. They will have to approve any such projects and will have a major say in determining both the choice of practitioner and the terms of reference. The internal group will thus have every incentive for helping the success of the engagement and, more importantly, for implementing the findings effectively.

Provided that the internal group is well thought of and is seen as accepting the real need for external consultants, then their assistance in such activities as preparing requests for tender, interviewing and assessing consultants, setting terms of reference and monitoring progress and costs should be accepted as a valuable part of the internal consulting activity.

Conversely, if the situation is one where the desire to use external consultants is both seen as reflecting adversely on the internal group and, indeed, stems from a lack of confidence in that group, then the internal and external workers will be antagonistic to each other with a corresponding loss of effectiveness for the engagement.

Among the most successful exponents of business process re-engineering is a US insurance company which, initially, employed several consultant companies to identify and start up their re-engineering work. However, they have steadily expanded their internal consulting function to work with the external people and now only use external consultants for specific expert needs. They attribute their continuing success with re-engineering to the continuity and expertise provided by the internal consultants.

Funding

The final major topic is funding of the internal consultancy. As with most other support or service activities, the options range from a function which is fully funded centrally as an overhead, to a fee earning position, where any work is paid for by the department concerned by means of a cross-charge (that is, a transfer of budgeted funds from the department concerned to the consulting group). The group may even have the capability of seeking income from work outside the parent organisation. Experience indicates that the extremes are undesirable. If no payment is made, the work is all too often undervalued, while the cost of the resource loaded on to all departmental expenses will often be seen as unacceptable. On the other hand, a fully commercial consultancy has been shown not to work: first, because the attractions of external consultancies (at similar cost) are often preferred; and, second, because the ability to perform outside work is usually more attractive to the consultants than is inside work with its limitations and frustrations.

The best examples of excessive 'commercialisation' of an internal function come from information systems functions. In a number of cases, a conflict has arisen between the need for financial profits by the commercialised function and the specific needs of the parent organisation. This has resulted in the information systems group being floated off as an independent company – and an in-house function being restored.

The recommendation is that a charge *should* be made to any internal department which uses the consultancy and that this charge should relate to the work done and at least partially cover the cost of the resource. However, it is not recommended that any profit element should be included since this will introduce an artificial commercial element and a motivation other than simply achieving the best possible result for the organisation as a whole.

CASE STUDY: THE BIG COMPANY RE-ORGANISATION

This case study is based on an actual engagement and is presented from the viewpoint of the manager of the internal consulting group. The Big International Group (BIG) Company is a multi-national company with sales offices and factories throughout Europe. European headquarters are in Brussels and HQ staff and management are of mixed nationalities. Each country company has a fair degree of autonomy, but product policy and overall organisational structure is determined by HQ.

The UK company has a flourishing consulting group, which mainly provides consulting services to its customers, e.g. as part of package solutions using its products. The Manager of the group reports to the Services Director, who has overall responsibility for consultancy and professional services. In addition the consulting group undertakes internal consultancy projects. These have been mainly within the UK but the group has occasionally worked for other BIG country organisations. It has a good track record within the UK company and is generally well regarded by UK management.

The project

In mid-September, 1994 the Manager of the UK consulting group was contacted by the Services Director and told that there was a possible requirement for his group to undertake a study concerning the new sales office organisation. For some months, BIG had been reviewing its sales office organisation. There had been discussion of alternative re-organisations at country and international executive meetings but no firm statements of direction had been issued.

Following a telephone conversation the Consulting Group Manager (CGM) met a member of the HQ staff (see Figure 4.2) and was briefed on the sales function. Until now, each sales office has been largely self-sufficient, with a good level of product and business expertise under its own management so as to be able to offer a complete range of products and services to its customers. HQ management believe that substantial savings could be made and a more knowledgeable service provided if the sales offices focused on specific industries and concentrated on building understanding and expertise relating to that industry (e.g. banking, retail, manufacturing etc.). They would rely on central, specialised groups to provide technical and product expertise for both selling and support. The central groups would each be responsible for a limited product range and would be measured on their success in selling their particular products.

Following the meetings and discussions involving country and HQ executives there was agreement on the proposed strategy but there was no plan for implementation, although it was proposed to move to the new organisation on 1 January 1995. An outside firm of internationally known consultants (Alpha Inc) had been asked to bid for the task of assisting HQ staff in formulating the implementation plan. However, their bid had called for a project lasting at least three months at a cost of $500,000. The HQ requirement was to complete the study by mid-November, in time to

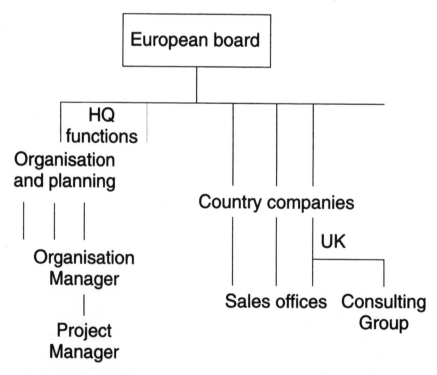

Figure 4.2 BIG organisation chart

present to the European board for approval on 20 November. Moreover, the staff group responsible for the project had a budget of only $100,000 and were reluctant to ask for such a massive over-ride.

The UK consulting group was therefore invited to undertake the work with the HQ team with the objective of presenting an implementation plan for approval to the board meeting on 20 November. The UK group would be funded at internal cross-charge rates and the request had the approval of UK management.

Several questions arise at this point in the case. First, should the CGM take the project? There are several pros and cons of doing so. In its favour is that it keeps out Alpha, raises the international reputation for the group giving high-level visibility and it also leaves some spare capacity for fee work. Against taking the project is the level of requester – how much support will there be up the line? Could the group get to the key players and is the new structure *really* agreed? Another issue is the time frame – if Alpha can't do it can the internal group? Other questions it raises are who wants a consultant involved – and why? What problems are likely if the group does undertake the project? How could these be guarded against – what differences are there compared with what would be done by an external consultant?

Terms of reference

After considerable discussion with the team, the CGM agreed to undertake the project on terms agreed with the Director of Organisation and Planning in Brussels. The CGM's team would conduct a series of interviews with country and HQ executives 'to establish their views on implementation' – but mainly to determine the degree of real commitment to the new organisation and the extent of common understanding of what was being proposed. A letter from the European Chief Executive would be sent to all of the relevant executives instructing them to make the necessary time available for these interviews. The interviews would be completed by mid-October and the findings at this stage would be presented to the Director of Organisation and Planning and to his reportee – the VP on the European board. The CGM's team would then work with the Project Team at HQ to draw up an implementation plan; the timetable for implementation was not part of the terms of reference of the consultancy study. And it was agreed that the workload and hence the cost of the implementation planning work would only be confirmed when the first phase is complete.

These terms of reference beg several questions: will they allow anything useful to result from the study? Will they protect the team and the CGM from possible failure?

Findings from the executive interviews

As was partly suspected, the executive interviews showed a very wide
divergence of views and opinions. Most, but not all, of the executives, had
been involved in discussions of the proposed new organisation, but only as
one of a number of possible options. Some, especially those responsible for
individual products, were enthusiastic about the direction although there
was great diversity in how responsibilities should be allocated in detail.
Country management in the larger countries (UK, Germany, Sweden etc.)
were often opposed to the plan; they saw it leading to poorer and more
fragmented contact with customers. Typical comments made were 'we'll be
back to twenty different salesmen calling on the customer selling him
twenty different solutions'; 'we will lose the benefits of local (geographic)
knowledge'; 'the Sales Office Manager will become redundant' and 'it's a
typical HQ staff plan'.

After some twenty interviews, the findings showed that the rationale for
the proposed re-organisation was not widely understood by Senior
Executives in the countries or in HQ. There was also considerable uncertainty about the details of what was proposed; this extended to matters
of importance such as reporting lines inside and outside the countries. A
substantial proportion of country executives saw the proposal (as far as
they currently understood it) as unworkable and undesirable. It also
became clear that implementation within the originally proposed timescale
would be very hazardous; little or none of the necessary staff work (e.g. on
re-allocation of customers and prospective customers) had been done.

Review with the 'sponsor'

The findings were presented to the Project Leader. She was reluctant to
allow the findings to be presented as they stood to her manager but this went
ahead as planned. It became clear that he, the Director of Organisation
and Planning, was most unwilling for any presentation to be made to his VP
which cast doubt on the proposed re-organisation. He gave the team to
understand that the plan had been fully approved by the European Chief
Executive and that the purpose of the study was to establish *how* not *whether*
the new organisation should be put in place.

As a result of this reaction, the way forward for the CGM was less than
clear. Several factors influenced what the CGM could and did do next. This
was clearly a political situation. Whose job was on the line and who was on
which side? Who was important to *the CGM* and his group? What was
best for BIG? The views, particularly of country management may not be
unbiased. The CGM also needed to consider the balance of his own career
with the best interests of BIG and the sheer practicalities of the situation:
i.e. could the re-organisation be stopped or delayed anyway?

Three options emerged for the CGM: first, to go up the line and say it can't be done and he wants out; second, to bear in mind what has been said but work flat out with the staff group to produce an implementation plan; and third, a compromise. If the Chief Executive really has decided, he would not appreciate being told that all his country people are against it – still less that it is a bad idea. On the other hand, if the CGM caved in and simply went ahead and helped develop an implementation plan and it resulted in chaos, as is likely, he would be blamed. So, somehow the CGM needed to combine going along with the principles of the re-organisation with warning of practical difficulties (and gaining credit for doing so).

The CGM had to recognise that the terms of reference for the study related to implementation of the re-organisation *and not to its desirability or appropriateness.*

However, the Director of Organisation and Planning also had to agree that the views and attitudes of country (and some HQ) executives were factors in achieving a successful implementation. The CGM therefore agreed on a presentation to the VP which highlighted the uncertainties and differing views on what is being proposed rather than on whether or not it is a good idea.

The presentation

The presentation to the VP covered the limited extent of awareness of the plans for re-organisation – consequently, limited amount of country preparedness. It also looked at the implementation difficulties and concerns identified during the interviews, arising from lack of preparedness e.g. local staff work needed to agree sales personnel re-assignments and customer re-assignments during the busy year-end period; there were incentive and payment issues to be resolved for sales personnel and re-structuring of information systems was needed to support the new organisation at sales office, country and HQ levels. The CGM and his team provided an assessment (agreed with the project team) of the *risks* involved in January implementation, and recommendations for what is required if implementation is to proceed. The latter included an early HQ meeting for country and other executives to spell out the new organisation and make it plain that it is a question of *when not whether*; a rapid review of whether initially a scaled down implementation can go ahead on 1 January and if so, what activities are on the critical path to achieve this. This review needed to include recommendations of phasing of the full scheme. The recommendations also suggested that the responsibility for implementation planning remained with the project team in HQ, with the consultancy team available to assist.

The outcome

The presentation to the VP went well. He was pleased to be warned of the risks but jumped at the possibility of a partial implementation as scheduled. His view was that 'we must put something in place at the start of the year'. He decided that he wanted the plan for phased implementation to be developed and for this plan to be what was taken to the board on 20 November. He asked the Director of Organisation and Planning to make the presentation with help from the Project Leader if needed. He decided not to ask the consultancy group to present. In the meantime he would go to the Chief Executive to express the concerns about the need to line up the country executives behind the plan.

The country executives meeting took place in early November and, predictably, the executives fell into line – at least verbally. They were given those outlines of the phased plan which had so far been developed and told to appoint country project leaders – who must be senior managers – immediately. The board meeting on 20 November agreed the phased plan after a minimal amount of discussion and the implementation was initiated.

Some real changes were put in place for 1 January. More 'cosmetic' changes were put in place – that is, existing sales branches were given new titles reflecting their supposed industry oriented responsibilities and some reporting lines were changed – without significant commitment to new ways of working. However, HQ staff acted as though the plan was in full swing and attributed stronger powers to HQ product managers. This inevitably led to local conflicts where, since country management continued to support their own sales branch people, the old procedures remained largely in place.

Outlook

Inevitably, as time passed and pressure from HQ was maintained, the new structure emerged more strongly. The short-term impact was, on the whole, adverse – because of the additional unresolved conflict and little opportunity to reap whatever benefits there might be in the new organisation plan.

Effect on the UK consulting group

In the end the group maintained a fairly low profile in the project – which was just as well. The Director of Organisation and Planning saw that good consultancy work had been done but that it was adverse to his interests. The VP concerned was quite favourably impressed but saw the work done as being at a low level.

Lessons

It seems clear that the overall effect of the reorganisation was not very good for BIG – at least in the short term. To the extent that the consulting group was seen as involved this result will not have been good for their reputation. Yet it is hard to see how the consulting group manager could have handled the situation differently. However, there are a number of general lessons which can be drawn, and these emphasise some of the differences between internal and external consultants and the pressures on the former.

The sponsorship for the engagement was at the wrong level. In effect, the sponsorship was by the HQ project team and the Director of Organisation and Planning, rather than the VP responsible for the re-organisation. An external consultant would have been in a much stronger position to insist that terms of reference were agreed with the VP and that the study was seen to be his project.

The expectations for the engagement were incompatible with the timescales set. It is clear that this was one reason for the much higher fee which was part of the bid by the external consultant. Again, an external consultancy would have been more strongly placed to ensure that the terms of reference and the timetable were compatible. The consulting group was brought in to the middle of the project with little opportunity to assess the real position before making a commitment. Although the project was presented as addressing an open question, it soon became clear that executive management had already taken the real decisions and that at least part of the reason for consultancy involvement might be to make it appear that a study had been carried out. It could be assumed that the internal group would accept the decisions which had been taken and would not be able to press for time to do an initial survey.

The remit for the consulting group was very narrow – although this was disguised. The ideal report from the internal group would simply have 'rubber stamped' the plans which had been made and would have given some guidance. A normal investigation, prior to bidding, by an external consultancy would have made this clear from the start.

All of these points are no more than standard issues for a consultancy undertaking an engagement. However, as has been seen, they presented great difficulties from the perspective of the internal consultant. While an external consultant would not necessarily have been able to negotiate better sponsorship, timescales, a wider remit, etc. they would have been unlikely to have undertaken the engagement on the terms available.

OVERCOMING THE CONSTRAINTS TO INTERNAL CONSULTING

Although many of the problems identified are fundamentally similar to those experienced by external consultants, the approach needed to overcome these constraints will often be different. In the end, the external consultant has the ability to 'walk away' from an assignment opportunity if it cannot be set up in such a way as to give a fair prospect of success (however unattractive doing so might be from a commercial point of view). On the other hand, the external consultant, once hired carries an aura of belief which the internal consultant has to struggle to attain.

Among the most frequently encountered problems in achieving a satisfactory basis for engagements are: 'political' pressures reducing objectivity; excessive client expectations, and achieving adequate sponsorship for engagements. Problems which relate to creating conviction include, in particular, image problems and marketing, building credibility, and sustaining and enhancing capability.

'Political' pressures reducing objectivity

Such pressures are seldom overt, indeed, sometimes they are accorded more fear by the consultant than need be the case. The principal way to handle these issues is by bringing the actual or potential pressures out into the open with the people concerned. It must be made clear who the client is and this will often suppress the pressures. If the *client* is unwilling to allow a clear field for an unbiased report then there is little option but to accept the limitations. The best approach in such circumstances is to agree (and document!) a change to the terms of reference which deliberately excludes the contentious topics. If the engagement has to be set up in such a way as to prove a point or support a predetermined case, then it may not be possible to refuse the work – but it is possible to make the nature of the engagement clear to all concerned and, again, to document what is being done.

Excessive client expectations

Here again, careful documentation is critical. This applies both to initial contracts and to subsequent reviews. Often, excessive expectations result from a multiplicity of clients for an engagement, each with their own agenda. Obviously, the identification of a clear client and a contract with that client will overcome this aspect of the problem. Some of the difficulties in this area, in particular, result from the culture of the organisation. Where this has emphasis on 'can do' – that is, employees are expected to say 'yes' to almost any demands – it is hard for the internal consultant to behave differently. The external consultant, however, finds it much easier to bring, and have accepted, their own culture which places boundaries on what is undertaken.

Achieving adequate sponsorship for engagements

The requirement here is not only that of identifying a sponsor at the right level to accept the findings and drive action, but is also the need to ensure that the sponsor, once found, understands and accepts the responsibilities of the role. Typically, the external consultant has the lever of money. The sponsor in this case is responsible for approving and being responsible for a significant expenditure and is usually very willing to do whatever is needed to ensure that the money will be seen as having been wisely spent. Without this lever, the task is harder but equally important. Indeed, it may be necessary, for long engagements, to plan for a succession of sponsors if the first is likely to move on during the work. Occasionally, it will be found helpful to have multiple sponsors for particularly wide-ranging engagements.

Image problems and marketing

This is closely tied in with the credibility issues, but before that can be questioned, visibility must be achieved – the group must be known to exist and the type of work which it can undertake must be understood. Visible sponsorship at the highest possible level in the organisation is a pre-requisite for being known and this is a key part of the strategic marketing plan which should be drawn up. Constant communication to potential clients must then follow *via* information sheets, fliers, newsletters and brochures as well as taking every opportunity to take part in internal courses and seminars. Finally, client satisfaction surveys should be run after every engagement, based on the agreed criteria for success.

Building credibility

The techniques for building credibility for the internal consultant are, fundamentally, the same as those for the external consultant. Credibility comes from favourable references from credible sources. If the only clients are internal, then the references must come from them although it may be more difficult to obtain such references if the work is confidential. This means that one of the factors in looking for assignments should be the likely impact of a favourable reference from a particular client. Similarly, the nature of early engagements should be governed by the need to be able to cite successes which will be attractive across the organisation – for example, in being able to initiate real change. Outside the organisation, publications and conference appearances have some value in convincing potential internal clients of the skills of the group.

Sustaining and enhancing capability

In an internal group, the range of skills and capabilities is usually limited and the opportunities for recruiting needed new skills may be small. Also there will be less chance to expand experience by working in a wide range of client organisations. This means that there must be great emphasis on staff competency planning and personal development plans and even more care than usual in ensuring that the necessary capabilities are available for specific engagements. Often, the capabilities of the group can be extended by the use of 'associates' from outside the organisation, who might be retirees or other freelance consultants. Academics can also bring specialist skills and experience to consultancy engagements. Perhaps the main task of the group manager is to ensure that there is the best possible match of expertise *and personality* for each engagement.

CONCLUSION

There are good reasons for instituting an internal management consultancy function. These include cost savings but are mainly concerned with the continuity and learning which accompany a successful function. However, successful management consultancy typically involves challenges to established procedures and structures and, as such, may be a difficult internal activity to sustain. There will be constant conflict between the need for independence of approach and findings and the normal line and staff relationships of the traditional organisation.

Moreover, it will usually be more difficult for an internal consulting group both to establish satisfactory terms of reference for studies and to ensure that the results of those studies are properly assessed at the necessary high level in the organisation. Despite this, there are very substantial potential advantages which a successful and well regarded consulting group can offer and these justify a sustained effort to achieve the necessary status and credibility.

Some of the issues are practical and concerned with formal structural and organisational matters, but the 'political' ability of the management of the internal consultancy is likely to be the determining factor in creating and sustaining the group.

REFERENCES AND FURTHER READING

Bloomfield, B. P. and Daniels, A. (1995) 'The role of management consultancy in the development of IT', *Journal of Management Studies*, 26–38.

Eden, A. (1991) 'The internal consultant: resisting the undertow', in R. Casemore (ed.) *What Makes Consultancy Work – Understanding the Dynamics*, South Bank University Press, 229–33.

Hall, E. A. *et al.* (1995) 'How to make re-engineering really work', *The McKinsey Quarterly*, 37–48.

Hardaker, M. and Ward, B. K. (1988) 'How to make a team work', *Harvard Business Review*, 848–60.

HMSO Publication (1994) *Getting Value for Money from Management Consultants*.

Lindon, L. and Rathborn, S. (1991) 'In search of synergy: the relationship between internal and external consultants', in R. Casemore (ed.) *What Makes Consultancy Work – Understanding the Dynamics*, South Bank University Press, 269–79.

Steele, F. (1982) Selections from *The Role of the Internal Consultant: Effective Role-shaping for Staff Positions*.

Chapter 5

Ethics in management consultancy

C. Paul Lynch

THE PROBLEM

The initial question a client asks is:

> 'Where can I find a management consultant with the knowledge and experience to help me to solve my business problem?' This is followed closely by, 'Which of the consultants are best for me and my company?' and, 'Which consultant can I trust to handle confidential information about my company with integrity and in a trustworthy manner?'

The first question is often answered by asking around. Anecdotal evidence of work carried out for other clients can be obtained through business colleagues, the Chamber of Commerce, Institute of Directors, CBI and similar bodies. Another way is to approach the Institute of Management Consultants' Client Support Service. This service provides a shortlist of three or four consultancies which could respond to the client's needs.

Armed with this information the client company should contact three or four consultancies with relevant experience and invite them to make proposals to assist the company to develop its business. During the process of getting to know each other, the client will be able to answer the second question and get a feeling for the culture of each consultancy, and its *ethos*. No doubt the client will choose the consultant based on many criteria including: the ability to demonstrate an understanding of the problem; the capability to develop practical solutions to meet the client's needs; the comfort with the style of the individual consultants assigned to the client; the nature and timing of the deliverables promised; the demands they will make of the organisation; and last but, not least, the cost.

One of the most difficult judgements clients have to make, however, is in answer to the third question – judging the integrity of the consultants involved. Consultancy is not a regulated profession, so there is nothing to stop anyone setting up in business as a management consultant. This ease of entry attracts people, who may be uncommitted to the process of consultancy and who see an easy living in ripping off unsuspecting clients.

In some cases, the activities of these rogues can border on the criminal with fraudulent intent. Such activities include the production of client reports, purporting to represent a tailored solution for the client. Whereas, in fact, it is an exact duplicate of a standard report with only the client name changed. Another ruse which some consultants have used to extend their involvement with a client, is to threaten to report questionable business practices to the Inland Revenue.

Such consultants are lacking in ethics. They are regarded as cowboys, charlatans and crooks. They are here today and gone tomorrow. Their behaviour contrasts with that of reputable and ethical consultants. In their case, such questionable practices are beyond their experience. Ethics has been described as the 'hidden spine of long term relationships'. Clients return again and again to reputable consultants, and many are proud to claim that more than half of their annual fee income derives from satisfied repeat clients. This emphasises the need not only to find competent experienced consultants but also to find those who behave in an ethical manner.

AN ETHICAL ENVIRONMENT

There are those who argue that society today should have as much freedom as possible, there should be few, if any, constraints on behaviour. This, it is argued, provides the impetus to creative freedom and the ability to change with a fast-changing world. These people argue there are few constancies.

However, if this argument is followed to its conclusion, will there be a civilised society left? Who or what prevents one from stealing, lying or more grave intrusions into our neighbour's space or possessions? If, for no other reason, we need to have an understanding of what is expected of us, and what we may expect of our fellow human beings, there must be some 'cement' to bind society. This was described as 'the social cement theory of ethics' by Professor Jack Mahoney during one of his Gresham College lectures in the late 1980s. How can society function without such implicit, and even explicit understandings of behaviour.

Just as such understanding may be needed for the working of society, the same applies to that part of society called business. It was often said that 'an Englishman's word was his bond'. And this principle has persisted to the present day. Now, however, we see this understanding breaking down when more and more agreements are being tested in the courts. This, in turn, requires that comprehensive and binding agreements be drawn up, before commencing a business relationship, so that all parties understand their duties and obligations within the confines of the contract.

We see in the media, almost daily, the exposure of personal behaviour which takes advantage of the unspoken rules: Members of Parliament who accept fees clandestinely as consultants, and submit questions in the Houses of Parliament on behalf of their secret clients: Members of the American House of Congress who cash cheques, which subsequently are dishonoured: businessmen who misapply and even steal funds entrusted to them, such as pension funds and banks deposits.

We are appalled at these revelations. But, as each case develops in the media, over time, we become confused. The balance of right and wrong becomes more difficult to discern. The waters are muddied by the arguments of clever advocates. We become uncertain about whether something is ethical but illegal. Or is it unethical, but legal?

A simple diagram (Figure 5.1) may help to clarify our thinking in this regard. Frequently people say 'if its legal, it must be ethical!' But would this apply to the apartheid regime in South Africa? It may have been legal to exclude persons of a different colour from certain social activities – but was this ethical? It may have been legal for the pension funds of the *Daily Record* to be applied as they were – but was it ethical? It may have been legal to pour poisonous effluent into the sea – but is it ethical?

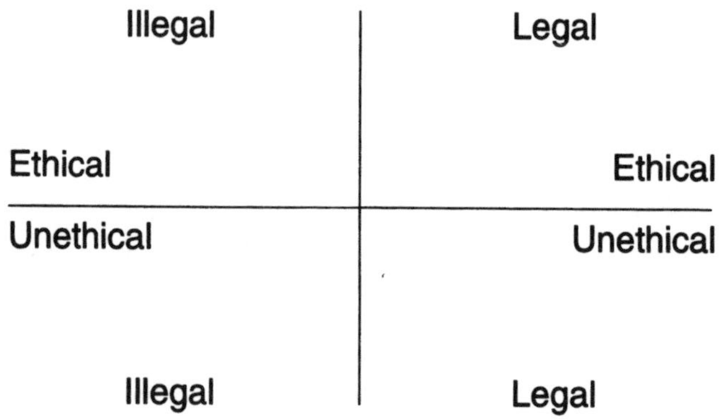

Illegal	Legal
Ethical	Ethical
Unethical	Unethical
Illegal	Legal

Figure 5.1 Legal–ethics matrix
Source: Henderson 1992

Figure 5.1 shows how desirable it is to have actions assigned to the top right quadrant, the action is not only legal, it is also ethical. In the case of management consultants there are several examples. If a consultant fails to provide a clear proposal document, while their actions may be legal – could they be taking advantage of a vulnerable client and acting unethically? If a consultant over-books time to a client, and pads out expense claims, while it may be difficult to prove – it is certainly unethical. If the consultant practices such small deceptions as a matter of habit, it won't be long before they go on to larger deceits.

A simple story may help to illustrate this point. It was quoted by Kenneth Blanchard and Norman Vincent Peale in *The Power of Ethical Management* (1988).

'It's OK, Son, Everybody Does It' by 'Jack Griffin'

When Johnny was 6 years old, he was with his father when they were caught speeding. His father handed the officer a twenty dollar bill with his driver's license. 'It's OK, son,' his father said as they drove off. 'Everybody does it.'

When he was 8, he was present at a family council presided over by Uncle George, on the surest means to shave points off the income tax return. 'It's OK, kid,' his uncle said. 'Everybody does it.'

When he was 9, his mother took him to his first theatre production. The box office man couldn't find any seats until his mother discovered an extra $5 in her purse. 'It's OK, son,' she said. 'Everybody does it.'

When he was 12, he broke his glasses on the way to school. His Aunt Francine persuaded the insurance company that they had been stolen and they collected $75. 'It's OK, kid,' she said. 'Everybody does it.'

When he was 15, he made right guard on the high school football team. His coach showed him how to block, at the same time grab the opposing end by the shirt so the official couldn't see it. 'It's OK, kid,' the coach said. Everybody does it.'

When he was 16, he took his first summer job at the supermarket. His assignment was to put the overripe strawberries in the bottom of the boxes and the good ones on the top where they would show. 'It's OK, kid,' the manager said. Everybody does it'.

When he was 18, Johnny and a neighbour applied for a college scholarship. Johnny was a marginal student. His neighbour was in the upper three per cent of his class, but he couldn't play right guard. Johnny got the scholarship. 'It's OK, son,' his parents said. 'Everybody does it'.

When he was 19, he was approached by an upper class man who offered the test answers for $50. 'It's OK, kid,' he said. 'Everybody does it.'

Johnny was caught and sent home in disgrace. 'How could you do this to your mother and me?' his father said. 'You never learned anything like this at home'. His aunt and uncle were also shocked. If there's one thing the adult world can't stand, it's a kid who cheats.

This story illustrates clearly how to behave in an unethical manner. It is not always easy to go against the flow and do something unfashionable. The same thing applies in consultancy. William A. Cohen in his book *How to Make It Big as a Consultant* (1991) refers to some typical ethical problems which consultants may face.

The client who already knows the solution they want to the problem. Should a consultant accept such an assignment or not? Some say it doesn't matter. The consultant is being paid to do the study.

The client who wants you to omit information from your written report. Some will refuse to do so as they feel it would compromise their independence. Others feel that it may be alright since the client is paying and 'the customer is always right'.

The client wants proprietary information that the consultant has learned while employed with another client. Most consultants will refuse to comply with such a request. However, another approach may be that the consultant will seek permission from the first client.

The client wants the consultant to lie to the boss. This usually involves a lower level manager or it could be the managing director who wants you to lie to the board of directors, or someone else outside the company, for example the bank manager. Some consultants say it depends on the lie, and that they might go along with a 'white lie' to protect someone's feelings. Other lies can be more questionable. Other consultants would simply refuse to lie under any circumstances.

A recruitment consultant is asked to recruit a member of a client's staff. Normally this would not be considered under any circumstances. However, some may regard the client as no longer off-limits after two years or some other suitable period. Alternatively, the consultant could seek permission from the individual's boss.

The client asks the consultant to invoice more or less than the actual amount. This is an other example of a lie. It should also be noted that it is probably involving tax law.

A balance must be struck between clients' interests and consultants' interests in such a way that the client receives competent and honest advice. If the consultant places his own interests first, the client is unlikely to receive objective help, because the consultant will always have regard for his own benefit before that of the clients. He will structure his advice to ensure that he, the consultant, benefits no matter what he advises. On the other hand, if a consultant places a client's needs before his own there is a greater chance that the client will indeed receive correct and objective advice. It is not over-stating the case to say that clients will return to a consultant over and over again, because they have learned to trust that consultant. Ethics provides the foundation for a long-term relationship between clients and consultants. Until management consultancy is a regulated profession, consultants themselves must promote high standards of personal behaviour. Many of the larger well-known consultancies are off-shoots of major accountancy firms. These firms operate to standards laid down by bodies such as the Chartered Accountancy Institutes. This can give confidence to clients that their management consultant will operate to their high standards.

Independent consultancies may be members of the Management Consultancies Association, which itself lays down a code of conduct. Again clients can have confidence that management consultants employed by these firms will operate to known and understood standards of personal behaviour.

Small firms and independent sole practitioners of consultancy often do not have overt rules, regulations, or codes of conduct, but they still need to offer clients some assurance of their probity. The term 'Certified Management Consultant' is internationally recognised, and consultants can offer this as some assurance. They obtain this title by applying to their national body which has the right to qualify individuals. In the United Kingdom, the relevant body is the Institute of Management Consultants, and it has a well developed Code of Conduct for members to adhere to.

A CODE OF PROFESSIONAL CONDUCT

The IMC's Code of Professional Conduct is founded on three basic principles, dealing with: meeting the client's requirements, integrity, independence, objectivity, and responsibility to the profession and to the Institute.

These principles are underpinned by detailed rules shown in Table 5.1. These are specific injunctions, and practical notes, which either, lay down conditions under which certain activities are permitted, or indicate good practice and how best to observe the relevant principle or rule.

The principles, rules and notes of the code apply not only to the members personally but also to acts carried out through a partner, co-director, employee or other agent acting on behalf of, or under the control of, the member. Members are liable to disciplinary action if their conduct is found, to be in contravention of the code, or to bring discredit to the profession or to the Institute.

This code has now been adopted by the International Council of Management Consulting Institutes (ICMCI). Individual consultants who belong to their respective national bodies, such as the Institute of Management Consultants in the United Kingdom (IMC), and the Dutch Association of Management Consultants (Ooa), which are Members of ICMCI, are entitled to be called 'Certified Management Consultant' (CMC). These initials are now recognised in some twenty countries, with

Table 5.1   IMC Code of Professional Conduct

Meeting with client's requirements	*Integrity, independence, objectivity*	*Responsibility to the profession and to the Institute*
A consultant shall regard the client's requirements and interests as paramount at all times. *Competence*: A consultant will only accept work that the consultant is qualified to perform and in which the client can be served effectively; a consultant will not make any misleading claims and will provide references from other clients if requested.	A consultant shall avoid any action or situation inconsistent with the consultant's professional obligations or which might in any way be seen to impair the consultant's integrity. In formulating advice and recommendations the member will be guided solely by the consultant's objective view of the client's best interests. *Disclosure*: A consultant will disclose at the earliest opportunity any special relationships, circumstances or business interests which might influence or impair, the consultant's judgement or objectivity on a particular assignment. This requires the prior disclosure of all relevant personal, financial or other business interests which could not be inferred from the description of the services offered. In particular this relates to: any directorship or controlling interest in any business in competition with the client; any financial interest in goods or services recommended or supplied to the client; any personal relationship with any individual in the client's employ; any personal investment	A consultant's conduct shall at all times endeavour to enhance the standing and public recognition of the profession and the IMC. *Annual affirmation*: A member will provide the Institute with annual affirmation of adherence to the Code of Professional Conduct. *Continuing professional development*: A member will comply with the Institute's requirements on continuing professional development in order to ensure that the knowledge and skills the member offers to clients are kept up to date. (A member will encourage management consultants for whom the member is responsible to maintain and advance their competence by participating in continuing professional development and to obtain membership of the Institute.)

Table 5.1   continued . . .

in the client organisation or in its parent or any subsidiary companies; any recent or current engagements in sensitive areas of work with directly competitive clients; any work for a third party on the opposite side of a transaction e.g. bid defence, acquisitions, work for the regulator and the regulated, assessing the products of an existing client.

Agreement on deliverables and fees:
A consultant shall agree formally with the client the scope, nature and deliverables of the services to be provided and the basis of remuneration, in advance of commencing work; any subsequent revisions will be subject to prior discussion and agreement with the client.

Conflicts of interest:
A consultant shall not service a client under circumstances which are inconsistent with the consultant's profes-sional obligations or which in any way might be seen to impair the consultant's integrity; wherever a conflict or potential conflict of interest arises, the consultant shall, as the circumstances require, either withdraw from the assignment, remove the source of conflict or disclose and obtain the agreement of the parties concerned to the performance or continuance of the engagement. It should be noted that the Institute may, depending on the circumstances, be one of the 'parties concerned'. For example, if a consultant is under pressure to act in a way which would bring the consultant into non-compliance with the

Professional obligations to others: A member shall have respect for the professional obligations and qualifi-cations of all others with whom the member works. A member referring a client to another management consultant will not misrepresent the qualifications of the other management consultant, nor make any commitments for the other management consultant. A member accepting an assign-ment for a client knowing that another management consultant is serving the client will ensure that any potential conflict between assignments is brought to the attention of the client. When asked by a client to review the work of another professional, a member will exercise the objectivity, integrity and sensitivity required in all technical and

Table 5.1   continued . . .

Code of Professional Conduct, in addition to any other declaration which it might be appropriate to make, the facts should be declared to the Institute.

Sub-contracting: A consultant shall subcontract work only with the prior agreement of the client, and, except where otherwise agreed, will remain responsible for the performance of the work.

Inducements: A consultant shall not accept discounts, hospitality, commissions or gifts as an inducement to show favour to any person or body, nor attempt to obtain advantage by giving financial inducement to client or client staff. Payment for legitimate marketing activity may be made, and national laws should be respected.

Fees: A member will negotiate agreements and charges for professional services only in a manner approved as ethical and professional by the Institute. Members are referred to the Institute's 'Guidelines on charging for management consulting services'.

Confidentiality: A consultant will hold all information concerning the affairs of clients in the strictest confidence and will not disclose proprietary information obtained during the course of assignments.

Privacy of information: A consultant shall not use any confidential information about a client's affairs, elicited during the course of an assignment, for personal benefit or for the benefit of others outside the client organisation: there shall be no insider dealing or trading as legally defined or understood. When required or appropriate a consultant will establish specific methods of working which preserve the privacy of the client's information.

Publicity: A member, in publicising work or making respresentations to a client, shall ensure that the information given: is factual and relevant; is neither misleading nor unfair to others; is not otherwise discreditable to the profession. Accepted methods of making experience and/or availability known include: publication of work (with the consent of the client); direct approaches to potential clients; entries in any relevant directory; advertisement (in printed publication, or on radio or television) or public speaking engagements.

Table 5.1 continued . . .

Non-poaching: A consultant will not invite or encourage any employee of a client for whom the consultant is working to consider alternative employment, unless it is the purpose of the assignment.

Due care: A consultant will make certain that advice, solutions and recommendations are based on thorough, impartial consideration and analysis of all available pertinent facts and relevant experience and are realistic, practicable and clearly understood by the client.

Communication: A consultant will ensure that the client is kept fully informed about the progress of the assignment.

Communication: A consultant will encourage and take note of any feedback provided by the client on the performance of the consultant's services.

Respect: A consultant will act with courtesy and consideration towards the individuals contacted in the course of undertaking assignments.

Objectivity: A member will advise the client of any significant reservations the member may have about the client's expectation of benefits from an engagement. A consultant will not indicate any short-term benefits at the expense of the long-term welfare of the client without advising the client of the implications.

Personal conduct: A member shall be a fit and proper person to carry on the profession of management consultancy. A member shall at all times be of good reputation and character. Particular matters for concern might include: conviction of a criminal offence or committal under bankruptcy proceedings; censure or disciplining by a court or regulatory authority; unethical or improper behaviour towards employees or the general public. A member shall not wilfully give the Institute false, inaccurate, misleading or incomplete information.

Source: Institute of Management Consultants, London

more joining ICMCI each year. If the consultant retained by a client has CMC as part of his or her qualifications, then the client can be reassured in dealing with someone of competence and integrity.

Ethical issues for management consultants

In recent years the perceived lack of individual ethical behaviour has received increasing publicity and scrutiny in the media. The public response seems to have been an increased level of expectations of higher standards from public servants, elected representatives and professional advisers.

Apart from media attention, which almost invariably focuses on lapses in behaviour, there has been an increasing volume of publications which concentrate on ethical issues in business. Many deal with corporate ethics or the ethics of those in public life and aim to inform and increase sensitivity to ethical issues. To help consultants in this area the IMC's Code has been extended by the addition of two important ethical principles embodied in guidelines. These guidelines pose a number of questions designed to assist individual consultants to gain an objective insight to their quandary. Having considered these questions, a consultant may feel the need to discuss the problem with someone else, and IMC provides access to a Confidential Ethical Helpline.

Basic guidelines

A consultant should consider, with some basic guidelines, the interests of a wider number and range of 'stakeholders'. The word 'stakeholders' has become common usage in ethical circles, and refers to those individuals or organisations who have an interest, or stake, in the situation. Stakeholders may include the general public and the national interest. *Transparency and vulnerability are two basic touchstones or tests to use.*

Transparency means the degree to which there is openness in the situation. That is, how much knowledge or information has been made available to the stakeholders? If there is not full and complete openness, the reason for such lack of transparency should be carefully examined by the consultant.

Vulnerability refers to the extent to which each of the stakeholder's interests are at risk as a result of the proposed action (or inaction). It may be that a client or a third party is vulnerable because of ignorance, incompetence or financial weakness. A consultant must give due weight to stakeholders' interests before acting. However, the client comes first, and a consultant's ethical concerns, and any resulting actions, must be capable of explanation to the client.

Some questions for testing ethical dilemmas

Below are some questions designed to assist consultants to consider how to deal with an ethical problem. They are not equally applicable to every situation and discretion should be exercised in selecting those that are relevant. It is important to try to place dilemmas in context, and the initial questions are designed to obtain facts about the situation.

Have you defined the circumstances accurately?

This means 'pulling together' the facts as objectively as possible. It also means including other relevant issues which may be less tangible and less easy to evaluate, such as the motives or aims of stakeholders. These may have a bearing on the influences involved.

Often dilemmas arise suddenly and consultants can find themselves involved, or invited to be involved in a dilemma. It is at such a time that a consultant's basic training should be brought in to play. One way of doing this is to write down the facts as objectively and completely as possible. Sometimes this process can resolve the dilemma since the solution may become obvious. At other times it may help to identify the core of the dilemma more clearly and assist the resolution by balancing the conflicts of interest.

How did this situation occur?

The circumstances surrounding the events leading up to the present situation, need to be considered carefully. This can be helpful in determining the motives of those involved. The facts obtained in answer to the question on circumstances may show that the consultant has no role in the situation. On the other hand, the consultant may be at the heart of the quandary. In which case, knowing the reason for the ethical dilemma arising may assist in its resolution.

What is your role in this situation?

Have you contributed to the circumstances wittingly or unwittingly? What have you to gain – or lose? What do others in the situation think is your role? Note that if you have a stake in the situation, you are probably breaking the IMC Code of Conduct. As with any consulting engagement it is vital that the consultant's role is clearly understood by the client and the consultant. Clearly defined terms of reference can help. The consultant's role in such a case is no different and unnecessary intervention should be avoided.

How does your intention compare with the probable results?

Samuel Johnson said in the eighteenth century, 'The Road to Hell is paved with good intentions.' It's as true today as it was then. One of a professional consultant's strengths is the ability to construct complex solutions for clients. This skill should be brought to bear in analysing the likely effect of proposed actions (or inactions). The answer to this question may lay bare the real core of the dilemma – how will you appear to your peers, the public, and the other stakeholders? Should you be influenced by such a consideration? Perhaps by the very act of your decision becoming public, the nature of the dilemma changes. Olivier Roux, the Bain consultant working for Guinness in the late 1980s, may not have worked through such a rigorous questioning before embarking on some of the questionable practices which came to light later.

Are you confident that your position is as valid over a long period of time, as it seems now?

With the passage of time, the dilemma may disappear, or it may be exacerbated. Perhaps the potential action (or inaction) will add to the complexity or introduce new factors. Will the solution still seem relevant? Solutions proposed by consultants often address a client's immediate needs, and perhaps make room for development in the medium term. It is difficult enough to implement workable solutions, which take account of the balance of strengths and weaknesses present in a client. Sometimes therefore, the need to address a problem and create a short-term and long-term solution is unfamiliar territory for a consultant. For example, advice on capital projects can affect the client business, the community in which the client operates, and even the surrounding geographical area. The investment may be a sound financial one, but the long-term effects on the community may not be desirable. Where does the consultant stand in that dilemma?

Under what conditions would you allow exceptions to your stand?

If you can arrive at an acceptable solution (in your judgement), it may be that there can, and should, be exceptions. You must be careful about such a conclusion, since it is then a very short step to justifying a self-serving decision, on the basis that you are the exception. A consultant may be asked to divulge confidential information about his client by a potential new owner. The quid pro quo is the guarantee of work after the take-over. The consultant may persuade themselves that this is an exceptional case and breach the confidentiality rule. They are merely serving their own longer-term interest. Part of the dilemma may be that the act of divulging is itself in the client's own interest. But is this a judgement the consultant can or should make?

Up to this point a consultant will be acting not unlike the way any professional management consultant should. Namely, independently and objectively establishing the facts of the situation and bringing to bear an informed and experienced judgement. This process itself may bring a different perspective to the matter, which may result in the potential dilemma dissolving without further action. The very act of seeking objective facts may expose the core of the problem and thus its potential resolution. Some consultants may find that progressing each of these questions with a trusted colleague or associate may help to clarify the answers and make the action to be taken easier to identify.

However, the clearer understanding obtained as a result of the self-questioning process may serve to heighten the dilemma and expose a more difficult challenge. The following questions are suggested to help consultants formulate a solution.

What options do you have as an adviser?

It is important to attempt to see the situation as objectively as possible. Yet this may be difficult since ethical dilemmas by their nature are not normally publicised, and it is not normally practical to talk the issue over with a third party. Because you are probably the only one in possession of all the facts and who understands that a dilemma exists, you are almost certainly the only one who can understand what options there are.

For example, a consultant may have possession of the raw data of a staff attitudinal survey. The client Managing Director may demand to have a sight of the original questionnaires which had been completed by hand. The consultant had given an undertaking publicly to the staff that only non-attributable feedback would be given to the board of directors. The choice for the consultant is to break faith with the staff, or to lose the confidence of the client Managing Director (and the opportunity for further fee paying work).

What opportunities do you have to discuss the issue with a colleague or third party?

If you are a sole practitioner or part of a small firm you can be more vulnerable than if you work in a larger firm. If you have such opportunities, you can test your opinion against that of a knowledgeable trusted colleague. However, even in a larger firm it may not be appropriate to discuss a dilemma with a colleague because the consultancy firm itself may be part of the dilemma. The IMC has recognised this predicament and established an ethical helpline.

What are consequences for each stakeholder of your action – or equally important – inaction?

The consequences may be apparent, but sometimes they are not easy to divine. There may be damaging consequences, no matter what course of action is taken, and the dilemma rests in making a decision which results in the least damage (at least in your judgement).

The Managing Director of a client may confide in you as the consultant that no one has any confidence in the Chairman. The Managing Director then seeks your support in a scheme aimed at removing the Chairman. In your judgement, however, it is the Managing Director who has lost his colleagues' confidence. Your dilemma is associated with choosing between a number of difficult options. You might chose to back your own judgement and tactfully decline the Managing Director's invitation; or, you might choose to sabotage his efforts; or, you might choose to report the situation to the Chairman; or, you might choose to do nothing. In a publicly quoted company the effects of any choice could have far-reaching consequences.

To whom and to what, do you give your loyalty as a person and as a member of the organisation?

Often the dilemma is coloured, or at least tinged, with person and/or poor client relationship. In business, one must make decisions, which can affect careers, and which can be seen to be disloyal or even hostile to a particular superior. This may result in an uncomfortable working environment, and could contribute to the nature of one's decision.

One example of such a dilemma could be the way in which you as an individual judge what is best for the client. You may choose to provide a minimum cost service to your client because they are weak financially. Your director or partner, on the other hand demands that you seek every opportunity to maximise fee earning from this client regardless of the ultimate potential outcome of receivership or liquidation. In a multi-disciplined accountancy firm, the liquidation or receivership may be the longer-term goal of the partner. To work against the partner's objective could have detrimental results for the consultants career with that employer.

Could your actions withstand cross-examination in court by an eminent barrister?

This question is proposed as the strictest of all public credibility tests. The example referred to above, involving Guinness and Olivier Roux, may be a case in point. There are few instances of consultants being cross-examined in court, but in his case he was granted immunity from prosecution in return for turning Queen's Evidence.

This second group of questions is aimed at helping individual consultants to formulate an objective understanding of their quandary and to understand where the vulnerabilities lie. The next few questions are focused differently, and are concerned with transparency. If a consultant feels uncomfortable about any of the answers, they should probe more deeply into the reason(s) for this.

Can you discuss the problem with the client before you make the decision?

The answer to this question, indicates to what extent the principle of transparency is present. If there are circumstances existing which make such a discussion unlikely, you need to consider why this is so. Is it possible that such a discussion could perhaps expose something with which you are uncomfortable or even weaken your legal position?

One consultant took an engagement to recruit a new Managing Director on behalf of the client Chairman. This seemed a perfectly straightforward assignment, until the Managing Director, who represented the majority family shareholders asked the consultant to undertake a search to replace the Chairman. Should the consultant be transparent in this situation? And if so who should he share the facts with?

Would you feel comfortable explaining your behaviour to your family? Your friends? Your fellow workers?

The purpose of this question is to explore the degree of comfort you have with your behaviour. If you feel uncomfortable with the answer, you must seriously question your behaviour.

Some years ago Dr E. M. Goldratt and Geoff Cox (1986) published a book titled *The Goal*. During the course of solving a production problem the hero of the book neglects his home life. The dilemma for the hero is whether he can risk his marriage for the sake of saving his job and those of the employees. He was very uncomfortable in explaining his behaviour to his family. However his fellow workers thought he was indeed a hero.

Would you feel comfortable if your actions were announced on television or printed in a newspaper?

Although you may feel comfortable with handling your family and friends, you may still be uncomfortable when faced with the possibility of having to explain your actions in the media. Does this have a bearing on your behaviour?

Would you feel confident that the action you propose to take
(or not to take) would be viewed as proper by your peers?

While you may be confident that you can rationalise and explain your actions to your family, your friends, the stakeholders and to the media, what about your professional peers? They are more likely to understand the issues involved and to be able to reach an informed point of view.

The IMC has a clearly defined disciplinary procedure so that consultants allegedly breaking the Code of Conduct can be sanctioned. However, to assist consultants in their service to clients, the IMC ethical helpline is aimed at providing a peer feedback in a confidential and non-judgemental manner.

CONCLUSION

Consultants are responsible for their own actions, and these testing questions are offered as help for consultants to manage their own resolution. The questions are not exhaustive or exclusive, and other questions may suggest themselves during the course of working through the process.

The 'older' professions generally have well developed and widely understood ethical standards, the medical profession, with its Hippocratic Oath, probably being the best known. The oath demands high personal standards of integrity which place the patient's interests first and foremost. These standards continue to inform the behaviour of medical practitioners all over the world today, as that profession faces challenges and dilemmas which were unimagined even ten years ago.

Management consultancy, as we know it, is a twentieth-century phenomenon and consultants need to aspire to their own high personal standards, if clients are to continue to engage them. For management consultants, ethical behaviour is undoubtedly a key part of the foundation for rewarding long-term client relationships and repeat business.

REFERENCES AND FURTHER READING

Blanchard, K. and Peale, N. V. (1988). *The Power of Ethical Management*, New York: Fawcett Crest. The authors are better known for their individual best-selling books – *The One Minute Manager*, Kenneth Blanchard; and *The Power of Positive Thinking*, Norman Vincent Peale. In this jointly written book they set out to prove that ethical decision-making in business is practical and effective – and why integrity pays.

Brigley, S. (1994) *Walking the Tightrope*, London: Institute of Management. This reports the results of a survey of a wide cross-section of UK managers' awareness, attitudes and experience of ethics in the workplace.

'Business ethics – a European review', *Quarterly Journal*, Oxford: Blackwell Publishers.

Cohen, W. A. (1991) *How to Make It Big as a Consultant*, New York: Amacom. This book, written by a professor of marketing at California State University, Los Angeles, sets out a lifetime of experience in consulting which is useful in its own right. His chapter on ethics in consulting is simple and to the point, and some of the ideas have been used to illustrate consulting dilemmas.

Goldratt, E. M. and Cox, J. (1986) *The Goal*, New York, North River Press. *The Goal* is about the OPT principle of manufacturing, and about people trying to understand what makes their world tick, so that they can make it better. As they think logically and consistently about their problems they are able to determine 'cause and effect' between their actions and the results. The book describes in a novel format the search by the 'hero' for an answer to his business and personal problems. This makes for a more interesting read than is usual with business books.

Henderson, V. E. (1992) *What's Ethical in Business?*, New York: McGraw-Hill. This book introduces the concept of an ethical algorithm, which can be used as an analytical framework for dealing with dilemmas in which executives are caught up. It also provides an opportunity to test readers' 'Ethical IQ'.

Institute of Management Consultants (1993) *Professional Code Of Conduct* (1994) *Ethical Guidelines*, London.

Lynch, C. P. (1993–7) *Dilemmas Column, Management Consultancy*, London: VNU Business Publications.

Mahoney, Professor J. (1988–92) *Gresham College Public Lectures*, London: Gresham College.

Sternberg, E. (1994) *Just Business*, London: Warner Books. This work focuses on the broader area of business in general, and defines the purpose of business in a specific way, namely, 'to maximise owner value over the long term by selling goods or services'. Following from that, an ethical decision model is featured which can be used to manage ethical problems.

Toffler, B. L. (1991) *Managers Talk Ethics*, New York: John Wiley & Sons. The author talked to 33 American managers about tough day-to-day issues in the workplace, including kick-backs, fudged reports, love affairs and forced retirements. They related how they wrestled with these issues, usually without the benefit of any source of guidance other than their own conscience.

Vagneur, K. and Evers, S. (1996) *Ethical Business in Britain*, London: London Society of Chartered Accountants. This report was produced by a multi-group working party sponsored by the London Society of Chartered Accountants. The group included representatives from the Institute of Management Consultants, HM Treasury, the Holborn Law Society, the Institute of Chartered Accountants in England and Wales, the Institute of Management, the Royal Institution of Chartered Surveyors, London Business School and the UK Society of CPAs. It contains recommendations for improving organisational practice in organisations, public policy and professional bodies and identifies current ethical issues for business.

Part II

Considering psychodynamic approaches

Considering psychodynamic approaches: Introduction

The editors have brought together four chapters for the second section of *Developing Organisational Consultancy*. Each chapter addresses the use of a depth psychology with organisational clients for the purpose of helping them to achieve meaningful and lasting change or development. Depth psychology refers to those theories that, as a central proposition, assert the existence of an inner psychic world within human beings that motivates their observable behaviour. Two approaches which apply depth psychology – psychoanalysis and Gestalt – are presented here.

What we are advocating as editors, through the vehicle of our authors, is a continuous process of attending to the psychological complexities of the consultancy situations in which consultants find themselves. Even if a consultant is not working with psycho-social processes as his or her consultancy domain, psycho-social dynamics will affect the process and outcome of the consultancy. These dynamics will be relevant to many different relationships during the work: the consultant–client relationship, the group and departmental relations, and other significant institutional and inter-organisational relations.

The fact that there are limitations to logical decision-making, that non-rational forces can influence not only individual and group functioning but also organisational strategy, culture and structure is becoming more widely accepted. Psychodynamic approaches add depth to political and sociological perspectives by examining covert psychological processes. They invite scrutiny of the boundary between what is inside the individual (or the pair or the group or the organisation) and what is in the social system outside, and the interaction across the boundary. They legitimately raise questions about contradictory behaviours, paradoxical intentions and multiple forms of resistance.

The utility of a psychoanalytic approach is illustrated in the opening chapter of this section, 'Organisation-in-the-mind'. Jean Hutton presents a tool that helps to uncover the individual client's internal representation of the organisational situation. This representation, while powerfully influencing the client's action, is usually unknown to them. By bringing the organisation-in-the-mind into their awareness through a process of organisational role analysis, the consultant helps the client to analyse and learn from their experience and to bring about change. The chapter illustrates how a consultant working within this model frees managers from thinking about the way things ought to be, and helps them to engage creatively with the way organisational life is.

The theme of working with the 'here and now' continues with Bill Critchley's chapter, 'A Gestalt approach to organisational consulting'. The application of Gestalt to consulting is based on three principles. It is phenomenological, with a primary goal of awareness as a source of energy for change. It emphasises dialogical existentialism; that is, change happens in dialogue and through interaction. It is holistic, founded on the human process of creating meanings by the perception of wholes and the need for closure. The chapter presents a strong argument for the relevance of Gestalt for consulting to organisational conditions of turbulence and uncertainty, and to situations of 'stuckness' and resistance.

In the third chapter of the section entitled, 'Becoming a psychoanalytically informed consultant', the authors speak to the advantages of this approach to consulting and present some aspects of its application in action. Howard Atkins, Kamil Kellner and Jane Linklater report on their experience, at two UK universities, in helping consultants who are developing competence in using psychoanalytic theory to inform their practice. Five different degrees of take-up of the competence are illustrated with individual case scenarios, and elements of an effective developmental strategy described.

The last chapter in this section, written by Petruska Clarkson, concerns 'Consulting in rapidly changing conditions of uncertainty'. She offers an extensive 'kitbag' of metaphors for understanding and re-framing situations, useful attitudes, necessary skills and facilitative behaviours. These ways of thinking are intended to assist clients and consultants in becoming more 'future fit', and in recovering from the stress, fear and deep upset characteristic of many employees and managers working in, what Clarkson calls, the late twentieth-century organisation. She draws on depth psychology, cultural theory, post-modernism and quantum physics in crafting this advice for developing consultants.

These four chapters offer only a sample of approaches to organisational interventions that take the psychological reality of organisational life as the major focus of attention. These approaches do not deny the significance of other, more 'objective' or 'real' features of organisations. But by conceptualising organisations as complex, dynamic social systems, they offer consultants a way of getting access to the issues which underlie the more visible concerns which clients present. The material presented here suggests that an appropriate awareness of and attention to the deeper underlying issues results in more robust and effective consultancy work.

Chapter 6

Organisation-in-the-mind

Jean Hutton, John Bazalgette and Bruce Reed

This chapter introduces a way of thinking about organisation which is a significant tool for leadership and management in institutions, and for consultants in working with their organisational clients. It focuses on the organisation as it is being experienced by the manager, and looks at how his or her internal picture is related to external events and assumptions.

There are two key factors which every manager has to consider in taking up a managerial role. The first is to do with the organisation that is 'intended', i.e. what is the planned aim and structure of this enterprise. The other is to do with the organisation that is actually happening, which will inevitably differ from the intentions, since it involves human beings who bring a variety of responses to the situation derived from their own ways of seeing the world – from previous companies in which they have worked, from past history within the organisation, from the vantage point of their particular discipline or skill, and so on.

Organisations are people behaving: the question is *how* they behave. Managers have to address this continually, both with regard to their own behaviour in the way they take up their roles, and with how they lead and motivate others to behave in ways which achieve the aim of their institution or department.

In The Grubb Institute we have developed Organisational Role Analysis (ORA) as a way of working with managers which enables them to stand back and explore their ongoing experience of their organisation and their own roles, through working with the concept of 'organisation-in-the-mind'. It enables managers to discover the realities of their working situation, and thus to make choices and take action. Their reasons for approaching the Institute can be varied. It may be because:

- They are running into difficulties with their management teams, or with colleagues.
- They have recently taken up a new role and are seeking to make the most of the new opportunities.

- Rapid expansion of the business calls for new structures and they are hesitant to make the changes without being clear about the implications for the present ways of working.
- There is conflict between well established staff and newly appointed managers, or between professional values and business objectives.
- Constant reorganisation due to external forces is leading to inefficiency and de-motivating staff.
- The working culture of the organisation needs to change to meet new demands and to improve quality performance.

ORGANISATION-IN-THE-MIND

'Organisation-in-the-mind' is what the individual perceives in his or her head of how activities and relations are organised, structured and connected internally. It is a model internal to oneself, part of one's inner world, relying upon the inner experiences of my interactions, relations and the activities I engage in, which give rise to images, emotions, values and responses in me, which may consequently be influencing my own management and leadership, positively or adversely. (Both here and elsewhere in this paper, the terms 'I' and 'me' are used in an illustrative way to refer to the individual's inner world.) 'Organisation-in-the-mind' helps me to look beyond the normative assessments of organisational issues and activity, to become alert to my inner experiences and give richer meaning to what is happening to me and around me.

'Organisation-in-the-mind' is about what is happening inside my own head – it is my reality – and has to be distinguished from any other reality 'out there'. It is the idea of the organisation which, through experiencing and imagining, forms in my inner psychic space and which then influences how I interact with my environment.

In applying this concept to those in management and leadership roles, we, the consultants, are making four assumptions.

1 Managers/leaders habitually and naturally construct organisational models within themselves which can only be tested by reflecting on and analysing their experience.
2 The more effective and experienced such a leader/manager is, the more the process of conscious imagining takes place; he or she can only function as a manager if they have such a model, whether they consciously make use of it or not.
3 The model the individual holds in their mind can be brought into view as they become sensitive to their own reactions, feelings and experiences, and reflect on these – which puts them in touch with the 'organisation' that is actually happening in their experience. (Very often this is best understood metaphorically. In The Grubb Institute we make

considerable use of mental pictures in our work with clients, inviting them to draw the organisation as they see it, with themselves in it.)

4 'Organisation', in the sense of understanding the pattern which is linking different activities and relations in an institution to achieve desired results, does not exist outside the mind at all – it is not a *thing* out there – it is a set of experiences held *in the mind*.

Figure 6.1 shows two people in the same organisation, interacting with each other. Why is it that A thinks he is communicating with B, when B evidently hears something different and then acts on what he thinks he hears? The two people have a reason for relating and communicating, which is the common system they are operating in, and they both want to communicate with each other. One reason is that A is making the assumption that the 'picture' of organisation he carries in his own head is the same as B's, and vice versa. When he speaks to B he is thinking 'square' but B thinks 'triangle' (see Figure 6.2).

A's picture is made up of an amalgam of ideas and experiences which are unique to him and which form and shape themselves in a particular pattern in A's head. He has his inner experience of the activities, relations, planned intentions, dynamics, culture etc. which form the pattern of activities we call 'organisation' and which for him are 'square' shaped.

B's inner experience of the same environment is unique to him because it is filtered through his way of seeing but is 'triangle' shaped and experienced differently. We are seeing *two* kinds of difference here:

- the differences in *A's and B's minds*;
- the difference between the picture of *'organisation-in-the-mind'* and the *institution as it is intended to be* by those who planned it.

In some ideas of organisational theory it is assumed that the intended organisation *is* the way things are, but the squares and triangles model refutes this.

Why these two ways of seeing?

We need to explore more precisely why there is a difference between A's and B's pictures of the same institution. Why do A and B organise their experiences so differently that 'organisation-in-the-mind' is a square for one and a triangle for the other?

Here we draw first on the work of Melanie Klein (1963) to help our understanding.

As I work in an institution – I introject (take into myself) aspects of what is happening to me from people and events to form internal *objects* and *part objects*. These are symbols of my external world which are what I use to think about my surroundings. These are real to me, but are not the

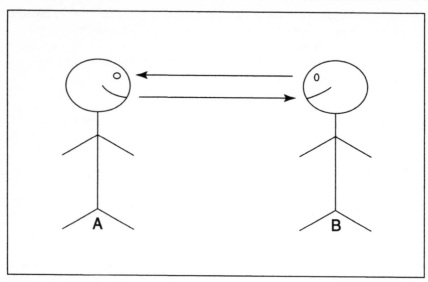

Figure 6.1   A and B interacting
Source: Bruce Reed, The Grubb Institute

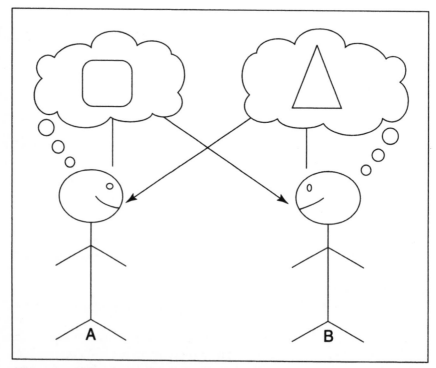

Figure 6.2   Different pictures in A's and B's minds
Source: Bruce Reed, The Grubb Institute

same as the 'real' people and things in my environment. Some of these objects will give me pleasure, others pain and discomfort; some I will keep in front of me consciously, others I will try and forget, suppress into unconsciousness. However, even if I suppress them they are still objects in my inner world and affect my behaviour.

As I face the fears and anxieties of engaging with the real world I respond to these internal objects – I feel, I think, I act as prompted by them. I modify these internal objects which I draw upon (wholly or partly), or suppress (wholly or partly) into my unconscious. In order to know how to act, to make decisions and to work with others as a leader/manager, I try to make sense of everything which I am conscious of inside me – all my thoughts, feelings, ideas and 'hard data' available to me. This process includes my aims, plans and intentions, instructions from others, regulations, responses to changes in the context, my memories of earlier work environments and roles I have taken, and so on. Exactly the same process is going on in those around me with whom I work.

What the squares and triangles model illustrates is that, as human beings interacting with others in our environment, we monitor and control, for a variety of reasons, what we take account of in ourselves, and in others. We are then taken by surprise when we come up against some blotted out features which are active and powerful, because they have been internalised unconsciously. We find ourselves suddenly angry, guilty, pleased or excited and may not always know why. We also trigger unexpected reactions in others, which may be constructive or destructive.

It may be that we have suppressed them so much that they are not immediately accessible to us. Christopher Bollas (1987), in his book, *The Shadow of the Object* has the wonderful expression of the *unthought known* to refer to those things which inside us we 'know' are affecting us but we have not yet brought to consciousness. These are things that are obvious when brought to our attention but until they are surfaced, we have not given thought to them. (This is of course often very clear in group settings where no one refers to the obvious, e.g. the significance of an empty chair in a group).

Why do we suppress these experiences in so much of our organisational life? Because as a person-in-role I have my own needs and desires, fears and anxieties into which come the experiences from my workplace. I 'monitor' consciously and unconsciously what I will allow myself to 'know' and perceive, for the sake of the organisation, for my own survival's sake, or for ambition's sake, or for other reasons.

The idea of 'organisation-in-the-mind' alerts us to the fact that there is data here which has to be accessed if we are to take up roles effectively and enable others to do so. The organisation that is happening is not just out there – it is in me. I have the *workplace within*, to use Larry Hirschhorn's (1990) description. If I take its existence seriously, and study 'organisation-in-the-mind' within me, I can begin to understand why some things which *are* happening in the organisation are happening. Links and connections can be made which help me to see the organisation as a whole with myself in it, and which lead me to consider choices about my own behaviour-in-role, and also what I expect of others. The same can be true in my work with a client, if I am a consultant.

Transitional phenomena

This is where the world of psychoanalytic thought helps us, and we refer again to Melanie Klein (1963), and also to D. W. Winnicott (1971).

If I am a good-manager, I recognise I want to relate effectively with that outside world of which I am a part. So I become caught up in what Winnicott (1971) describes as *transitional phenomena*. In a formal sense, these phenomena may include defining aims, organising groups, making plans, having discussions – and from these plans and encounters I formulate my actions and behaviour toward the actual situations of my work as I perceive them in reality. In fantasy I may have dreams and visions which impinge on me and affect my decisions and behaviour.

But these things may not harness my real feelings, anxieties, fears and aspirations. The drive from my inner world may be unable to engage effectively with the real situation 'out there'.

In Winnicott's terms I need to discover a *transitional object* which can carry my inner feelings, thoughts, imaginings etc., to surface my internal objects and bridge the gap between my inner world and the world outside me, in which I have to act. Just as a teddy bear enables a child to handle his anxieties about discovering his own separate identity from the reality which is his mother, this transitional object is for me, an adult manager, something that enables me to cope with the stresses and uncertainties of making decisions, taking risks and being accountable for what I do. 'Organisation-in-the-mind' is for me the transitional object which I need to contain both my irrational thoughts and ideas as well as my rational ones.

The transitional object is itself paradoxical in that it is both *created* by me (it emerges from my own internal imaginings about the pattern I give to the components of 'organisation-in-the-mind') and *discovered* by me (the pattern presents itself to me as if it were independent of me), often in unexpected, surprising ways and places. Thus the transitional object is essentially a *possession* both created and discovered by its owner. The transitional object therefore contains aspects of irrationality because of its paradoxical nature and because of my inner contradictory feelings and anxieties.

Hirschhorn (1990: 116) makes the important point that in the process of management training, '*technique can function as a transitional object*, which helps adult learners make the transition from feelings of incompetence to feelings of competence', and 'the working alliance between trainer and learner can create *a transitional relationship*'.

Alongside the idea of the transitional object, I want to refer back to the ideas of Melanie Klein (1963), who describes how, when our anxieties about the dissonance between the things we love and rely on and those we fear and hate becomes too great and unmanageable, we split them into good and bad objects. We then project these splits into the realities of our environment. She calls this inner emotional state that of being in the 'paranoid/schizoid' position. In this state we see our surroundings in polarised terms, e.g. idealised some and despised others. However, in everyday life working as managers on tasks, we have to face the reality of a continuous, changing flow of interacting events, and it is predictable that this polarisation begins to crumble. We begin to realise that the world is not black and white, but that we have made it so. From this position follows the search for a way of resolving the dilemma of how to handle the *real* relation between the split-off bits of ourselves, splits which exist initially inside ourselves but we project and reify them in our context.

During the process of resolving, the person looks for something which will 'hold' the situation while sorting out the complexities and moving forward. If the holding is successful, it enables him or her to understand the splitting which has taken place and to recognise the anxieties which lay behind it: to own the bad, unrealistically negative split-off parts and re-introject them with the good, unrealistically positive parts, and thus come to a realistic understanding of the situation in which decisions are made and actions taken which are based on reality. Klein considers that the energy to be creative and decisive, derives from the person seeking to make reparation for what has been done to others through the processes of splitting and projection. She calls this state the *depressive position*, the position from which one recognises that the *good and bad* belong together, and are in reality parts of *me*. In recognising that position for oneself as a manager, I find that I do not need to get caught up in the dynamics of blame and punishment but I can work realistically with my colleagues and staff to find a way forward, working through the negatives and positives which are facts of life.

The roots of this area of Klein's thinking lie in infancy (1963: 1–22) and early family experiences. But few managers will be willing or in a position to regress to dependence in a classical psychoanalytic process. Amongst other things, the necessary pace of their life will not normally accommodate such a lengthy process. What a manager needs in order to function in role is to get in touch with the processes of splitting and projection as features of organisational rather than familial behaviour. Where in a classic analytic setting the family provides the organisational frame for exploration, for a manager in role it is the company, the hospital, the school, or the agency; hence the manager's need to get in touch with his or her own 'organisation-in-the-mind' of the actual institution.

Taking this as the background then, we come back to how working with clients on their 'organisation-in-the-mind' has released them to find and take their roles in new ways.

Organisational role analysis

A core process in The Grubb Institute's work is what we call Organisational Role Analysis (ORA). This is a one-to-one method of reflective consultation for senior executives which consists of a series of two-hour sessions between a client and a consultant held at regular intervals, preferably away from their workplace.

In Winnicott's (1971) terms the ORA session provides the occasion for transitional phenomena to be engaged with. The work is to explore the internal objects that have been patterned by the client to form his or her 'organisation-in-the-mind'. This is then examined against the external phenomena in the workplace through a process of hypothesis building and testing. The hypotheses are formulated in an open ended way to bridge the gap for the client between his or her ideas and feelings and the experiences of their institution. Following Hirschhorn (1990), the *transitional object* is the 'organisation-in-the-mind' which is surfaced with the client through the ORA process, while the *transitional relationship* is that established between the consultant and the client.

Because the material surfaced in the ORA process is powerful and potentially volatile, it is necessary that the structure which contains the work is resilient and strong. In Klein's terms, the holding is done in the management of the working relation between the client and the consultant. The fixed time, the secure boundaries, meeting in the same room with the same furniture arrangement, together provide the facilitating environment of the ORA. This enables the client to relax and to allow those inner, symbolic representations of the organisation to come to the surface. The holding is done in such a way that the client is willing to regress to dependence on the consultant, to let go of their own wish to manage the situation or suppress their 'organisation-in-the-mind' phenomena, to allow their feelings, anxieties, thoughts and ideas about their institution and its workings to emerge and to be looked at. When this clarification of what is inside them happens, the client can begin to test the external realities of their situation, and work at how they can be addressed – taking note of the real state of the institution or department, the processes by which it sustains itself in its context, and considering all those involved. The client can then move to a position where they can truly take up their role as a manager.

Our experience as ORA consultants is that, in a session with a client, the culture the client induces around them, the way they relate to the consultant (the transformer), the kinds of incident that are recounted – all provide evidence which enables 'organisation-in-the-mind' to become manifest to both. That enables the client and consultant together to devise ways of testing what is going on in the external world of the institution and why the client experiences their role in the system in the way they do.

CASE STUDY

A client could not understand why, when he and his colleagues on their own initiative presented their department's business plan to the board, just as everyone else in the organisation had done, the board members refused to discuss it, dismissing it almost out of hand. He felt that, despite not having been asked to submit such a plan like all the other departments, his department had behaved in a fashion that showed managerial responsibility and for which they expected praise. Instead they were subjected to what felt like an attack on the work of their department such as they had never experienced before in the previous ten years.

The fact was that this was the Chaplain's Department in an internationally known mental hospital and he was the joint Head of the Department. He had come to The Grubb Institute with several things he was determined to understand so that he could behave effectively as a manager of a significant part of the overall system of the hospital:

- He was being used extensively to run support groups for nurses across the hospital, but these were treated with suspicion by hospital managers though they did nothing to stop the groups.
- The behaviour of the board and many managers towards the department and its work was very different from how he wanted it to be treated.
- He was deeply concerned about some of the practices that were being adopted by nurses, especially towards adolescent patients, which verged on violence at times and which was being concealed from the hospital management.

In the early sessions of ORA, the consultant found himself being filled up with religious imagery and theological concepts. He felt that he was being used as some kind of priest, while in the material being introduced into the session the client was presenting himself as some kind of psychotherapist. By questioning aspects of how the client spent his week, the consultant elicited that the client was indeed an experienced psychotherapist who did some therapeutic work in the hospital. Not only this, it became clear that he felt considerable jealousy towards the consultant psychiatric staff in their white coats. This, along with the incident about the business plan, gave a strong clue to how the client was picturing his 'organisation-in-the-mind' and his own part in it. He was apparently suppressing his clerical responsibilities, training, appointment and original vocation to the priesthood, and only felt justified in his roles as a therapist and a departmental manager.

In investigating this further it emerged that he felt ill-equipped and unsupported as a chaplain, and unable to justify his existence as a chaplain in conventional management terms in the hospital. However, he hoped that he could find an acceptable identity for himself within the non-religious structure of the hospital. Hence his suppression of the Chaplain's Department and its unique place in the hospital, under the conventional structures which seemed to him to be more acceptable. That was his 'square'; however the 'triangle' in other people's heads shaped things differently: hence his puzzlement at the treatment by the board of his voluntary presentation of a business plan which might keep him in line with other managers, who appeared only to see the Chaplain's Department as something outside the conventional structures and ways of doing things.

The work that followed the uncovering of this picture of the chaplain's 'organisation-in-the-mind' was to direct attention to some of the details of his experience and to relate his department to other parts of the hospital system.

One important detail was that he felt that some of his psychotherapeutic work was arid and ineffectual with some patients showing little development or change, while others advanced by leaps and bounds. It emerged that the more successful sessions took place within the Chaplain's Office, which was clearly labelled, while his ineffectual sessions took place in other consulting rooms.

Further questions focused attention on the services taken by the chaplain. He discovered that he had in the past conducted rather conventional services paying little attention to the context of the mental hospital. By drawing upon experiences of the actual life of the hospital and the issues being faced by those patients who came to the services, a new vitality grew up. Patients now began to participate in the service in ways that were then reflected in their progress towards health. One of the most remarkable cases was of a schizophrenic patient who had hit the national headlines when he ran amok while on short-term release. He had made little advance in the normal treatment but after he started to attend the new style of services began to make striking progress which had not been evident before.

Attending to the experience of having his business plan rejected, it became clear that in this hospital the expectation of the board was that the Chaplain's Department should 'hold' the mystery of human life for the institution as a whole. They were not expected to justify the money spent on their work – nor were they expected to be 'effective' in conventional value-for-money terms. The chaplain's problems about his own faith and its significance in the hospital had caused him to come to suppress his religious function and to deny how he and his department were being used in the overall system of the hospital. However, things were happening despite his denial, e.g. his successful work with patients in his office and the fact that patients and staff came to his uninspired services. Whatever he might have thought consciously, other members of the hospital could see things about him and his department of which he was apparently unaware.

Things came to a head when there was a rash of suicides amongst the hospital's out-patients which led to a sharp increase in the demand for the services of the Chaplain's Department. Because he had begun to see the value of what he was actually doing, he was able to apply his belief in ways which were not simply therapeutic but which handled the spiritual dimension of the presenting problems. This had important results for patients and staff in that it enabled them to handle appropriately their feelings of grief, guilt and failure about the crisis.

Rediscovering his role as chaplain in the system of the hospital, he was able to establish new relations with the nurses in the groups he was supporting. In particular he enabled them to re-assess their experience in the heated moments of being confronted with dangerous teenage behaviour. The nurses worked at developing ways of drawing their difficulties to the attention of senior hospital staff. Senior staff in turn, could then begin to draw up new programmes of treatment which stood greater chance of succeeding, as well as creating new robust support structures for the nurses on the wards.

Reflections on the case study

The case study illustrates the shift for the chaplain in his way of understanding how to take up his roles in the hospital. It was as if he had only been working with a partial picture of the hospital as a system and himself within it. By listening to the accounts the client was giving of his experience in the various interactions and relations day by day, the consultant in the ORA enabled him to see the significance of the Chaplain's Department as a sub-system within the hospital, and to discover his primary role in that department and its relation to his roles in other sub-systems of the hospital. He was able to understand the reactions he had been getting from other managers, and to appreciate their 'triangles' and his 'square'. It is interesting to reflect on the presenting negative experience of the uninvited business plan, and how that negative power was turned into positive results, by being explored and understood through the medium of 'organisation-in-the-mind'.

It was only by becoming alert to his own 'organisation-in-the-mind' that the chaplain could use it as a transitional object to facilitate his working relations with others. It has been our experience in The Grubb Institute that in the cases where our clients have become alert to their own internal objects, especially in the form of 'organisation-in-the-mind', they have become more effective. This is because it has freed them to interact with others in their institutions which enabled them in their turn to surface their 'organisation-in-the-mind', thus enhancing their work.

GUIDANCE FOR CONSULTANTS

The value of working with the idea of 'organisation-in-the-mind' is that it frees managers from thinking about the way things *ought* to be, so they can engage creatively with the way organisational life actually *is* in order that future plans and intentions can be more realistically planned and achieved. The case study shows the practical outcomes of working with this tool, and the usefulness of the ORA method as a way of helping clients to reflect on their experience, to analyse and learn from it, in order to bring about change. It is worth commenting on some of the factors involved in taking up the consultant's role in the ORA process. These include the following.

Keeping alive the idea that there is 'organisation-in-the-mind' for the client to discover and that this is informing and influencing his or her behaviour in his or her role(s)

This starts with the consultant explaining the process and describing the idea of 'organisation-in-the-mind'. The client is invited to start at any point – with the presenting issue, or with a critical incident, or by describing or drawing a picture of the organisation as he or she sees it with himself or herself in it. The consultant listens and reflects back and in due course presents hypotheses about what is going on. This is a cyclic process throughout the ORA. The client can test the hypotheses for himself, and seek more evidence in the intervening weeks to prove or disprove the hypotheses.

Providing the dependable holding environment for 'organisation-in-the-mind' to be exposed as fully and richly as possible

Dependability is provided both physically and psychologically. The consultant tries to keep to the same room arrangements, to start and end on time, and to avoid altering dates. For the client to learn to 'see' the organisation in his own mind, it is important that the consultant works in a way which reflects back to the client the impressions and implications he is conveying. The consultant can also be a 'memory' for the client in later sessions, when new happenings and events in the client's workplace may blot out material which needs to be recalled.

Using the consultant's own experience of working within the ORA pair as a resource

The consultant sometimes finds that he or she is developing strong feelings about the situation, which on examination can be seen to be reflecting what is going on in the client's situation. In ORA this transference is worked with in terms of 'organisation-in-the-mind', not as evidence of individual psychology.

Assisting the client to remember, to notice, to make links between what is in his/her head/mind, and the external events, experiences and structures of everyday working life which have to be checked continually with the internal picture

The consultant models this process for the client in the early stages, until it becomes a mutual process. The consultant also makes brief notes in the session, and spends time reflecting on these afterwards in order to develop further hypotheses.

Making connections between apparently unrelated pieces of data by thinking systemically

Thinking systemically involves taking account of the whole system in which the client is involved, and recognising that there is a relatedness between all the parts and between the system and its context.

Remembering that working life is a dynamic, ongoing process and that meeting with a client over time means never taking for granted that 'organisation-in-the-mind' has stayed the same

Each new ORA session is a fresh start. The consultant cannot assume that the client is at the point where the last session finished. Many other things will have happened in-between, and the picture of 'organisation-in-the-mind' which the client brings in this week may have altered. It is important that the consultant always invites the client to start from where he or she wants to. Recapping can be dangerous because it can throw the client back, instead of allowing change to be noticed and worked with.

REFERENCES AND FURTHER READING

Bollas, C. (1987). *The Shadow of the Object: Psychoanalysis of the Unthought Known*, London: Free Association Books.

Hirschhorn, L. (1990). *The Workplace Within: Psychodynamics of Organizational Life*, Cambridge, MA: MIT Press.

Klein, M. (1963) 'Our adult world and its roots in infancy', in *Our Adult World and Other Essays*, London: Heinemann.

Reed, B. and Palmer, B. (1972) *An Introduction to Organisational Behaviour*, Working Paper, London: The Grubb Institute.

Reed, B. and Armstrong, D. (1988) *Notes on Professional Management*, Working Paper, London: The Grubb Institute.

Winnicott, D. W. (1971), 'Transitional objects and transitional phenomena', in *Playing and Reality*, London: Tavistock Publications.

Chapter 7

A Gestalt approach to organisational consulting

Bill Critchley

I started my career in consultancy immediately after completing my MBA. Like many of my contemporaries, I thought consultancy offered an obvious opportunity to apply my newly gained knowledge. It seemed unlikely that many companies would give me, someone who had spent ten years in sales and marketing, a highly paid job in their finance department, or any other function of which I had no direct experience. Yet that was the hope of many people taking their MBAs, that they would be able to jump the functional barrier. Consultancy offered the best possibility, but even then, the most attractive offer I was able to get was in a specialist marketing consultancy.

The prevailing consultancy paradigm at that time, and it probably still is to a large extent, was based on the assumption that the consultant would have greater knowledge or skills in a particular functional or technical domain than the organisation. The methodology of this paradigm is a linear-analytic one in which the consultant diagnoses the problem, and writes a report with recommended solutions, although these days he/she would be likely to get involved with the process of implementation.

This approach is fine where the assumption is justified, but far too often it is not, and the consultant has to engage in some skilful promotional and selling activity in order to promote an essentially spurious claim to expertise over and above the client's. Clients often collude with this at some level, because they would like a 'solution' to a 'problem' which they feel they have identified.

The client's collusion is based on a second shared assumption: namely that organisations work in a linear fashion, in which cause–effect relationships can be objectively ascertained, and hence problems correctly identified. There is much to suggest, from both recent and current research, that this view of organisations is extremely limited in its ability to handle the complex phenomena which managers and consultants are experiencing in their attempts to improve organisational effectiveness. Sticking with the old paradigm serves merely to sustain the myth of certainty and predictability in an essentially chaotic world.

The Gestalt approach on the other hand has field theory as its central premise, a way of thinking in which the total situation is appreciated as a whole, and there is acknowledgement of 'the organised, interconnected, interdependent, interactive nature of the whole' (Lewin 1952). Taking this view, all events and phenomena only have meaning in their context. This view seems to me to be a particularly helpful way of conceptualising organisations, and a useful starting point for thinking about a consultancy intervention. It also places emphasis on fully experiencing the 'here and now', the notion that by going fully into the experience of the present, the possibilities for action come clearly into focus. This emergent way of working seems a more appropriate method of engaging with complexity and uncertainty than attempting to predict and plan for it.

THEORETICAL OVERVIEW

The assumption which underlies a Gestalt approach to organisational change, is that change is a naturally occurring phenomenon which we cannot control. What we can do is enhance the organisation's capability to *respond* to its changing internal and external environment, to release its capacity to experiment and to initiate. For most managers who are trained to set objectives, and construct milestones to reach them, the idea that change cannot be 'managed' in the same way comes hard.

Furthermore there is an obvious implication that change is inherently unpredictable, and therefore attempts to 'plan change' in the way managers, brought up in the conventions of 'scientific management' assume they should, are futile. Stacey (1993) argues that elaborate planning procedures are merely a defence against anxiety, 'a denial of uncertainty itself'.

A further assumption of the Gestalt approach is that human beings and organisations have an inherent capacity to creatively adjust to their environment. This capacity to stay in healthy relation to one's changing environment is referred to in Gestalt terminology as *'self-regulation'*.

This natural capacity for self-regulation is liable to be interrupted by environmental interferences, events and experiences which are neither bad nor good in themselves, but whose cumulative impact induces a fixed rather than a flexible and creative response. Hence any impairment of the capacity for self-regulation broadly defines the problem area in a Gestalt intervention.

The main purpose of a Gestalt intervention is to increase *awareness* of the field and the client's relationship with it, through paying attention to and emphasising the processes and interactions taking place *in the present*. This focus is predicated on the 'paradoxical theory of change' (Beisser 1970), whereby 'change occurs when a person becomes what he or she is, not when he or she tries to become what (s)he is not'.

The act of fully exploring and *experiencing* phenomena as they presently are, will lead to spontaneous self-organisation. This is the Gestalt theory of change, which is contrary to most prevailing theories of organisational change. It does not depend on evangelism, visions of the future, re-engineering or top–down cascades, but on a fundamental view that human beings and the organisations they construct, have an inherent capacity to creatively regulate and organise themselves in response to their changing environment, if that capacity is nurtured and sometimes released. Leaving the final word with Beisser (1970), 'change does not take place through a coercive attempt by the individual, or by another person to change him, but it does take place if one takes the time and effort to be what one is – to be fully invested in one's current position'.

Foundations of Gestalt theory

The essential underpinnings of the Gestalt theory of change, are drawn broadly from the fields of science, Gestalt psychology and philosophy. Clarkson (1989) explains that 'in Gestalt, the whole is always greater than the part and any part refers to the whole. Most core Gestalt concepts overlap'. It is rooted in existential philosophy, it is explicit in complexity theory, and is predicated on the Gestalt psychology theory that it is characteristic of human perceptual processes to create meaning by the perception of wholes and the need for closure.

Clarkson suggests a clustering of three theoretical concepts: holism (organismic wholeness), change (cyclic flux) and process (dynamic inter-relatedness). Yontef (1980) uses three principles to define the application of Gestalt which seem to be particularly helpful in understanding the role of the practitioner.

- *Principle one*: Gestalt practice is phenomenological; its only goal is 'awareness' and its methodology is the methodology of awareness (the change principle).
- *Principle two*: Gestalt practice is based wholly on dialogic existentialism, i.e. the I–Thou contact/withdrawal process (the process principle).
- *Principle three*: Gestalt practice's conceptual foundation or world view is based on holism and field theory (the holism principle).

Furthermore, any of the three properly and fully understood encompasses the other two. I now intend to elaborate briefly on each of these principles, and in doing so it is interesting to notice the overlap between them – their essential indivisibility.

Phenomenology

Phenomenology has been interpreted as the method of faithful description of phenomena in order to get 'to the things themselves'. It places description first in the process of investigation, before experimental or other forms of data reduction take place. To be critical of one's own assumptions is a prerequisite of unbiased description, and in that respect it is a critical science. Husserl (1970) warned the investigator 'not to hunt deductively after constructions unrelated to the matter in question, *but to grant its right to whatever is clearly seen*'.

As the science of meaning, phenomenology holds that every experience of reality is an experience of unities of meaning. This derives from the concept of intentionality which is central to phenomenology. Intentionality means that any human experience or action has an object which is *conceptually* distinct from that experience or action, and may or may not exist independently. That which I see over there, the pain which I feel within, the theory which I hold to be true, are all objects of my present acts of seeing, feeling, believing and as such they are said to be 'intended' by these mental acts. They are *intentional correlates* in contrast to the Newtonian notion of objective reality in which subject is separated from object, and reality is chopped up into supposedly scientific manageable proportions.

Phenomenology is the methodology of *existential philosophy*, which is not a doctrine but a style of philosophy in which the subject holds the truth, not the object, in which the subject is the existent in the whole range of his existing, and which tries to express the *whole spectrum* of existence known directly and concretely in the very act of existence. Phenomenology is the tool by which the existentialist explores her passionate, subjective experience, by which she becomes aware of her presuppositions, prejudices, her interpretational process.

The phenomenological exploration, on the one hand focuses on, and gives prime value to, the unique and unshareable differences in every person's experience of their world. Unshareable in the sense that one person can never *fully* know the experience of another, or at least they can never be certain whether they know or not, and the assumption is that each complex interaction between a changing person and their changing environment will necessarily be unique. On the other hand, the essence of a person's experience may well correspond in many cases with that of others, and so the troublesome notion of 'reality', expressed in the Descartes/Newtonian paradigm as a concern for objective, robustly logical/analytical definition, is transformed into a process of subjective, consensual validation.

While psychology traditionally focuses on the individual, phenomenological psychology is *situation centred*. The primary emphasis is on the person–world relationship. No analysis of behaviour is complete without an adequate description of the place in which and with respect to which behaviour 'takes place'.

Field theory

Field theory is particularly relevant for those of us who are interested in organisational change. Kurt Lewin (1952), who originally introduced the idea into social systems thinking, said that field theory is not a theory in the usual sense, but a way of 'looking at the total situation' rather than looking at it piecemeal. There is acknowledgement of 'the organised, interconnected, interdependent, interactive nature of complex human phenomena'. The theory emphasises the 'interconnectedness between events and the settings or situations in which these events take place', and describes how human actions and experience are a function of the organisation of the field as a whole. With a field theory outlook *we abandon looking for single causes*, and we also abandon viewing phenomena in terms of cause and effect thinking. Lewin drew upon Maxwellian field theory in physics in which the fundamental 'unit' is no longer a particle or a mass, but a field of force. Within a field, there is a constantly changing distribution of forces affecting things in the field. Events are determined by the nature of the field as a whole, which is constantly in flux.

This concept of 'field' however, while having a scientific basis in physics, can only be viewed as a useful metaphor when applied to social systems. Gestalt practitioners have always had some difficulty in explicating it as a proper 'theory' of organisation, hence Lewin's reservation that it is not a theory in the usual sense, rather a way of 'perceiving'. What is more, it is a way of perceiving that tends to have more currency with intuitive, than with rational–analytic modes of thinking which have tended to predominate in organisations. Fortunately for Gestalt practitioners, with the growing awareness of the inherent complexity in organisations, the ideas contained within field theory now have more face validity, and the emerging theory of complexity itself seems likely to provide a more robust theoretical foundation for a field view of organisations.

Resistance to change

As with individuals, organisations are maintained by a system of beliefs, about how to survive, how to relate to their environment. Indeed we might argue that the essence of an organisation is the system of beliefs and perceptions that constitute it. The balance sheet may be what defines it for an accountant, but for those who work in it, it is a phenomenon, part shared and part personal. The shared beliefs are what is often described as 'the glue'. Edgar Schein (1985), talks about 'basic assumptions' as the roots of organisation culture, which inform all transactions both internally and externally and give rise to *stable patterns and routines*. While stable patterns and routines are both useful and necessary for effective organisational functioning, when they become fixed, they inhibit capacity for adjustment and renewal. The basic assumptions began as conscious choices which led to success, so that these stable patterns and routines are therefore embedded in powerful, historically validated assumptions, which often lead to valiant efforts to defend and maintain them.

They also provide a certain cohesiveness and meaning to members of an organisation, so attempts to change them give rise, not unnaturally to what is often labelled as 'resistance'. However, as Nevis (1987) points out 'it is a label applied by those who see themselves as agents of change, and is not necessarily the phenomenological experience of the targets; most of the attempts to understand resistance are made from the perspective or bias of those seeking to bring about change'. From their point of view the most common reasons are likely to be:

• a desire not to give up something of value;
• a misunderstanding of the change and its implications;
• a belief that the change does not make sense for the organisation;
• a low tolerance for change.

All but the last give credence to the fact that there may be legitimate differences in the way various members of the organisation see the same situation, and what we have come to label 'resistance' can alternatively be seen as a variety of different views on the desirability of the particular change, rather than an undifferentiated blob of 'resistance'. This is often created by imposed change, starting with the manager's articulation of some change objectives, or desired future state, and continuing with a planned set of activities to bring about the change, opposition to which is seen as a challenge to his/her legitimate authority. (Nevis also observes that resistance as a concept or as a manifestation has meaning only where there are power differentials among people.)

As a result of trying to 'manage change' in this way, we have come to assume that resistance is natural, that everyone is reluctant to change. This is not surprising if we are pushed, sometimes implicitly threatened, or if the process requires that the present reality is denigrated so that those involved in creating and striving to maintain it inevitably feel bad about themselves. Gestalt starts from the proposition that people and organisations are what they are for good reasons, and that these good reasons need to be respected and taken into account in any change process. Donald Klein (1976) observes that without resistance to change, every new idea would be acted on immediately. There would be no continuity or stability, so we would be caught up and destroyed by chaos. Even our cells would burst because of the absence of resistant membranes to contain their substance. From this perspective, resistance is essential to life as we know it.

While Gestalt assumes that change is natural, and a potential source of energy, paradoxically, change cannot occur without a necessary degree of stability and containment. A Gestalt practitioner will pay equal attention to the routines, procedures, rituals and boundaries which are necessary to provide stability, as to what is needed to release the natural potential for innovation and change within the organisation.

Organisations as complex systems

I want to introduce a final piece of theory because I think it is totally compatible with Gestalt, and also offers some extremely important and useful new thinking about organisations. This is emerging from the study of *complexity theory*, which is as yet in its infancy, and we are developing it and modifying it as new theoretical insights are combined with our experience of working with organisations. It appeals to me both because it helps me make more sense of my current experiences with organisations, and also because it provides some potentially more rigorous theoretical underpinnings to field theory. Here is a brief overview.

Organisations are non-linear, dynamic feedback systems, driven by simple feedback laws, capable of generating behaviour so complex that the links between cause and effect, action and outcome, simply disappear in the detail of unfolding behaviour. Feedback can have either an amplifying or a dampening effect, and it is impossible to know which of those two possibilities will occur. When a nonlinear feedback system is driven away from stable equilibrium towards the equilibrium of explosive instability, it passes through a phase of bounded instability in which it displays highly complex behaviour. There is what we might think of a border area between stable equilibrium and unstable equilibrium, and behaviour in this area has some important characteristics:

- It is inherently unpredictable.
- It displays what has been called a hidden pattern.
- It is in permanent flux.
- The implicate order emerges.
- The system in this phase is inherently self-organising (Stacey 1992).

The principle is demonstrated when plotting a simple relationship, say between profit growth and the percentage of profit invested in advertising, by continuously increasing the profit variable. For a while the curve is stable, then it bifurcates, while remaining predictable, and then it becomes unpredictable within a boundary; there is pattern, but never any repetition. Beyond this phase, the system goes totally unstable.

So between the phases of stability and instability is the phase of 'bounded instability', within which lies the opportunity for optimal creativity and regeneration within the overall limits of a stable system boundary. This is the phase of disequilibrium which managers need to be willing to embrace. It does not mean abandoning the principles of stable state management for managing the short term; it requires that leaders are able to both manage the short term, and simultaneously live in the domain of bounded instability.

This represents a paradigm shift in our way of conceiving organisations in Kuhn's (1970) sense of the word, and as managers come to adopt it, and to learn a new type of behaviour, so they will become liberated from the forms of recurrent 'stuckness' defined by Watzlawick *et al.* (1974) which I describe at the end of this chapter.

THE GESTALT MODEL OF INTERVENTION

The notion of *presence* is core to a Gestalt model of intervention. By this I mean the way in which the interventionist *is* in the organisation. He essentially joins the organisation, becoming part of the field; he does not attempt instrumentally to 'do something to' the organisation, but rather to have an impact in the field through the quality of his or her presence. The interventionist provides a presence which may otherwise be lacking or discouraged in the system. Specifically this means:

- being authentically present in such a way that encourages others to be fully who they are;
- modelling a way of solving problems which pays attention to the emergent, self-organising properties of the field;
- helping to focus client energy on the reality of things as they are, rather than as they would like to believe they are, through a process of deep dialogic exploration;
- facilitating dialogue across rigid boundaries, in such a way as to permanently loosen those boundaries.

From this stance, the consultant teaches the client system those skills necessary for functioning better in carrying out the functions of awareness, mobilisation, action and contact.

These functions form part of the Gestalt cycle of experience, which is one of the cornerstones of the Gestalt model (see Figure 7.1). It describes the process by which people, individually or collectively, become aware of what is going on at any moment, and how they mobilise energy to take some action which allows them to deal constructively with the possibilities suggested by the new awareness.

The notion of a cycle, starting from rest and moving through a phased cycle of energisation back to rest, is a powerful metaphor for the life process. The cycle describes the essential nature of the interaction between an organism and its environment. It is a natural cycle and individuals move through its phases with or without help; or they may get stuck. The cycle (see Figure 7.1) describes a flow and ebb of energy in the continuous process of need fulfilment essential to an individual's survival and growth. We move from rest through a series of phases to full contact with our food,

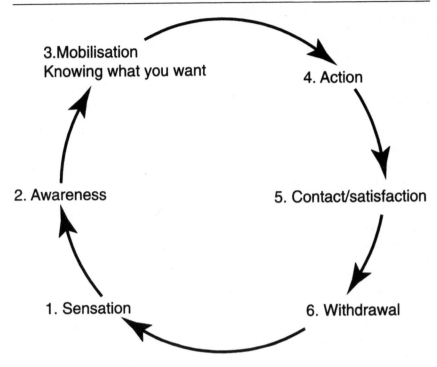

Figure 7.1 The Gestalt cycle

with our friends, partners or colleagues or issues which we need to tackle, followed by satisfaction and withdrawal.

The first phase, as a new experience begins to emerge, is internal sensation; as we begin to focus the sensation on to something or some person in our external environment, we attach meaning to the sensation; this is described as 'awareness'. As we become aware of what the sensation is telling us – as we give it meaning – we begin to mobilise our energy towards the external object through clarifying the nature of the interaction we want. We then take concrete action to bring about contact: at some point when the fullness of the experience is realised, we achieve satisfaction, and then finally we withdraw from the experience and another cycle may begin. That is no more than the briefest outline of a rich and insightful model. It is not possible to do justice here to Gestalt theory with all its very practical principles and useful axioms. Many readers will be familiar with Gestalt and for those who want to dig deeper, the literature is very accessible (Goodman *et al.* 1972).

CASE STUDY

I was working with some colleagues for a reasonably large engineering company, which had grown by a series of acquisitions and needed to respond to some of its large car maker customers' demands that it become more integrated in its capability to respond. This was expressed in the jargon of the day as a requirement to be a 'global player', a 'virtual company'. In this case the natural boundaries defined by a country or a site which had previously defined the business entity, which people saw as the source of their livelihood, and for which they strove to win orders, often in competition with other members of the same group, were now seen as an impediment by an emerging group of powerful global customers. These customers threatened to withdraw their business unless this supplier 'got its act together'.

Our way of working with this organisation was to start by holding a two-day workshop for about fifty managers to begin a dialogue about what becoming 'global' would entail. We had two process principles in mind; one was to create opportunities for people to start talking and addressing problems in groupings that crossed their normal country, site or national boundaries, and the other was to challenge the boundaries of their thinking, to provoke them into experimentation with innovative ways of working. For example, as engineers they tended to tackle problems with 'project groups', with defined terms of reference, clear statement of goals, milestones and methodology. This is fine for many types of problem, but it was very much part of their existing culture, and while it solved problems incrementally, it was not capable of radical innovation. Their view was that the company was facing radical change and our view was that it therefore needed to learn innovative ways of working.

A number of change initiatives formed out of this first workshop, and we interacted with each one to help them define what was *really* important in the broad area they had chosen, what could usefully be a project, and how to tackle what could not be turned into a project. The group concerned with customer service, for instance, started by defining four parameters of customer service. They then identified the processes which had the greatest impact on these parameters, what was needed to improve each of these processes and ended up with an impossible list of projects! They then tried to prioritise the list, and then ultimately came to realise that the final outcome of all this work would be to solve a few problems. The question then became how to have a wider impact, how to *engage everyone* with the issue of customer service, so that everyone started to think of what they did in terms of its impact on the four parameters. The members of this group began to get themselves invited to operations group meetings, to explain their analysis, point out some of the problem areas in specific terms to specific groups. Some groups accepted the analysis and initiated their own activities to tackle the problems, and other groups were less willing to 'own' their problems, but such is organisational reality. Nevertheless the members of the customer service group now saw themselves as leaders of a change initiative rather than members of a project team.

One member of our team was less exercised by the need to release innovative potential, and felt the need to pay equal attention to incremental improvement in the engineering, project-based culture. He worked with one group to help them rationalise their production systems, and another to establish an efficient and effective pan-organisation costing system. Organisations need to feel sufficiently secure in their ability to get things done *via* the formal systems before they can embrace innovation in their business processes.

Commentary on case study

This case study serves to highlight the importance of maintaining both stability and creative instability in organisations, and therefore the need to both honour and challenge 'resistance'. In working on the boundary between stability and instability, we were drawing on the principles of complexity theory.

We started with a reasonably large grouping, which we kept working in one large room (we did not have break-out rooms) in order for people to have a better sense of the 'field' of the organisation. Within some broad parameters we invited them to explore their reality, to discover what the issues were, as opposed to giving them a diagnosis and asking them to work on the problems (the approach which was first mooted by the client), and we allowed groups to form around the issues which emerged rather than attempt to assign individuals to issues (self-organisation).

It is interesting to observe that senior managers did not think that the 'right' issues had been identified, but we encouraged them to let this rather messy process of self-organisation unfold rather than have them impose their own change agenda, and many of the groups subsequently redefined the issue they were working on, thereby demonstrating their capacity for creative self-regulation.

Finally, we realised how important it was that senior managers did in fact join the change groups but not as the group leader. They were thus not excluded from the process as they would have been in a 'bottom–up approach', but were able to influence it by participating in the informal processes of the organisation, as opposed to exerting their influence through their formal leadership role, evoking compliant responses to the exercise of formal power, and inhibiting the system's potential for innovative self-organisation.

BEYOND STUCKNESS IN ORGANISATIONS

In most organisations there is much talk of the need for change, and much of the response to the change imperative seems to consist in trying to do things faster, in Draconian 'cost cutting' measures, in programmes to improve customer service, in delaying initiatives and their like. One organisation counted up to eighty six current initiatives! Organisations are talking about 'initiative exhaustion' because most of the work is additional to the everyday work load.

It would seem that this frenetic activity is creating exhaustion without solving 'the problem', and is in many cases making matters worse. Managers are experiencing a new phenomenon which is not susceptible to conventional management techniques, where a fundamental shift in their assumption base is required. It has always been understood that management is about improving things, but the techniques of improvement are not applicable to fundamental change. Organisations tend to tackle fundamental change by applying improvement techniques, so what results is more of the same, including more work and more stress. At a recent workshop with Richard Pascale, who is a proponent of the need for a fundamental shift in what he calls the organisation's 'context – the underlying assumptions and invisible premises on which its decisions and actions are based', one manager eventually burst out: 'I don't believe in breakthroughs – fast incremental change is what gets results.'

Watzlawick *et al.* (1974) defined 'stuckness' as repeated attempts to solve a problem which only succeeded in reinforcing the problem. They described four archetypical patterns of stuckness: 'trying harder', 'if only' solutions, 'utopian' solutions and 'setting paradoxes'. These types of stuckness are described in detail in the book, but essentially the stuckness is created by the attempt to solve the problem. For example, if an organisation's revenue is insufficient to generate a required level of profit, it has a problem, but it is not stuck. If repeated attempts only succeed in raising revenue, reducing margin, increasing effort and consequent fatigue and frustration, and not increasing profit, then it is stuck.

The reason for repetitive failure, if we discount pure incompetence, must lie in the inappropriateness of the underlying mindset or paradigm which informs our attempt to solve the problem. Since the industrial revolution we have tended to view organisations as machines, which can be 'set a direction', monitored, and controlled. Cause and effect links are assumed, and 'rational' behaviour is expected.

The technologies which derive from this objectivist, mechanistic paradigm, such as planning processes, project management techniques, continuous improvement, re-engineering, performance management etc. are well known and can only work *within* the current paradigm, and because they derive from it, they are not capable of changing it. They are nevertheless widely applied to bring about fundamental change, that is, change which probably requires a radical shift in both the way its members understand, and work in the system, and in its way of relating to its external environment. The most frustrating experience for managers engaged in change initiatives is that despite their best endeavours, they do not experience the real shift they had planned for; *plus ça change, plus que c'est la même chose.*

It is of course very hard for managers who have struggled to the top of their organisations, to accept that the rules by which they played need to be fundamentally changed. They are usually willing to make substantive changes to the way work is done, often involving what appears to be quite major restructuring, but they are understandably unwilling to question the fundamentals, such as the distribution of power, the inherent hierarchy and related principles of reward; the role and purpose of management, the purpose of the organisation, in effect the deep cultural patterns, routines and assumptions of the organisation which lie at the heart of the current paradigm.

A major part of the job of any Gestalt intervention is to help organisations respectfully understand and work with these patterns of stuckness, to enable them to see and understand better the properties of social systems, and to work more effectively in them.

REFERENCES AND FURTHER READING

Beisser, A.R. (1970) 'The paradoxical theory of change', in J. Fagan, and L. L. Shepard, (eds) *Gestalt Therapy Now*, New York: Science and Behaviour Books.

Clarkson, P. (1989) *Gestalt Counselling in Action*, London: Sage Publications.

Goodman, P., Hefferline, R. F. and Perls, F. (1972) *Gestalt Therapy*, London: Bantam Books.

Husserl, E. (1970) *The Crisis of European Sciences and Transcendental Phenomenology*, Evanston, IL: Northwestern University Press.

Klein, D. (1976) 'Some notes on the dynamics of resistance to change: the defender role', in W. Bennis, K. Benne, R. Chinn and K. Covey (eds) *The Planning of Change*, New York: Rinehart and Winston, 3rd edn.

Kuhn, T. (1970) *The Structure of Scientific Revolutions*, Chicago: University of Chicago Press.

Lewin, K. (1952) *Field Theory in Social Science*, London: Tavistock.

Nevis, E. C. (1987) *Organisational Consulting, a Gestalt Approach*, New York: Gardner Press Inc.

Schein, E. (1985) *Organisational Culture and Leadership*, San Francisco: Jossey-Bass.

Stacey, R. (1993) 'Strategy as order emerging from chaos', *Long Range Planning*, 26.

Watzlawick, P., Weakland, J.H. and Fisch, R. (1974) *Change – Principles of Problem Formation and Problem Resolution*, New York and London: W. W. Norton.

Yontef, G. M. (1980) 'Gestalt therapy: a dialogic method', unpublished manuscript.

Chapter 8

Becoming a psychoanalytically informed consultant

Howard Atkins, Kamil Kellner and Jane Linklater

This chapter explores the conceptual basis and benefits of a psychoanalytic approach to organisational consulting. We demonstrate how the approach offers a unique understanding of the important non-rational aspects of organisational life, and thus complements other more traditional, rational conceptual frameworks. This approach, therefore, is a valuable addition to the theoretical framework which informs consulting practice rather than an exclusive theoretical perspective. The chapter suggests a process whereby consultants can develop capability in this area, drawing on the authors' experience of training and supervising psychoanalytically informed practitioners.

Consultants are now becoming increasingly sophisticated in their application of diverse models to understand organisations as intrinsically human entities and social systems. Many are becoming aware that the pre-dominantly rational models of organisational behaviour are inadequate and are unlikely to generate interventions which result in a robust long-term change.

The psychoanalytic approach to understanding and intervening in organisations is a relatively new response to the growing awareness of the complex nature of organisational life. Organisational literature informed by psychoanalytic understanding – the work of writers such as Bion, Jacques, Levinson, and Miller – arrived on the scene later than contributions from sociology and psychology, and was initially seen as rather esoteric, somewhat separate from mainstream management theory.

However, more recent psychoanalytically informed work by the likes of De Board, Hirschhorn, Kets de Vries, Levinson, Merry and Brown and Zaleznik has found favour amongst practitioners and academics in search of new ways to understand and intervene in organisational life. A psycho-analytic perspective has established its worth in providing practitioners with a distinctive insight into organisational processes.

A central concern for the organisational consultant wishing to make use of a psychoanalytic perspective is how to go about acquiring such expertise. Of course, gaining sufficient training is problematic in all disciplines, but the problems associated with consultant training in a psychoanalytic approach appear particularly great. In particular, there is potential for the inexperienced or insufficiently trained consultant to cause danger both to themselves and to clients through the inappropriate use of the approach.

PSYCHOANALYTIC APPROACH TO ORGANISATIONS

The central theme of psychoanalytically oriented organisational theory is that irrational and unconscious processes play a significant part in organisational life. They become more pronounced in cases where there is risk and anxiety – real or perceived – in taking up a role and fulfilling an organisational task.

Psychoanalytic theory (Klein 1959) asserts that the adult's unconscious and self-protecting defences have their roots in childhood. Anxiety and stress in every day life can cause unconscious regressive acts which distort perception of the difficult reality and thus provide a way of coping. These personal defensive strategies, inappropriate for dealing with the real situation, are unconscious and are out of normal awareness. Therefore they are very powerful. Examples may be splitting of 'good' and 'bad'; projection of our bad feelings onto others; denial of aggressive feelings or thoughts; or excessive feelings of hopelessness, depression or paranoia.

These unconscious processes have an impact on role effectiveness, group identity, decision-making, political behaviour in the workplace, and relationships with other organisations and the external environment. The resulting irrationality generates collusive fantasies about how we relate to others and provides a distorted mindset which informs often inappropriate and dysfunctional behaviours and actions.

There are several significant concepts for considering the psychodynamics of organisations.

- *Anxiety*, a source of emotional stress, causes various degrees of psychological disturbance.
- *Ego defences against anxiety* attempt to stop the emotion of anxiety from being overpowering. However, these emotions 'leak' and get unconsciously projected onto others and can take the form of splitting, denial, projection, and other defensive behaviours.
- *Work* acts as counter-defensive behaviour – it is healthy and productive for the individual or group and provides an opportunity for reparation and growth. Task, or primary task is the *raison d'être* or purpose of the system, be it a workgroup or an entire organisation. Authority is the system's investment in the role to carry out various tasks and functions on its behalf. Role sets the authority of the member in a system in relationship to others and in relationship to the system's requirements.

- *Boundary* defines the limits and scope of the system; these may be loosely or tightly defined. Social defences are collectively and tacitly shared fantasies within the organisation in the form of organisational defensive routines in decision-making, group myths and rituals

Psychodynamic model of organisational dynamics

Hirschhorn (1990) argues that organisations are driven by a primary task, which is their main goal or purpose for being. The primary task often demands managing risk, engaging with uncertainty and exercising aggression – it therefore generates anxiety. These anxieties evoke powerful unconscious dynamics, which may lead to dysfunctional organisational behaviour, distortion and defensive routines in the form of poor decision-making, irrational politicking or regressive individual and group dynamics (see Figure 8.1).

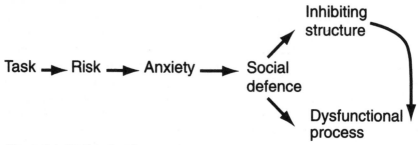

Figure 8.1 Dysfunctional process
Source: Adapted from Hirschhorn 1990

Making the environment 'safe enough' so that it acts as a 'container' of anxiety supports the development of functional group and organisational behaviour. Doing 'work' and acting on the desire for reparation also counteracts regressive tendencies (see Figure 8.2). Thus, Hirschhorn's model suggests that where the risk is managed appropriately through an 'authority boundary', this provides a facilitating structure for containing the anxiety of the task, and channels energy into useful 'work'. An example

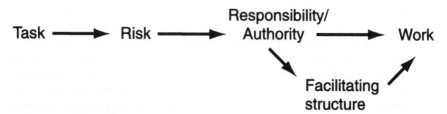

Figure 8.2 Facilitating structure
Source: Adapted from Hirschhorn 1990

of an appropriate authority boundary might be a manager taking difficult decisions and not blaming others or avoiding responsibility, while at the same time recognising the difficulty and pain the outcome might cause to colleagues in the workplace.

Consulting with a psychoanalytic perspective

This model offers consultants a framework for examining the internal relations in the form of the group dynamics and authority relations. It also examines the external boundary through the organisational task and integrates the diagnosis by considering structures. The task of the consultant is to recognise the defensive behaviours and processes, help the client to understand what is going on, to reframe the situation and to direct the organisational effort towards task activity.

The recognition of defensiveness is generated by the consultant's ability to reflect upon and interpret her own experience for both diagnosis and design of intervention. For example, a consultant is 'messed around' by a client who cancels some meetings and is late for others – the consultant feels unwanted and undervalued. For the psychoanalytically informed consultant the experience provides not a justification for feeling angry or frustrated, but valuable diagnostic material. She will explore her experience of the interaction for an understanding of the client system. The consultant with this orientation will seek to interpret the experience and may get clues to the experience of staff of the organisation, or the relationship of the organisation to its external stakeholders, management style or some aspects of organisational culture. Psychoanalytically informed understanding of the situation (arising from a backstage 'self-consultation' or a consultation/supervision on the consulting task) are invaluable for processing and using such information.

CASE STUDY ONE: PSYCHOANALYTICALLY ORIENTED CONSULTATION

This case study is an account by an organisational consultant employing a psychoanalytic perspective. In particular the account attempts to illustrate how the personal experiences of the consultant are valued as important diagnostic information about the client organisation.

'I was contacted by a member of a local all women organisation which worked with women escaping domestic violence. Her description of what they wanted was brief and incomplete. "We work as a collective and are looking for a consultant to work with us on conflict resolution and also to help us work together as a more effective team. Please send us a proposal." My heart sank. I had many years previously worked with similar organisations and I felt I knew the issues well. Organisations such as this work in potentially life threatening situations; basically the workers are there to understand and work with male violence. It is dangerous, under-resourced work which relies heavily on the commitment of volunteers. Training and supervision of the work rarely happens, it is pure crisis intervention. I spent days agonising over whether I wanted to tender for the work – "Do I need this?" I asked my long suffering supervisor, a group analyst. I knew that it would be amongst the most challenging and difficult work that I had ever done, or was likely to do.

'Having been given the job I embarked upon the process of diagnosis. I was not going to plan any work until I felt I had a reasonably clear picture of what it was like currently to "be" in this organisation. Through open confidential letters to each staff member I began to build that picture. The main issue and concern was that any challenge or "feedback" would be experienced as violent and damaging. Through the written word they expressed their fears: previous members had left in an angry and harmful way. Their "past" was painful and there were fears that the present and future were not going to be any better or different. Working collectively was a deeply held value and it brought with it real difficulties. How can women challenge one another and survive? Is it possible to be positively powerful and not take power away from others? What do they want from me as consultant? They wanted to tell me everything so long as I too maintained the "secret", and made everything better without any challenge.

'I booked extra supervision time with my supervisor. I have a background in social work and have always valued the ability to give and receive supervision – which comes from that professional base. It is something I always raise when working with other consultants: Who do you *talk* to about your work? Who do you *think* with? Together we began to unravel the "story" together and thought about ways in which to intervene.

'My contract with the organisation was for an initial diagnosis and then a two day weekend workshop. From the start I talked with them about the importance of ongoing consultation, regular opportunities to review their working practices together with someone from outside. I faced the usual consultant dilemma of not wanting to appear to be digging for more work for myself whilst giving them what I thought was sound advice. They seemed amenable to the idea and we left it until after the weekend was over to decide where to go next.

'We arrived for our weekend, a delightful environment away from our work settings, and one could feel the anxiety in the group. My supervisor and I had decided that the main focus of my work was to help them acknowledge the past and to begin to understand their own projections and those projected on to them by the women who used their service. Their view of the world was obviously shaped by their own experience as working-class women, many of whom had not had the benefits of further education. Their lives were shaped by poverty and inequality and by the abuse of power relationships, both in the wider political system and with their male partners. My psychoanalytic perspective was not one that they shared, understood or valued. My task was to bring my own framework into the situation without using exclusive and intrusive language or ideas.

'Day one concentrated on the past and workers who had left. What feelings had gone with them and what had been left behind that they hoped would have gone but had stayed. We also spent a lot of time trying to understand the fear of feedback and challenge. I then drew what I hoped was a useful cycle of processes I understood were taking place:

- Women clients come into the organisation with a fear of violence and an inability to challenge that violence.
- They pass on (project) that fear on to the workers.
- Workers pick up that fear.
- Workers take on the fear and behave "as if" it is their own fear.
- Workers become unable to challenge each other for fear of attack from colleagues.
- This lack of challenge and feedback leads to ineffective working practices.
- This then leads to ineffective working relationships in the organisation, so that when . . .
- Women enter the system and project their fear of violence and so on.

'There was some resistance to linking what was happening in their own internal system to what was happening in their wider system. Their primary task was to deal with anger and violence and seeing this as something which was inevitably mirrored in their own working system was initially difficult.

'The projective identification processes were also clearly at work. The constant fear of attack was defended against by attacking behaviour in the group. Abuses of power were also mirrored – quieter members felt intimidated and powerless in the face of stronger, more articulate members. The role of "victim" could easily be identified: "Like me", "Save me", "Be nice to me" – as victims looked around for rescuers who so easily turned into persecutors and again round and round we went.

'Unravelling these processes was difficult and painful and we managed to do quite a lot of it. The question of further consultation arose – we all acknowledged that it would be too easy for the success, and indeed any failure, of the event to lie with me and that "back at work" it would be hard to sustain the changes. So, I have been asked to provide ongoing consultation for them and have met them once since the weekend. They reported there have been improvements and that they are aware that letting go of old behaviour is very difficult. Some of the old power games have been re-emerging. I talked with them about the importance of my own supervision

– the need I have to discuss my work with someone outside the system – to some degree I am now a part of that system – who can help me understand and make sense of what is going on for myself and them.'

DEVELOPING PSYCHOANALYTIC CONSULTING CAPABILITY

We have developed our thinking on training and development of psycho-analytically oriented consultants from the experience of designing and teaching two academic programmes which train organisational consultants in the application of psychoanalytic theory to organisational work (MSc in Human Resource Development at South Bank University and MSc in Organisation Development at Sheffield Hallam University) and our work as supervisors of consultants who wish to develop their psychoanalytic capability.

Process for development

In recognition that a little knowledge can be dangerous for both consultant and client, we start from the premise that there are necessary conditions and features of consultant training required to create an adequate minimum level of capability. We have found that there are three elements which are of prime importance for this to happen: psychoanalytic theory base, critical self-reflection, and supervised practice (see Figure 8.3).

The *theoretical base* provides a conceptual and experiential grounding in core psychoanalytic processes of transference and counter-transference, projection, introjection and projective identification (see Table 8.1). This is

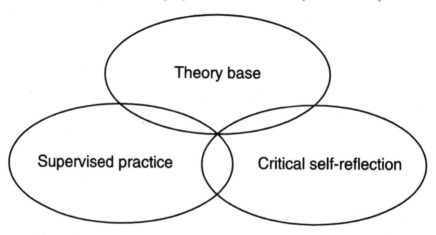

Figure 8.3 The elements in consultant development

Table 8.1 Core psychoanalytic processes

- *Transference*: When the feelings of an important past relationship (usually family and/or authority) are transferred on to a current relationship; we then behave 'as if' the present relationship is that of the past; for example, when someone in the present reminds us of a parental figure and we behave 'as if' that person is our parental figure.
- *Counter-transference*: The mirror image of transference, the feelings raised in the other party in response to the transferred feelings; for example, we become parental in response to transferred feelings of parental authority.
- *Projection*: Aspects of the self which are difficult to own, either positive or negative, which are projected on to others and become their's; for example, a projection of competence or anger.
- *Projective identification*: Aspects of the self which are projected into another and then attacked in order to ward off these aspects.
- *Introjection*: Our parent messages; the feelings we take in (introject) and turn into rules.

followed by exploring applications of the core concepts to key organisational arenas: peer couple, managerial couple, groups and teams, intergroup activities, the organisation as a whole in its environment, the consultant–client relationship. The resulting conceptual framework is sketched above. The exposition and accompanying experiential learning builds on participants' organisational experience, their knowledge of consulting theory and practice, and their personal development. This approach provides consultants with a greater depth of understanding, particularly important for the 'backstage' reflection which informs their 'public' performance.

An ability and willingness to engage in *critical self-reflection* is an essential part of the training. It means examining one's feelings, thinking and behaviour in relation to one's own history and to relationships with and within the client system. Many consultants have gained this experience in previous exposure to humanistic personal development or counselling, while others may have developed reflective skills through religion or other reflective belief systems. This capability is developed to assist consultants to recognise and interpret the projective and transference processes. Experiential learning – the cycle of activity, reflection, conceptualising and experimenting, is an important process here.

Supervised practice refers to the necessity of ongoing reflection and learning for consultants making use of a psychoanalytic framework. Consultants with a base in counselling or social work will be familiar with such supervision, those from management or academic backgrounds often have some difficulty with the concept. We have found that receiving ongoing consultation on organisational work is important for learning in general, and particularly important for practitioners developing a psychoanalytic approach. It creates an arena for internalisation of the theory and integration into everyday practice.

CASE STUDY TWO: PENNY'S STORY OF DEVELOPMENT

This case study illustrates one consultant's journey from a rational, managerial stance towards becoming a psychoanalytically oriented consultant. It illustrates how she learnt by utilising the three core elements: psychoanalytic theory base, critical self-reflection and supervised practice.

'I decided a couple of years ago to make a career change from that of an internal training consultant in the Health Service (NHS) to that of an independent consultant, having a go on my own. I am a graduate member of the Institute of Personnel and Development and I have a degree in Public Administration. My initial NHS experience was within personnel management and I then made a slight transition to become a training and development co-ordinator. I am only in my early thirties and wanted to follow a different career path. I realised that over time I was moving away from uncritically following the management line to wanting something different – a chance to be more independent in thought and action, a desire to discover different perspectives on my work in organisations. I was frightened about the prospect of launching myself off into independent work immediately and decided to do a postgraduate degree as a way of managing that transition and also to develop those more critical and wider skills.

'I opted for Masters in Organisation Development. A major component of the programme was the regular group dynamics workshop where we tried to understand psychodynamic principles through use of theory and also by participating in an unstructured group – to put theory into practice. I found this aspect of the course useful, interesting and very much an eye opener. Our group consultant gave us a grounding in Bion (1959) as a way of understanding group behaviour and then ran the group using a group analytic model favoured by Foulkes (1975).

'I found the experience of being in the group both challenging and stimulating but also alarming, as I became aware of my own anxieties which seemed to shoot through the ceiling as a result of this unstructured situation. I realised that the central issues we were dealing with were around our own feelings of power and authority – what is my power and authority as an individual in this group and how can I maintain myself as an individual in the group. The group consultant then led us through the practice and the theory to link this to behaviour in the wider context of our lives and to the work which we were doing in organisations. I was very clear that the psychodynamic framework allowed me to understand in a very different way how individuals and organisations are driven by their need to have and to hold on to a sense of power and authority. It is these powerful primitive feelings that drive us and force us into defence activity. How can a small voice of dissent make itself heard and understood when the large group or organisation is travelling down a path the individual neither wishes nor cares to follow.

'Our group consultant told us of her own "supervision" of the work she did with us. Part of using the psychoanalytic framework – being a psycho-analytically oriented consultant as she called herself – was always to take her work to an external supervisor, someone who could help her unravel the complexities of, in this instance, working with us as a group. She has a group analyst as a supervisor.

'The idea of supervision was new to me – was it mentoring? What was it? It intrigued me. Our group consultant certainly seemed to benefit from it, I was impressed by her competence and felt safe in the sometimes unsafe setting of the group. There were moments when I experienced a real threat to my identity! Her way of helping us understand the dynamics and par-ticularly the projective processes, and the authority issues, seemed very helpful to me and I could see how they could be also useful in work with organisations. I began to think about some of my past experiences through this framework and found different insights. After finishing the course I decided that I would ask her for supervision of my first piece of work.

'I took a job as a project worker at a high security hospital. I was glad to find a piece of work that would be stimulating and challenging. It was a 12-month contract with a brief to start the process of multi-disciplinary team working within one of the directorates of the hospital – one responsible for patients with learning disabilities. My team leader was the psychiatrist, male, who had been at the hospital for some years. He worked closely with a business manager and a nurse manager. We were to start the process of multi-disciplinary team working in this hospital, which I knew, was entrenched in its old culture – it was only fairly recently that the staff had become nurses rather than prison officers, and did not wear prison uniforms. My experience of the Health Service meant that I was not surprised by its rules and regulations, and adherence to procedures and protocol. The doctors were "god", the nursing staff were lacking in confidence and were determined to stay in their old way of working. I was an internal person, they saw me as a middle manager with no clout and no authority. I realise now how difficult it is for the internal consultant to acquire the level of authority to be able to bring about change in an organisation.

'My "client" was the psychiatrist, who was unwilling to have me, and did not want multi-disciplinary team working (MDTW); certainly not in the way in which I envisioned it. There were clearly authority issues between the two of us. The doctors working with him were even more resistant to change – the atmosphere in the hospital was dire to say the least. I was struck immediately by how people working in this environment, caring for patients who had committed some of the most horrible crimes – murder, poison, rape, etc., somehow built their day around a series of "tasks" and minutiae. It was a place where feelings generated about working there were never raised.

'I took my work to supervision. Together we began to look at the issues involved in working within this context. One of the most useful things for me was to understand the consequences of the context in which the hospital operated (with dangerous people who had to be locked away "forever" from society because of their violent crimes against themselves and others) – the effect of the primary task on the organisation. The anxiety raised in the light of such a context led them into defensive activity away from dealing with the task. We looked at the pain, the denial of feelings, the management or non-management of vulnerability and anxiety.

'Interestingly it was the supervision which caused immense pain in the organisation! If I had not taken my work to an external person I would have given the organisation what it wanted, a bland "audit" of current procedures and a "checklist" of "how to do it" rather than trying to work with them over a piece of work which was raising anxieties and much resistance, particularly with the doctors. As the internal person I had no clout, was constantly undermined, felt awful. I became increasingly stressed. Supervision helped me to unravel this, I realised that in many ways I had been given an impossible brief. The "ownership" of MDTW was not there at a high enough level and in a sense it was a sop to a central government directive which dictated that MDTW was to be put in place. With supervision I tried hard to maintain an external focus, a neutrality, not being drawn in. Without psychoanalytic supervision I would have become more stressed, ill, taken time off and become like my colleagues – depressed, unhappy.

'The organisation was completely inert, seeing me as forced upon them. I really began to understand the issues of authority through the experience of powerlessness in my own role. I used supervision to reflect on what was going on for me in the work and was shocked when I realised that the psychiatrist was not able to reflect and use the psychoanalytic model himself. That was a great surprise and revelation, I was unprepared for his defence against introspection.

'I was consistently surprised at how my supervisor seemed to have the capacity for seeing behaviour as something that always gave more insight into the dynamics of the organisation. I have a tendency to judge and it was so useful to begin to reflect on my experience and interpret the information instead.

'Inevitably I felt rejected along the way by the organisation, the projective processes were certainly finding their way into me. Having the opportunity to talk about the work with someone who believes in you when the organisation seems to be entirely rejecting of everything you are trying to do is tremendously valuable. It is so hard to maintain that "sense of self" when one is confronted by the extreme defence mechanisms of a large vulnerable institution.

'I am now working independently, struggling with all the complexities and anxieties of "making it on my own". I am clear that psychoanalytic thinking underpins my practice now, I use it in all my work. I continue to use supervision and always find it a learning, supporting and challenging process.'

BECOMING A PSYCHOANALYTICALLY INFORMED CONSULTANT

A psychoanalytic approach to consulting is not right for everybody, however powerful and useful it may be. The journey towards becoming a psychoanalytically informed consultant is a very individual one and depends on previous consulting practice, past clinical experience and history of personal development. Some consultants find that it really works for them, for some it remains a foreign language, others take parts of the journey and incorporate particular aspects of the model into their practice at their own pace.

Typically, outcomes of the developmental process can be categorised as:

- no impact;
- sophisticated client;
- skilled diagnostician;
- psychoanalytic practitioner;
- dangerous consultant.

The first four 'types' are, for many consultants, steps along the way towards psychoanalytically informed consultation; the last one is the potentially problematic outcome of the developmental process. There are two dimensions which distinguish these 'types': willingness to use a psycho-analytically informed approach, and the degree of sophistication in application of psychoanalytic theory.

The model in Figure 8.4 illustrates that the key to an appropriate integration of psychoanalytic theory into a consultant's practice is the maintenance of an appropriate balance between 'willingness' and 'sophis-tication'. A low level of sophistication in psychoanalytic knowledge is not in itself wrong or dangerous for consultant or client, provided it is countered by a cautious approach to its application. When those who cannot maintain such a balance develop an interest in this way of working, their pseudo-competence becomes potentially dangerous.

Psychoanalytically oriented consulting demands both intellectual and emotional energy. The development of the capability is therefore facilitated by both cognitive and emotional capacity to 'take up' psychoanalytic organisational theory and practice. Past clinical work (counselling, social work, etc.) or personal development activities, particularly if in a psycho-dynamic framework, often provide a good grounding for development of self-reflection and the integration of cognitive and emotional material.

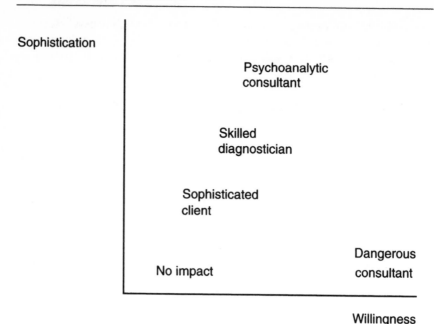

Figure 8.4 Developmental outcomes

In the following discussion we highlight the key features of each 'type' and offer a short case example for illustration.

No impact

Some consultants make no use of a psychoanalytic framework in their future work. Two reasons are commonly expressed for this. Either the consultant lacks interest due to a different theoretical orientation, or reacts to it as too deep and complex for their task, or threatening and potentially dangerous.

Tim came to the Sheffield programme as an experienced management consultant who had recently completed an MBA. At the time of his arrival on the programme his model of consulting was located firmly at the 'expert' end of the continuum, and his understanding of organisations was dominated by a technical, rational systems perspective. On finding that training in psychoanalytic concepts was part of the course, he expressed severe reservations, arguing that he was not at all interested. Tim recognised that psychoanalysis did not fit into his past experience or his plans for future consulting work. When asked by a potential client for a psychoanalytically informed approach, he was able to decline and recommend a consultant who he knew was able and willing to use such an approach.

The sophisticated client

For some consultants the training results in them becoming consumers of consultancy services provided by psychoanalytically informed consultants. They are interested in making use of a psychoanalytic perspective to effect change in their organisation. As their moderate level of sophistication is matched by an appropriate level of interest and safety they choose to contract with (and learn from in the process) a psychoanalytically oriented practitioner.

Gerard was seconded onto the South Bank programme by his organisation – a large financial institution. He was the Training and Development Manager, a position he had held for twenty years. Much of his work had been fairly routine, managing a large team providing training programmes, mostly technical. Gerard had always been interested in people, but the psychoanalytic perspective offered him an entirely new way of viewing the world. In particular, it helped Gerard make sense of the increasing pressures his team was facing from the wider organisation. He attached a magical quality to the skill of psychoanalytic insight; he valued and learned from psychoanalytically oriented supervision of his research project. Consequently he wanted some of the 'magic' to be brought into the work of his training and development team.

Gerard thus became a psychoanalytically oriented client. He had a basic understanding of the core concepts, recognised their validity, and wanted to 'see it in action' in his own organisation. The resulting psychoanalytic interventions were experienced as extremely effective by him and his staff.

Skilled diagnostician

Some consultants gain a sufficient level of understanding of key concepts, typically around projection and transference, and apply them in an eclectic way to provide an additional perspective to inform their diagnostic work.

Ruth arrived on the Sheffield programme from the Far East, where she was a senior training officer in a large financial institution. Most of her training experience was technical and highly prescriptive. When exposed to psychoanalytic theory she had great difficulty in making links with her experience of training in the 'real world', and the theory was largely rejected. She re-evaluated her reaction to psychoanalytic theory when she was trying to make sense of some of the client behaviours she had encountered in her research project, and found that the application of psychoanalytic theory gave her great insights. Her use of psychoanalytic theory was largely in terms of *post hoc* reflection and diagnosis rather than active intervention in the client situation.

Ruth's willingness to use this approach was related to her own background in Buddhism. She was able to make links and explore differences between psychoanalytic theory and Buddhist philosophy, and came to an awareness of the value of such theory in understanding groups and organisations. She is clear that her competence in self-reflection, integral to her Buddhist faith, promoted and supported her understanding and use of psychoanalytic theory. It is likely that Ruth will continue to employ this approach.

Psychoanalytic practitioner

The consultant's work is strongly informed by psychoanalytic perspective. Diagnosis is influenced by a range of psychoanalytic concepts and inter-pretations; and change interventions are based on psychoanalytic tools and techniques.

Charlie trained some years ago as a social worker, worked also as a community worker, and undertook training in family therapy. He pro-gressed into local government politics and became chair of personnel of a local authority. He is highly intelligent and took up the psychoanalytic perspective with alacrity. He made much use of psychoanalytic theory in understanding his previous social work and his ongoing involvement in local government. His research project was focused on the dynamics operating within a small family firm, and he made extensive use of both the family systems theory and organisational psychoanalytic concepts in undertaking his diagnostic work. As a result of his work on the Masters programme he decided to continue his research into organisations with the supervision of a psychoanalytically oriented supervisor.

Dangerous consultant

A few consultants develop a limited or confused grasp of the theory and its application, but persist in applying analytic models to their work. Problems may arise from lack of clarity over boundaries, misdiagnosis, inappropriate interventions, or inexperience in dealing with the consequences of inter-vention.

Paul is a senior army officer. Having risen through the ranks, he has been in an internal OD consultancy role for some time. The organisation has employed external consultants who use the psychoanalytic model for their practice on a number of projects in which Paul has been involved. As a consequence he became convinced of the supremacy of this way of working and claimed that this was now his approach to consulting. Peter had been an enthusiastic and helpful member of the course group and a champion of the psychoanalytic aspects of the programme, although he tended to use the psychoanalytic concepts somewhat inappropriately. Surprisingly he also challenged the leaders by claiming that the process of experiential work was persecutory and manipulative.

His research project was ostensibly framed within the psychoanalytic paradigm and he was therefore offered a psychoanalytically oriented supervisor. He found it difficult to make use of this model of supervision, and contracted with another supervisor who had some appreciation of psychoanalytic thinking and who recommended multiple perspectives. Peter rejected this advice and used psychoanalytic organisational theory as the only framework for his research. His misuse of the framework resulted in a problematic project requiring many revisions. He continues to practise as a change agent believing that he is a psychoanalytically oriented consultant.

GUIDELINES FOR DEVELOPING PSYCHOANALYTIC EXPERTISE

Psychoanalytic perspective is no longer the preserve of an élite, gradually it is becoming integrated into broader management thinking. This powerful approach to achieving change in organisations is available to external consultants and internal change agents through relatively modest training and ongoing supervision. The outcome of the development results in a significant increase in the capacity of the consultant to make a real impact on an organisation in transition. To develop and maintain expertise in this arena, consultants may wish to consider the following opportunities.

Foundation training programme

A practising consultant who wishes to develop psychoanalytic consulting capabilities may need to start with a training programme. The programme should establish a useful level of competence in application of the core psychoanalytic concepts in organisational work and, importantly, help the participant to assess accurately their own competence. The enthusiasm to use this model needs to be balanced with capability. Hence such programmes stress the reflexive learning in ongoing consulting groups and in supervision. They typically consist of some version of the following elements:

- *Workshop (3–5 days)*: The workshop provides conceptual frameworks for understanding individual and group behaviour and the dynamics of organisation. Participants apply these frameworks to their current work situations through exercises and live consultancy. The workshop learning is supported by recommended reading.
- *Ongoing consulting groups*: Groups of approximately six participants who meet regularly with a consultant for an agreed period of time. The purpose is to enable participants to apply theoretical concepts to their own consulting/change projects. The group also provides the opportunity

for continued development in the understanding and management of groups and group dynamics as well as growth in consultancy skills.

• *Personal consultation with tutors and peers*: This enables participants to clarify and develop their professional role, diagnose their personal behaviours and styles in order to become more effective change agents. Ideally this becomes an ongoing practice.

Supervision of consulting practice

Supervised consulting practice is a highly desirable learning process for integrating psychoanalytic theory into consulting work and for utilising and understanding the projective processes in the client system. Consultants who aspire to use a psychoanalytic orientation are recommended to work with a psychoanalytic supervisor – someone who is outside the client system and who therefore can provide the necessary reflection on the work. Working alongside colleagues who have a similar orientation is a recommended way of furthering learning, as long as that pair or alliance also avails itself of external supervision.

Use of transference

An appreciation of and an ability to work with transference and counter-transference is important in effective consultation (Hirschhorn 1994). The sophisticated consultant or change agent needs the capacity to use their own experience in order to sense and interpret both conscious and unconscious communication with and within the client system. They need to consider all relationships as containing elements of transference/counter-transference and projection (see Table 8.1) and inform diagnosis and intervention by this (often painfully gained) data. Supervision is central to the effective use of transference and projective processes. Working with colleagues who have a psychoanalytic orientation as a consulting pair or a team is also valuable.

Academic programmes

There is an increasing provision of (usually postgraduate) programmes which offer longer-term developmental opportunities for consultants; some now incorporate psychoanalytic perspectives, or another equally demanding depth of psychological orientation with regard to organisations and consulting. In the UK we are aware of several providers including: Ashridge Consulting (Berkhamsted), Cranfield School of Management (Cranfield), Sheffield Business School, Tavistock Clinic (London), The Tavistock Institute (London), University of West England (Bristol); in the USA the William Allanson White Institute (New York).

International Society for the Psychoanalytic Study of Organisations

This society is based in USA but has a strong European representation. It welcomes participation and application for membership from consultants interested in the psychoanalytic approach to consulting. (Information about membership and events can be obtained from Dominic Volini: tel +1 908 754 5100, fax +1 908 754 7086, e-mail domvolini@aol.com.) It is an interdisciplinary organisation which provides a forum for consultants, academics and clinicians to discuss their organisational consultation and research. It explores the application of psychoanalytic theory to the study of organisations, is committed to the research and development of theory and practice in psychoanalytic approaches to organisations, and provides an opportunity for debate, critical appraisal, mutual support and education. The society holds an annual event, usually in June, which includes professional development workshops, a three day symposium, and a members' meeting.

REFERENCES AND FURTHER READING

Bion, W. R. (1959) *Experiences in Groups*, New York: Basic Books.

Burrell, G. and Morgan, G. (1979) *Sociological Paradigms and Organisational Analysis*, London: Gower.

De Board, R. (1978) *The Psychoanalysis of Organizations*, London: Tavistock.

Foulkes, S. A. (1975) *Group Analytic Psychotherapy: Method and Principles*, London: Gordon and Breach.

Halton, W. (1994) 'Some unconscious aspects of organizational life', in A. Obholzer and V. Zagier Roberts (eds) *The Unconscious at Work*, London: Routledge.

Hirschhorn, L. (1990) *The Workplace Within*, London: MIT Press.

—— (1994) 'Transference, the primary task and the primary risk', in R. Casemore *et al.* (eds) *What Makes Consultancy Work?*, London: South Bank University Press.

Hirschhorn, L. and Barnett, C. K. (1993) *The Psychodynamics of Organizations*, Philadelphia: Temple.

Kets de Vries, M. F. R. and Miller, D. (1985) *The Neurotic Organization*, San Francisco: Jossey-Bass.

Jaques, E. (1972) *A General Theory of Bureaucracy*, London: Heinemann.

Klein, M. (1959) 'Our adult world and its roots in infancy', *Human Relations*, 12: 291–301.

Klein, M. (1975) *Envy and Gratitude and Other Works*, London: Heinemann.

Levinson, H. (1972) *Organisational Diagnosis*, Cambridge, MA: Harvard University Press.

Menzies, I. E. P. (1960) 'A case-study in the functioning of social systems as a defence against anxiety', *Human Relations*, 13: 95–121.

Miller, E. J. and Rice, A. K. (1967) *Systems of Organization*, London: Tavistock.

Morgan, G. (1986) *Images of Organization*, London: Sage.

Obholzer, A. and Zagier Roberts, V. (eds) (1994) *The Unconscious at Work*, London: Routledge.

Reed B. D. and Palmer, B. W. M. (1972) *Introduction to Organisational Behaviour*, London: Grubb Institute.

Schein, E. H. (1987) *The Clinical Perspective in Fieldwork*, Newbury Park, CA: Sage.

Stacey, R. (1993) *Strategic Management and Organisational Dynamics*, London: Pitman.

Zaleznik, A. (1989) *The Managerial Mystique: Restoring Leadership in Business*, New York: Harper & Row.

Chapter 9

Consulting in rapidly changing conditions of uncertainty

Petruska Clarkson

This chapter will theoretically and experientially explore the individual and organisational capacities and competencies currently proving most useful in dealing with the increasingly complex conditions as people and organisations move towards the third millennium. It draws from the cutting edges of psychology, cultural theory, organisational behaviour and the new sciences. It explores conceptually as well as from personal and organisational experience important principles of consulting, counselling, developing, training, surviving and even thriving in conditions of chaos and complexity by enlisting the productive, creative and satisfying aspects of psychological, organisational and cultural uncertainty. The chapter will cover relevant theoretical and practical knowledge and explore new paradigm attitudes, skills and behaviours. A composite fictionalised case study will be used throughout to illustrate, with fractal examples of the consultancy as a whole, the process at work.

THE PROBLEM

In a recent consultancy case, most people associated with a late twentieth-century organisation reported to the consultant that the organisation was disintegrating. The Managing Director had a vision of the future which required that the company be restructured, whilst it was in fact making more money than ever before, to reduce the workforce by 30 per cent over the next three years. Managers would be, for example, applying for their own jobs. Complaints of falling production, low morale, absenteeism and increasingly acrimonious top level management meetings were escalating. Eventually one of the senior partners decided to call in the consultant. The first work of the consultant was to clarify how the company wanted to focus the change effort. We used a counselling approach that recognised the stress the partner was under (Clarkson 1990) to start towards contract clarification.

What follows is what I think helped. It's called 'future fitness'. According to Darwin's ideas it is the fittest who shall survive. However, he did not mean strongest – which is the usual mistranslation and false meaning. He meant those organisms who are most adaptable to changing conditions.

I am writing these brief notes threading in the story of the late twentieth-century organisation in a post-modernist mood. It is not my intention to provide a new truth or even a new version of the old truths. This is a collage, juxtaposing the past and the present, the thoroughly digested with the half understood, intuition with knowledge, and experience with received wisdom. There is no intention to lead, or to prescribe; only to stimulate and ignite, to perhaps prompt towards recognition.

As a counsellor and psychotherapist, I have become increasingly aware of the large-scale disruptive impact current world conditions have upon my clients, most of whom are well-functioning and intelligent professionals. As an organisational consultant, I am increasingly perturbed by the depression, fear, anger and bitter disillusionment of many people with organisations, from which they are being 'out-placed', or fear being made 'redundant', or are undergoing yet another restructuring with greater and greater demands for productivity and profitability while in receipt of less and less resources.

The natural human need for security, control, certainty, and pre-dictability is abrogated again and again, as institutions go out of business, and economic conditions fluctuate unpredictably. What used to be a reasonable expectation, for example a lifetime of employment, is now constantly under review. No one can be sure of it, even in the last bastions of the public sector. When I first interviewed members of the middle management in the late twentieth-century organisation, they all told me versions of the following: 'We just don't know what sort of job we will have in the future, or in a few months' time. There seems to be no leadership. We are given impossible tasks. Our targets are increased, resources lowered, employer expectations seem to be escalating, and we feel crazy because we're expected to do what cannot be achieved.' I saw the anxiety in their eyes, in their breathing and in the discrepancy between their 'can do' postures in meetings with senior management members and their despair in their private interviews with me.

I saw sincere hard working committed people floundering and making many more mistakes (passing up opportunities, fluffing others) for fear of slipping up and being blamed. I was reminded of Pavlov's dogs who were rewarded for successfully differentiating between an ellipse and a circle. As the experimenters gradually shaped the ellipses into circles and the circles into ellipses, the dogs experienced the impossibility of the task and essentially went mad. This kind of craziness which is the result of trying to meet impossible and gradually more confusing demands is how these people were describing their current working conditions. As a consultant I experienced their anxiety almost viscerally. This empathy with their experience is the necessary ground and foundation from which I listen to their condition, reflect their situation as they see it and build the rapport which will be essential to our working alliance during my intervention.

At the same time as these conditions of precariousness, uncertainty and stressful anxiety become the norm for a very large section of our working population (including the top managers of the late twentieth-century organisation) there is an escalation in complexity on all fronts which leave many of the employees and managers feeling even more de-skilled personally as well as professionally. As one of the top-level managers said to me, 'Even if I don't change and don't want to change, change is being foisted on me from the outside. People may think that I'm driving it, but in truth, more likely it's driving me. Furthermore confidentially, and only between us: I don't have a clue where it's driving to!'

Continuity is over, and the 'management of change' has in a certain sense become a contradiction in terms. I heard this in the rueful and cynical laughter of the whizz-kids in the 'Management of Change' department. Long-range unpredictability has become the norm and the only constant now is change itself. I know that many managers confide such fears to their wives or their counsellors (which they keep well secret), but eminent organisational consultants are not ashamed to admit in learned journals that: 'We don't know what is happening and we don't know what we are doing' (Moult 1990: 77). However, such private sentiments on managers' part don't go too well with a clear vision and mission statement which the Executive Director felt he had to provide publicly for his company in order to inspire confidence and trust in his leadership.

We all now live in an organisational, cultural and scientific world where the old paradigms seem to have lost their usefulness, inspiration and sometimes their values. All of us are confronted with these rapid changes through the constant bombardment of the media, our children's developing lives, our economic upheavals. The nature of change itself, whether through evolutionary development or radical quantum leaps, has changed, and it appears that it will only continue changing. The quantity and quality of change itself is changing at the same time as the tempo of change is accelerating. Managers and consultants need to enable themselves and empower others to survive these turbulent, unpredictable conditions and transform them into opportunities for survival, if not development and growth. A consultant, as I explained to my client, can only undertake to facilitate such enablement or empowerment, not guarantee to make it happen for the late twentieth-century organisation.

THEORETICAL AND METHODOLOGICAL APPROACH

From my previous experience and the kinds of requests made of me as organisational consultant and consultant/trainer of consultants, it seemed to me a useful idea to put together what I have found to be the most essential tools for organisational practitioners. I don't think that there is any hope that the old paradigms can see us through (even though they may still be very useful on occasions). This client organisation had also realised this. I therefore set myself the task of identifying the few most useful conceptual and practical tools that I could teach or enable in the limited time available for this consultancy intervention, which could be of use to managers and developers not only for the late twentieth-century organisation, but also for many others.

I was (and am still) under no illusion that these ideas are some kind of cure-all, placebo or infallible prescription. The one single factor which causes the greatest pain as people struggle with these conditions whirling around us towards the end of this century is the Utopian fallacy – the child-like hope in each one of us that someone somewhere should have the answers, or that someone somewhere should come up with a solution which will alleviate, if not obviate, our distress. This is often the greatest danger for the consultant – an idealising transference onto the consultant which expects (or demands) the delivery of magic, childhood wish-fulfilment of security, unconditional love and unending supplies of goodies from the parents with no personal responsibility at all. Of course, this often results in envious attacks if the source of supplies keeps supplying, followed by total rage, cynicism and disappointment when the supplies fail to live up to the fantasised perfection – as any parent, consultant or organisation inevitably will. (For further discussion on the role of transference and counter-transference in prioritising organisational interventions see Clarkson and Kellner 1995.)

The tools are divided here into *metaphors, attitudes, skills and behaviours* in a reasonably arbitrary way, to be used, changed or discarded just the way one would real tools and equipment in a real kitbag (see Figure 9.1). There are of course many more which I could have included and sometimes do. However, skilfulness in the use and understanding of their application as well as the imagination to adapt them to life's infinite invitations to creative problem solving remain the user's responsibility.

Metaphors for enhancing understanding

The late twentieth-century organisation had built its products and reputation on scientific, cultural and organisational models from Newtonian physics, a rationality based on the laws of cause and effect, a hope for incremental increases in knowledge, component analysis and step-by-step planning, a hope for the ever upward-pointing arrow of progress reflected in the unending improvement of company profitability charts. These old models had proved very useful and people were quite fond of them as one becomes of things which no longer quite work, but is reluctant to throw

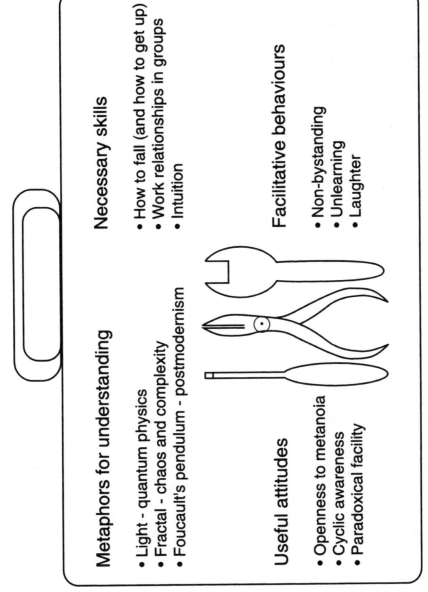

Figure 9.1 A small kitbag for the future
Source: Clarkson 1993b

away in case it some day comes in useful. However, the MD had seen the future and knew in his bones that future fitness for this company was going to require entirely new approaches – even though there may always still be valid occasions for using manual typewriters rather than state of the art word processors. But how to explain this?

Human beings learn best through stories and metaphors. They have ways of opening up the mind to new possibilities where reason and logic can sometimes restrict. Metaphors employ the right side of the brain (to use a simplified analogy) and stimulate creativity, the creation of new categories rather than the rote application of the well-established rules (like time-management) which everyone knows they should follow, but hardly ever do – and even then only for little while.

The first category of tools in any kitbag for the future would therefore be a set of new metaphors. They come from fields which few people will ever master, yet they affect each one of us profoundly as persons and as professionals. We can but proceed with intelligent discrimination and imagination using them as metaphors, not as actualities. On the other hand, originating as these metaphors do from physics laboratories and academic institutions, they may sometimes have a face validity for managers schooled in the old paradigms which can in some cases facilitate their acceptance if presented appropriately.

Light and quantum physics

The implications of the complex and disturbing field of quantum physics for the thinking and practice of the late twentieth-century organisation are potentially enormous. So I use the notion of a light in the kitbag to symbolise this. A light is simple, useful in the dark and the science of it passing mysterious. For example, in the words of Sir William Bragg, 'Elementary particles seem to be waves on Mondays, Wednesdays and Fridays and particles on Tuesdays, Thursdays and Saturdays' (Koestler 1972: 52).

'How is this possible?' asks anyone with everyday logic. Yet, one of the first lessons of quantum physics is that apparently contradictory views of reality co-exist. This metaphor invites the workers into a willingness to deal with simultaneous contradiction in the physical as well as the psychological and organisational world. It connects with the notion that the observer is always part of the field and that, therefore, ultimately all our so-called 'knowledge' is profoundly and ineradicably relative.

The new physics makes it untenable to consider an objective or value-free scientific approach, or the idea that a consultant can be 'objective' or 'neutral'. For example, it requires us to take on board fully the notion that there is nothing we can discuss or consider in isolation from ourselves or, for that matter, from the entire environment surrounding us. As a result the consultant is never truly separate from the organisation or neutral to the field. The importance and different natures of relationships in organisations is further explored by Clarkson and Shaw (1992) and is outlined in Table 9.2.

The next, vital aspect of quantum physics as it relates to organisational work which I find particularly helpful is Heisenberg's (1930) 'uncertainty principle'. For managers of the late twentieth-century organisation and for teachers of management and organisational behaviours, this implies that there are some things, no matter how accurate our apparatus or calibration, that we cannot ever know for certain.

Of course there will be some objections. Does that mean that just anything goes? No, of course there is much that we do know and can know. The new managers and new entrepreneurs have to develop the discrimination between these kinds of knowing and unknowing. It is more to do with acknowledging and valuing the inherent and intrinsic indeterminacy of human and organisational phenomena, thus challenging our hubris at the same time as extending our compassion for our inevitable shortfall from perfection. These were some of the conclusions from the discussion groups following the first presentation I did with the client organisation.

A fractal

What is a fractal? A fractal is a way of showing how things often display the same structure when you look at the same things on bigger and bigger or smaller and smaller scale. One could say that the whole is also always within each part and each part is also the whole. The word 'fractal' was coined by Mandelbrot (1974) to describe this kind of phenomenon in a repeating pattern – elements of the whole are repeated in every fragment, and spiral off each other towards creative evolution as wholes.

This preoccupation with wholeness of contemporary chaos theorists has of course existed since the beginning of time. It is merely a modernist phenomenon to try to reduce things to their constituent parts. For example, Briggs and Peat (1990: 75) state:

> The whole shape of things depends on the most minute part. The part *is* the whole in this respect, for through the action of any part, the whole in the form of chaos or transformative change may manifest.

This has peculiar, even amazing implications for consultancy to the late twentieth-century organisation – perhaps any segment of the organisation, however unrepresentative or unrelated it may appear, encodes the whole of the organisation. An intervention into any fractal of an organisation in this sense would be an intervention into the whole of the organisation, and may possess the solution for the whole. It is possible that our current limitations of habit and theory can evolve to take on the radically new possibilities which open up to organisational consultants and managers when we take this intuition of complexity seriously into our practice.

'Fractal geometry describes the tracks and marks left by the passage of dynamical activity' (Briggs 1992: 22). Just as the galaxy pulsates, so too does nerve tissue. The same is true for the human heart and so too, surely, for the late twentieth-century organisation. Instead of going off into 'syndicate groups' in different rooms for example, with the organisational client we experimented with keeping participants in large meetings within the same space. Instead of time-limited exercises, people attempted to simply 'flow' around the space, coalescing when mutual interests drew them together, finding out (within the informal structure) who had the information or resources they needed and being available in a similar way to other individuals or other spontaneously forming and unforming learning fractals (groups).

In a way which is difficult to describe the jerky rhythms of starting a task, the energetic focus of concentrated working at the task, the loosening pulse which follows peak performance could be felt in the conference room. Most obviously the volume, speed and intensity of speech would indicate these patterns. There was soon a kind of synchronisation forming as the group members got used to working in this way and became more skilful at mining such natural rhythms of group, individual and organisational energy.

Chaos and complexity

Chaos concerns the pattern within randomness (time or space) as an aspect of complexity (Waldrop 1992).

> The first Chaos theorists . . . had an eye for pattern, especially pattern that appeared on different scales at the same time. They had a taste for randomness and complexity, for jagged edges and sudden leaps . . . They feel that they are turning back a trend in science toward reductionism, the analysis of systems in terms of their constituent parts . . . they believe that they are looking for the whole.
>
> (Gleick 1989: 5)

Chaos sometimes convulses dynamic systems and sometimes simply resides in the background. From chaos often comes a new, more complex and differentiated order. Chaos has often been used as a negative word: sometimes chaos is a sign of incompetence, and the description of an organisation or teamwork as 'chaotic' has been a term of approbation. Chaos theory offers the late twentieth-century organisation a new meaning and a new way of looking at options for responding to chaotic conditions: not with an expectation of disintegration or panic at the lack of structure, but an openness to the emergence of novel and more creative outputs. For many of the managers in this consulting project, the notion that chaos is not necessarily 'a bad thing' proved helpful. Many saw chaos as a precursor to more developed, complex and creative order, the possibility that it can be survived – or even used productively – was a reframe of exciting value.

For others of course, it was simply nonsense and their reactions ranged from fear to anger – natural enough when faced with the upset of one's treasured world view! For the consultant it is vital to validate and accept such reactions without argument, not only for the progress of the learning to continue, but also to model and learn from the parallel process in the managers, how their staff may react and what may or may not be helpful to staff in turbulence.

Given the very complex and challenging economic and organisational conditions faced by the late twentieth-century organisation, creativity is required more than ever. Of course, everyone was in agreement with this proposition. But the new sciences have much to teach on this topic which goes against received wisdom and common sense. Creativity abhors balance, the middle way and a measured tread (Zohar 1990). Indeed, the literature of chaos normalises and values imbalances.

Most of us really have always known the uncomfortable fact that 'Creativity happens at far-from-equilibrium conditions' (Gruber 1988); it often needs the stimulus of deadlines, emotional turmoil or a change of setting to flourish. Chaos scientists have discovered that predictability and regularity can be a sign of illness – the only time the heartbeat is completely regular, for example, is shortly before a coronary. The healthy organism, and therefore the healthy organisation, is always *out* of balance and this process of flux is an intrinsic part of natural processes: the flexibility, the innovation, the capacity for finding novel solutions in rapidly changing unpredictable conditions. The biggest danger for the late twentieth-century organisation is a striving for the biologically impossible and probably destructive achievement of becoming stable in a highly unstable condition. Perfect balance on a surfboard means constant re-adjustment and often quite dramatic twists and turns to keep up the momentum and direction as the waves thrash about.

By applying the idea of wholeness from chaos theory to organisational life, the company in this case began to rethink its concepts about the relationship between the MD and the management team, between the individual managers and their teams. If such groupings are seen as momentary and changeable configurations of the whole organism which is the company, then leaders and followers become mutually reinforcing in a way which, potentially at least, challenges and undermines the prevalent but unproductive blaming mechanisms where either the bosses don't know what they're doing or we just can't get the workers to do it right (or variations on these themes). If the individual cannot be separated from his or her group context or organisational field, from the dynamic ebb and flow of organisational life and development, then it follows that there is no genuine separation of leadership from the group.

Leadership can be very much more complex (and perhaps more effective) than the management psychology books have described so far. It may be a hidden factor in the nature of the so-called 'strange attractor', the existence of which can but be imputed in chaos theory. As such, it is not directly identified or seen. The MD of this late twentieth-century organisation was willing to reconceptualise the function of his leadership not only in what he did but also in the way he was a person. Perhaps the most effective leaders create turbulent space within which they can act as an inferred attractor, from which a pattern can be discovered and form can develop. It is possible that as soon as the form rigidifies, when they stop causing turbulence in the field, the leaders are no longer functional. Leaders who are no longer maintaining themselves in disequilibrium may be part of an organisation in decay.

One of the other most disturbing discoveries of chaos theory is that small events can cause very large effects, and large events may lead to only very small effects. Unfortunately, we do not always know when these conditions apply, but we do know that they sometimes do. This sensitive dependence upon initial conditions is known in science as the 'butterfly effect': the idea that a butterfly stirring its wings in America can cause major storms in China. This notion makes the work of organisational consultants exceptionally difficult, particularly when they try to attribute positive changes to their consultancy intervention. However, it does mean that perhaps even small inputs into our world may have profound results.

Foucault's pendulum: the post-modernist turn

The title of Umberto Eco's novel is included in this symbolic kitbag as a symbol or metaphor for a post-modernist view of the world. Post-modernism is defined in contradistinction to modernism and is a way of describing the spirit of our current time – our *Zeitgeist*. Modernism was characterised by a search for an ultimate truth, a belief in incremental progressions in knowledge and clear boundaries between different disciplines; in effect a master text, such as Freud or Marx once provided (Adair 1993). Modernism was the idea that there was one answer to human ills or human progress or organisational development – and it is still with us even as we see the fashions in what is the one answer change. Postmodernism describes the state of mind so many workers in the late twentieth-century organisation share: there are no more heroes; there is no one truth.

Postmodernism is characterised by 'a diversity of purpose, a confusion of boundaries and an eclecticism' (Moult 1990: 173). New technology and discoveries have meant that the late twentieth-century organisation seems to have more simultaneously impossible realities to contend with. A new, more complex, technological language proliferated in the company with high hopes that it would explain it all, but failed repeatedly.

> We live in a world in which the authority of previous guides has apparently crumbled. They have become fragments, bits of a particular archive (of Western Europe, of the white male voice), part of a local history that once involved the presumption (and power) to speak in the name of the 'world'.
>
> (Chambers 1990: 81)

There is by now a widespread disillusion with the grand answers, the next organisation development fad; and yet employees cannot afford the luxury of despair (like the fashionable nihilism of the 1960s) because of the painful economic and cultural conditions which impinge upon them daily – if not personally, then through the media. In a culture of multiple narratives, many stories are true, and there is no longer one story. Yet, this meaning – individually and organisationally – never dies, however impossible it has become to fully satisfy it now with company slogans, vision quests and mission statements.

This kind of consciousness leads inevitably to an awareness of values and collective issues and it mandates everybody to be responsible for the 'whole thing' – nobody can say it has nothing to do with me any longer. 'There is no promise of utopias here, but the possibility of active and engaged participation in cultural process is significantly enhanced' (Gergen 1990: 33).

Useful attitudes

Alongside these metaphors I have also packed, into my consulting kitbag for the future, three attitudes which help to empower us in the face of an uncertain future.

Openness to enantodromia or metanoia

A useful concept is that of *enantodromia*. It is an ancient Greek word which means reversal into the opposite. It is similar to the flip-over effect in chaos theory or to the notion of metanoia. For Laing and Esterson (1972: 63), metanoia is 'dialectical rationality, a praxis of reconciliation and dynamic unity, an enterprise of continual and continuing reappraisal and renewal, constantly bringing forth new experience with deepening understanding and wholeness'. Metanoia is a turnaround, a change of heart that can only happen in openness to change and the disorientation it may bring.

Therefore we may need a positive attitude to change, an investment in evolution, and the willingness to bear the disintegrating and fragmenting forces without incapacitating ourselves. Implicit in the process of metanoia as viewed from a Gestalt perspective is the reversal of figure and ground. For instance, when looking at a picture, we can concentrate on the shapes created by the positive forms, or on the shapes created by the spaces between – the negative shapes. Future fitness in the late twentieth-century organisation requires not only one turnaround, but many, not one change of mind, but several, and not only one organisational transformation, but continuing commitment to unending organisational change.

Cyclic awareness: what goes around comes around

This leads to the next important attitude which is an awareness of the cyclic nature of most human and organisational phenomena. An attitude which embraces this cyclic awareness manifests in the willingness to do something again and again, knowing that the nature of change experience is cyclic (or resembles a spiral). The MD of our late twentieth-century organisation knew that although his company was doing exceptionally well – in certain ways – at the time he spoke to me, it would inevitably be followed by different harder times. And, the very same conditions, resources and strategies that had been successful in the past, would most likely not ensure continued success in the future. As breathing in and breathing out follow each other in the human body, so do cycles of economic growth and recession. Any attempt to conceptually or practically deny this rhythm results in serious consequences.

Heraclitus, whose wisdom has endured since 500 BC, postulated that the only thing in life of which we can be sure, is change. Furthermore, he said that the nature of change is cyclical. Everything is in a constant state of flux, and human experience is continuously trying to make meaning from the ever-recurring cyclic interplay between things staying the same and things changing. We may see even leaders take an evolutionary rather than revolutionary role in the way that the MD of the late twentieth-century organisation was attempting to do – pre-empt and prepare for the down-swing – rather than simply be in reaction to the predictable fluctuations in fortune.

Apparently, individual human beings as well as organisations need to enter the void again and again if we are to emerge more fully and completely. Structuring is followed by restructuring or destructuring and then the cycle commences again. The skilfulness required concerns riding the waves of change, not in futile attempts to iron out the natural rhythms of history and the body. In this sense we can say that linearity has reached the end of the line. The new era requires that we bring back the right hemisphere of the brain (the non-verbal side of us that works in flashes of images rather than in words) which is our source of creativity, of lateral thinking, of intuition and linking leaps of faith.

Paradoxical facility and the end of causality

Unknowability and uncertainty of many 'facts' means the end of simplistic cause and effect links and particularly the end of specific attempts at long-range predictability. However, the organisation may not yet have equivalently useful conceptual or experiential structures to replace and/or augment the old notions of linear and sequential causality. Any working kitbag must contain the belief that the past is past, consistency is flawed, and, more often than not, contradiction is *in*. This necessitates a positive attitude to change and an investment in personal experience of change, particularly during 'the dark night of the soul', which seems to be an essential requirement for any creative breakthrough, whether in art, organisations, psychotherapy or international change. It has become necessary to be comfortable with paradox, for managers to model such facility and for the rest of the employees to be encouraged, and even rewarded for 'believing six impossible things before breakfast' as the Red Queen said in *Alice in Wonderland*.

Necessary skills

Here follows a brief list of skills which, when added to the metaphors and attitudes in the kitbag, emerged and were adapted to equip people in the late twentieth-century organisation to cope better with the changing circumstances – systemic, societal and individual – in which they find themselves.

How to fall (and how to get up)

'Rolling with the punches' is another way of expressing a willingness to enter the fray, or maybe to enter the void, and to try to survive through flexibility and spontaneity, knowing that each individual influences the system as much as it influences each individual. Learning how to fall well, like a martial artist or a parachute jumper or a baby learning to walk, involves learning how to keep your physical and psychological centre of gravity low, so that you can rapidly change the vector of your force depending on how circumstances may change from moment to moment.

It has been said that skilfulness in life does not depend on whether you can stay up on your horse, it all depends on how well you get up after you have fallen down – again and again. This kind of skill concerns the psychological and physical ability to mobilise energy and intelligence in any direction, like a tennis player preparing to return serve. A high and unstable centre of gravity is associated with a person who gives out more than they take in (or vice versa). Empathic listening is therefore an essential low gravity habit, whereas needing to be right all the time is not.

Flexibility in this sense includes the willingness to feel emotions of love, grief, anger, joy, rather than to suppress or deny them. Of course, this does not always mean saying what you feel like to whom you feel like when you feel like it. It also concerns discrimination between feeling and acting, between authentic experiencing and appropriate behaviour. The skill of falling and getting up, of surrender and yielding again and again includes knowing how to make mistakes and admit defeat – and 'start all over again'.

Over and over again, executives complained that they were afraid to make mistakes, afraid to own up to this fear and constantly 'guarding their backs' in case someone were to find out that they were bluffing. I have elsewhere (Clarkson 1994) described and explored the pseudo-competency (or the Achilles syndrome) when pretence or covering up substitutes for true competence and confidence and the fear of making mistakes plus the cover-up results in failure to risk appropriately, but specifically in hamstringing creativity and preventing learning in the individual and in the organisation.

For the late twentieth-century organisation, it is essential to overcome the fear of failure and for management to instil, by practice and precept, an attitude which welcomes and embraces failure. The story is told that someone commiserated with Edison that it took him some 1000 attempts before he succeeded in making the light bulb – it must have been discouraging to have so many failures. Edison replied: 'No, I did not have failures, I had 999 successes in finding out how *not* to make a light bulb.'

Creating new paradigm relationships in groups

This will be a vital skill if we are all to pool our resources in a living example of dynamic interrelatedness. As it becomes increasingly clear that the old paradigms are outdated, even the way groups operate may also be in flux. The classical model of groups has been a deterministic one, defined in stages and generally model-oriented. Basic assumptions have been made about the group, and so its process and eventual outcome could be anticipated. Developmental phases in the group life have been considered to unroll in a relatively specified sequence. Of course this has some validity when the group is a closed system remaining together over a considerable period of time in the same space.

The late twentieth-century organisation does not work like this anymore. The ebb and flow of task focused short timespan teams, the sheer unavailability of everyone to attend all relevant meetings seem to have made the classical models, and prescriptions of team building, the counsels of impossible perfection.

Now, however, we are more aware that groups are probabilistic rather than deterministic; they are not simplistically based on cause and effect, and therefore they have an uncertain outcome. We see that any group creates itself through its own dynamic process. The consultant co-creates the reality while differences emerge through contact within the group, not based on pre-conceived or static assumptions made about roles, types or previous patterns. Instead of leadership issues coalescing around dependency/independence, the leadership function becomes more like a strange attractor – not exclusively attributable to one individual or even to one part of the system – but an effect which indicates that leadership is being created between members of the organisation.

Everything is open to possibility – particularly the notion that every-thing we are considering here may be completely wrong. The influence of members of the group on each other is an integral part of the process, both during the group time and continuing beyond – and hard though this may be to imagine – perhaps throughout life. Patterns emerge from the group which, like fractals, hold all the potential of the group, for all things are related and nothing exists in isolation. The organisation works holistically and existentially while acknowledging the influence of the past and future on the present state (Clarkson and Clayton 1992).

Intuition

Intuition is a sense of the impending. It is not based on obvious logic, but probably the outcome of very fast processing of barely perceptible stimuli. Unfortunately members of male-dominated organisations often pooh-pooh intuition, associating it with women. And indeed, Anita Roddick's Bodyshop company makes it one of the competencies expected to be developed by staff.

However, successful entrepreneurs, whether men or women, are often highly intuitive. The development of successful business strategy is based on intuition rather than the linear logic of old-style step-by-obvious-step forward planning. A 'radar' system is needed that is the result partly of relevant experience, partly wise reflection and partly inspired guesswork. This radar system needs to operate in a trusted way in order for it to work quickly enough to be useful in fast-changing situations.

The appreciation and development of intuition is a skill which can be learned and developed at all levels of an organisation and is particularly to be valued wherever it is found. The late twentieth-century organisation in this case invested in some specific skills training in order to facilitate intuitive functioning and creativity development throughout the organisation.

Facilitative behaviours

No kitbag for the future of the late twentieth-century organisation, would be complete without the following helpful behaviours.

Non-bystanding (or responsible involvement)

A bystander is considered to be a person who does not become actively involved in a situation where someone else requires help. Where one or more people are in danger, bystanders therefore could, by taking some form of action, affect the outcome of the situation even if they are not able to avert it (Clarkson 1996). The most potent possibilities of change in many organisations lie with those who would disclaim such power – the bystanders. As we noted before, the observer is always part of the field. The new physics also contributed the idea of 'state entanglement' to the vitality of the relationship field, which simply means that we are always, irrevocably 'entangled' with others – even those we may never see again.

There are many ways of adopting the bystander role in professional and organisational life. The following 'slogans' capture the spirit of many rationalisations of this kind which individuals and organisations use to limit their creative capacities in response to their interrelationship with others: 'It's none of my business'; 'This situation is more complex than it seems'; 'I do not have all the information/am not qualified to deal with this'; 'I don't want to get burned again'; 'I want to remain neutral'; 'I'm only telling the truth (to others) as I see it'; 'I'm just following orders'; 'I expect it's six of one and half a dozen of the other'; 'My contribution won't make much difference'; 'I'm simply keeping my own counsel'; 'They brought it on themselves'; 'I don't want to rock the boat'.

The question becomes, 'What is the best way to be involved?' and that does not always mean doing something directly or immediately. Understanding and accepting personal responsibility for bystanding behaviour may be uncomfortable. There is a deep heritage in many organisations of covering your own back, turning a blind eye, allowing scapegoating and relishing the vicarious excitement of office politics. One important lesson is not to wait to see which way the wind is blowing, but to make choices while the story is still unfolding, to decide how to be and what to do before the scene is played out and while the result remains ambiguous.

We explored with this late twentieth-century organisation what the possible advantages of responsible involvement might be. At a personal level people reported the satisfaction of expressing one's energy in the service of integrity and responsibility rather than turning it inwards into sleepless nights, gnawing doubts, ulcers and heart disease. Also there was vitality of engaging in 'a struggle for what you believe to be right, rather than the vicarious excitement of political gossip'. Together we explored the many fertile opportunities for learning and increasing one's knowledge of how to be effective amongst the complexities of organisational life. This is at least one way of understanding the challenge that the call for an empowered organisational culture represents.

In today's turbulent world, it is neither ethical nor practical to maintain that things are not our business, or to deny that we influence outcomes. Nor is it enough to espouse values without enacting them. Righteous indignation becomes rather empty when devoid of action. It is the difference between what is called on the street 'talking the talk' and 'walking the walk'.

Unlearning

There is a contemporary preoccupation with 'the learning organisation' and the late twentieth-century organisation in our case had also felt the impact of this approach to organisational culture. However, in this company we came to the conclusion that the unlearning organisation is at least equally important. It became clear to large numbers of people of this late twentieth-century organisation that 'it is the extent to which we hang on to old habits that prevents us from recognising that previously effective solutions have now become problems in themselves and inhibit our capabilities'. I cautioned all of us to remember that any solution will contain the seeds of future problems and when those have solutions, the next problems will arise in their turn from the seeds of the previous solutions. In counselling individual employees, as in organisational consultancy, there is a lot of work to be done around letting go of the belief systems and old hierarchies and not maintaining traditionalism just for its own, self-perpetuating sake, or because the old way is perceived as being too difficult or costly to change.

Laughter: the cosmic giggle

Humour is acknowledged in folk wisdom as one of the best natural medicines, and maintaining the capacity to find humour in all life situations is a life-preserving and life-enhancing skill. When Abraham Lincoln was criticised for making jokes during the American Civil War strategy meetings, he replied, 'If I couldn't have these 20-second breaks, the horror of the situation would kill me.' It is not to deny the seriousness of our situation, but if we take the real issues seriously enough we can free ourselves to laugh as well, to see things in perspective and to find hope and courage even in the midst of the worst despair. One of the most important features of the whole late twentieth-century organisation's culture change programme was the laughter and the jokes and the irony.

GUIDELINES FOR APPLICATION

Guideline one: decide on the sequencing of consultancy interventions in a whole organisation (see Table 9.1)

Table 9.1 A framework for prioritising organisational interventions

	Consultant's considered response (counter-transference interpreted)	Consultant's knee-jerk reaction (counter-transference acted out)
Danger	Listen Acknowledge feelings Explore sources Explore nature Elicit emotional reality	Teach Falsely reassure Rescue Contract unrealistically
Confusion	Restrain action Clarify issues Clarify roles Clarify authority Assess impact/consequences Provide models and maps	Get sucked into confusion Oversimplify Accept one frame of reference Fight Take sides
Conflict	Learn its history Welcome and understand it Model conflict handling Value the differences Validate all parties Provide arena and referee	Pathologise it Fear it Minimise it Ignore it Take sides
Deficit	Establish what they have Find what worked before Find out what did not Start where they are Establish needs and wants Provide relevant input	Do it for them Work with solved problems Solve symptoms Give your favourite package Assume there should be a training solution

Source: Clarkson and Kellner 1995

Guideline two: decide on the positioning of consultancy intervention in whole in terms of the relationship modality where creative organisational energy may need to be unblocked (see Table 9. 2)

Guideline three: remember that we are always working with a whole kitbag – no matter how small the part we are focusing on at any single moment

Table 9.2 A framework for assessing relationships at work

Relationship	Contribution to the organisation	Human motivation	Some signs of dysfunction
Unfinished	Grit in the oyster	Completion Resolution	Fixed, disruptive patterns of relationship
Working alliance	Achieving organisational tasks	Doing Competence Productivity	Task-dominated culture Sterile, driven work climate
Developmental	Developing the organisation's human resources	Growth Learning	Neediness Burn-out Over- or under-protection of staff
Personal	Developing the organisation as a working community with a healthy culture	Intimacy Friendship Community	Uncontactful conflict and competition Fake bonhomie Loss of task focus
Transpersonal	Developing wider organisation mission and purpose	Being Meaning Connection	Meaninglessness Anomie Ennui Disregard of ethics

Source: Clarkson, P. and Shaw, P. (1992) 'Human relationships at work – the place of counselling skills and consulting skills and services in organisations'. *MEAD* (the *Journal of the Association of Management Education and Development*) 23(1): 18–29.

Perhaps any segment of an organisation, however unrepresentative or unrelated it may appear on the surface, encodes the whole of the organisation. A consultancy intervention into any fractal of an organisation would be an intervention into the whole organisation.

Guideline four: consider that everything is always changing – including ourselves and the tools we are using

'Given the novelty and the indefinite variety of the environment, no adjustment would be possible, by the conservative inherited self-regulation alone, contact must be a creative transformation. On the other hand, creativity that is not continually destroying and assimilating an environment given in perception and resisting manipulation is useless to the organism (or the organisation) and remains superficial and lacking in energy; it does not become deeply exciting, and it soon languishes' (Perls, Hefferline and Goodman 1951: 406).

Guideline five: notice that we are always in a dynamic relationship with the whole and with ourselves – that nothing exists outside of relationship

The closer we analyse some 'thing' the less it appears as a thing and the more it appears as a dynamic process (things in relationship). Consequently, relationships become a primary source of our knowledge of the world. This can be taken to the ontological extreme by stating that things do not exist . . . that, in fact, things (and organisations of course) ultimately *are* relationships (Cottone 1988).

TEMPORARY CONCLUSION

I end on a quote from an unknown author from whom I have remembered the following line: 'I must warn you against the unfortunate use of what I have to say.' I do know that all of these notions can be abused, misunderstood and used out of context. I also believe these embryonic ideas can be helpful in developing training, managers, organisational consultancy, personal counselling and national responses to people in need in the current conditions of the late twentieth-century organisation. I hope they also serve you well and that you will add to them freely forever.

REFERENCES AND FURTHER READING

Adair, G. (1993) 'Scrutiny: Freud slips into the shadows', *Sunday Times*, 9 May, London.
Bateson, G. (1973) *Steps to an Ecology of Mind*, London: Paladin.
Briggs, J. (1992) *Fractals: the Patterns of Chaos*, London: Thames & Hudson.
Briggs, J. and Peat, F. D. (1990) *Turbulent Mirror*, New York: Harper & Row.
Chambers, I. (1990) *Border Dialogues: Journeys in Postmodernity*, London: Routledge.
Clarkson, P. (1990) 'The scope of "stress" counselling in organisations', *Employee Counselling Today*, 2(4): 3–6.
—— (1993a) 'New perspectives in counselling and psychotherapy (or adrift in a sea of change)', in P. Clarkson, *On Psychotherapy*, London: Whurr, 209–32.
—— (1993b) 'A small kitbag for the future', in *Order, Chaos and Change in the Public Sector* papers from the third Public Sector Conference organised by the Association for Management, Education and Development 18–20 January, 17–27.
—— (1994) *The Achilles Syndrome*, Shaftesbury: Element.
—— (1995a) *The Therapeutic Relationship*, London: Whurr.
—— (1995b) *Change in Organisations*, London: Whurr.
—— (1996) *The Bystander (an End to Innocence in Human Relationships?)*, London: Whurr.
Clarkson, P., and Clayton, S. (1992) 'Quantum group dynamics', *Second European Groupwork Symposium*, 33–6.

Clarkson, P. and Shaw, P. (1992) 'Human relationships at work – the place of counselling skills and consulting skills and services in organisations', *MEAD*, 23(1): 18–29.

Clarkson, P. and Kellner, K. (l995) 'Danger, confusion, conflict and deficit: a framework for prioritising organisational interventions', *People and Organisations*, 2(4): 6–13.

Costello, D. (1993) 'Gestalt, astrology and the group dynamics of our time', *The Astrological Journal*, 35(2): 86–90.

Cottone, R. R. (1988) 'Epistemological and ontological issues in counselling: implications of social systems theory', *Counselling Psychology Quarterly*, 1(4): 357–65.

Cunningham, I. (1990) 'Beyond modernity – is post-modernism relevant to management development?', *MEAD*, 21(3): 207–18.

Gergen, K. (1990) 'Towards a post-modern psychology', *The Humanistic Psychologist*, 18: 23–34.

Gleick, J. (1989) *Chaos: Making a New Science*, London: Heinemann.

Gruber, H. (1988) 'Inching our way up Mount Olympus: the evolving systems approach to creative thinking', in Robert J. Sternberg (ed.) *The Nature of Creativity*, Cambridge: Cambridge University Press.

Guerrière, D. (1980) 'Physis, Sophia, Psyche', in J. Sallis and K. Maly (eds) *Heraclitean Fragments: a Companion Volume to the Heidegger/Fink Seminar on Heraclitus* Alabama: University of Alabama Press, 87–134.

Heisenberg, W. (1930) *The Physical Principles of the Quantum Theory*, New York: Dover.

Koestler, A. (1972) *The Roots of Coincidence*, London: Hutchinson.

Laing, R. D. and Esterson, A. (1972) *Leaves of Spring*, Harmondsworth: Penguin.

Latané, B. and Darley, M. (1970) *The Unresponsive Bystander: Why Doesn't He Help?*, New York: Appleton-Century Crofts.

Mandelbrot, B. B. (1974) *The Fractal Geometry of Nature*, New York: Freeman.

Moult, G. (1990) 'Under new management', *MEAD* 21(3): 171–82.

Perls, F. S., Hefferline, F. F. and Goodman, P. (1951) *Gestalt Therapy: Excitement and Growth in the Human Personality*, New York: Julian Press.

Waldrop, M. M. (1992) *Complexity: the Emerging Science at the Edge of Order and Chaos*, Harmondsworth: Penguin.

Zohar, D. (1990) *The Quantum Self*, London: Bloomsbury.

Part III

Applying organisational theory

Applying organisational theory: Introduction

The editors have brought together five chapters for this third section of *Developing Organisational Consultancy*. Each chapter demonstrates the use of organisational theory during consulting about changes which have implications for multiple aspects of the organisation. Organisational theories have their roots in various social sciences, for example: sociology, political science, social anthropology, industrial relations, management and leadership theory.

What we are advocating as editors, through the vehicle of our authors, is the importance of thinking about organisations as systemic wholes with inter-connected areas of technology and behaviour. The authors are experienced consultants who work in the domain of structuring work organisations, large-scale organisational changes and other interventions that span hierarchical, departmental and operational process boundaries. Whether they apply the same theories in different ways or apply different theories, they share a common concern with alignment of inter-connected systems or levels in organisations.

The first chapter, written by Eric Miller, provides a detailed case study of 'Effecting organisational change in large complex systems: a collaborative consultancy approach'. The case simultaneously illustrates a unique application of socio-technical systems theory to inter-organisational relationships, while using the tool of a 'working note' to present the case and reconstruct the client–consultant interactions. The author offers data from the actual material he presented to the client, as well as disclosing his own feelings of confusion and ambivalence as the project unfolded over several months.

Richard Holti, in the second chapter, summarises the lessons he has learned in 'Consulting to organisational implications of technical change'. He begins by re-evaluating some of the original insights of those who developed the socio-technical systems (STS) theory. He suggests reformulation in the light of other organisational theories and international economic developments in the last thirty years. Specifically, he criticises the lack of attention to conflict and to other aspects of organisation in the original STS work. Holti proposes four different conceptual levels that need to be taken into consideration during organisational change and technological innovation: the political and economic, the logistical and cognitive, the cultural and the psychodynamic. He offers a case from the manufacturing sector, illustrating the way that he had to draw on these conceptual levels during the re-design of social and technical arrangements.

Application of the socio-technical systems theory continues in the third chapter of this section, 'Assisting work restructuring in complex and volatile situations'. Enid Mumford reports on her visit to the very coal fields in which The Tavistock Institute researchers conducted early work. She explains in detail how the changes in social relations, necessitated by technical changes, resulted in difficult industrial relations conflicts. A useful illustration of a 'stepwise' approach to work re-design is offered. Mumford also compares socio-technical systems theory with 'business process re-engineering' and 'total quality management' as approaches to work organisation design.

William Schneider addresses the issue of inter-connectedness from a different angle in the fourth chapter, 'Aligning strategy, culture and leadership'. Making a strong argument for customising strategic level change in organisations, the author reviews recent popular management books on this topic. He reports his own research in working with corporations through which he has identified four 'core cultures': control, collaboration, competence and cultivation. There are strategic, cultural and leadership implications in each of these cultures. The two cases included in the chapter demonstrate different types of misalignment, while also discussing how the consultant worked with the clients to resolve the difficulty.

The last chapter in this section focuses on 'Developing organisational communication'. Authors Jon White and Helena Memory emphasise the importance of consistency in messages, of alignment between leadership behaviour and a particular change initiative. They make an important distinction between communicating to inform and communicating to transform. Their chapter points interested consultants in the direction of methodologies for communication consulting, as well as of what to look for during diagnosis with a client. White and Memory provide seven short case studies in order to demonstrate the relevance of communication in a wide range of organisational situations.

As editors, we are aware that these five chapters barely cover the surface of the many different organisational theories that a developing consultant might wish to apply. They do, however, go a long way towards showing that to be worthwhile in a practical setting an organisational theory must reflect the complexity and inter-connectedness of organisational reality. Our authors have extensive experience in both developing organisational theories and applying them. Many of the organisational theories on the market inspire as good ideas, but do not stand up to multiple attempts by consultants and managers to apply them. Those presented in these chapters do.

Chapter 10

Effecting organisational change in large complex systems

A collaborative consultancy approach

Eric Miller

In the management of organisational change it has often been said that deciding what the state of the future organisation should be is the easy part: 90 per cent of the problem is how to get there. This is an exaggeration perhaps, but none the less a salutary reminder. It seems perfectly rational to start by defining the desired outcome – the task for which consultants are often hired – and then to plan the requisite steps for implementation. Managers tend to discover, however, that the planned route is littered with unforeseen obstacles – not least, resistance to change – and all too often the result falls far short of expectations.

The collaborative approach to organisational consultancy treats the 'what' and the 'how' together. Consultant and client system are partners in the process of organisational analysis and design, and there is progressively wider involvement of the client system in designing and managing the successive phases of the change itself. Resistances are not eliminated but are respected and worked with as a natural accompaniment of ending past relationships and making new ones, and the overall process tends to generate the culture of an ongoing learning organisation.

This chapter explores the use of a *systems psychodynamics* framework (i.e. a model of open socio-technical systems informed by a psychoanalytic perspective) in the processes of collaborative consultancy with large client systems. It takes the form of an annotated case study of one of a number of such interventions in which I have been involved. The example chosen – organisation for water supply and drainage in Mexico City – is some fifteen years old. This has the advantage that confidentiality is not an issue; and also there is information about longer-term outcomes. It might be argued that the problems of the 1990s are different – for example, that today's enterprises are operating in a more rapidly changing environment; but in fact this particular case raised many issues that have continued to be relevant to privatisation of public services, and in any event both the conceptual framework and the consultancy processes have proved their usefulness in a wide range of settings.

CONCEPTUAL FRAMEWORK

The systems psychodynamic framework evolved at The Tavistock Institute in the 1950s and 1960s. It draws on the two strands of systems theory and of psychoanalysis with its illumination of unconscious processes in individuals and groups. Figure 10.1 sketches the 'genealogy' of the framework.

On the systems side Kurt Lewin was a significant influence on the founders of the Institute. It was he who first drew attention to the 'Gestalt' properties of human systems, with his proposition that 'the structural properties of a dynamic whole are different from the structural properties of subparts' (Lewin 1947: 8). He also drew attention to the tendency of systems to move towards a 'quasi-stationary equilibrium' (Lewin 1950). His use of topological representations of psychological and social systems (Lewin 1936) was taken up as an illuminating way of exploring the implications of alternative designs for organisation (Miller 1976c). Importantly too, with his proposition that 'the best way to understand a system is to change it' (cf. Trist and Murray 1993: 30), he was the founder of action research (Lewin 1946) which The Tavistock Institute adopted as its key way of working to achieve its goal of combining research in the social sciences with professional practice.

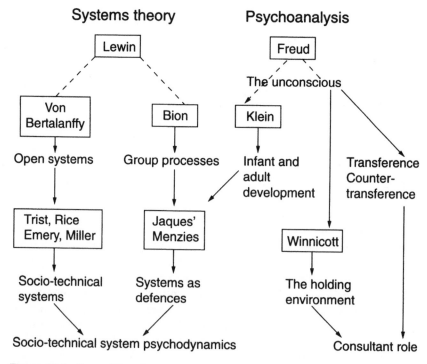

Figure 10.1 Genealogy of systems psychodynamics

The contribution of the biologist von Bertalanffy (1950a, 1950b) was *open system* theory. The model of the organism, which can exist and survive only through continuous interaction with the environment, as the source of its intakes and the recipient of its outputs, offered a much more satisfactory paradigm for organisation of the enterprise than the closed system model implicit in most previous theory of organisation. It was quickly adopted and developed in organisational analysis and change. In particular it underlined the significance of boundaries and their management. Thus leadership was seen as a boundary function, mediating between inside and outside (e.g. Rice 1958, 1963; Miller 1959; Miller and Rice 1967; Miller 1976c).

Emerging in the same period, and complementary to the open systems model, was the concept of the *socio-technical system*. As a reaction to the machine theory of organisation dominant in the earlier decades of the twentieth century the 1930s and 1940s had seen the emergence in the United States of the 'human relations' or motivational school of management (e.g. Mayo 1933; Roethlisberger and Dickson 1939). This drew attention to the informal organisation, which could sometimes support but often subvert the performance of the enterprise. Organisational effectiveness depended on meeting the needs – both overt and unrecognised – of the employees. The influence of this school was literally incorporated in the name of The Tavistock Institute of Human Relations and certainly the Institute's first major industrial project with the Glacier Metal Company (Jaques 1951) concentrated on the motives and drives of workers and managers with little attention to the technology and production processes themselves. It was studies of work organisation in coal mining (Trist and Bamforth 1951; Trist *et al.* 1963) that brought the mechanistic and human relations perspectives together, asserting the proposition that an effective form of work organisation was an organisation of two systems – psycho-social and technico-economic (cf. Emery and Trist 1960). This proposition was tested experimentally from 1953 onwards, initially in Indian textile mills with positive results (Rice 1958, 1963; Miller 1975). The application of the socio-technical system concept to the design of semi-autonomous group working has become widely disseminated. It has also been applied to organisational change of larger systems (Rice 1963; Miller and Rice 1967).

However, those developments in the 1950s and 1960s were also influenced by the other strand in Figure 10.1 – the psychoanalytic. Here a key figure was Melanie Klein with her theories of infant development and its continuing influence on adult relationships (e.g. Klein 1946, 1952, 1959). The infant is instinctively programmed to seek pleasure and comfort and to avoid pain and it polarises its world accordingly. The maternal breast is at one moment a good object to be cherished and at another a bad object to be destroyed. Early anxieties related to the splitting are complicated by discovering that the good and the bad are manifestations of the same person. The defences developed against these intolerable anxieties at this stage remain a permanent part of our psychic life alongside the emergent feelings of guilt, reparation and love. They find expression, for example, in processes of splitting and projection. To deal with the conflicts and complexities of our internal world we populate our external world with representations of good and evil, friends and foes, and the various other manifestations of 'not-me' or 'not-us' that enable us to hold on to a more consistent self-image.

This led to the notion that social systems, and in particular employing organisations, serve a function as defences against the unconscious anxieties of their members (Jaques 1955).[1] In other words the groupings and relationships designed for work not only carry a social component but are also channels for psychic projections. And actual ways of working may be not just used but distorted by defensive needs, particularly when the task of the enterprise, such as a hospital, itself generates anxieties among those who work in it (Menzies 1960).

Understanding of unconscious processes in groups and organisations is further enriched by the theory of *basic assumptions* (Bion 1948–51, 1961). Bion postulated that every group simultaneously operates at two levels. In effect it is two groups; it is a work group behaving rationally in pursuit of a task, but its members are at the same time combined together in one of three primitive shared assumptions. They may be suffused by dependency on a seemingly omnipotent or omniscient leader, often a person but perhaps a bible or its equivalent; by fight/flight in relation to an external enemy; or by pairing, which is a state of expectancy invested in a still-to-be-born saviour. These states are products of the inherent 'groupishness' of human behaviour – in Bion's words, 'man is a group animal' – as a vehicle for our equally primitive instinctive drives for survival – pleasure-seeking and pain-avoidance – and reproduction (cf. Miller 1993a). The emotions associated with these states may be consistent with the requirements of the work group: for example, the fight assumption may reinforce the competitive drive of a sales department. Often however the basic assumption gets in the way of effectiveness, as when uncritical dependency on a leader inhibits initiative and innovation.

Awareness of these unconscious processes helps in understanding the resistances that change can generate and in being prepared for them. Moreover, because uncertainty or ambiguity about the work task tends to make groups more vulnerable to basic assumption disturbances, definition of the primary task came to be seen as critical in organisation design (Rice 1958, 1963; Miller and Rice 1967).[2]

Taken together this set of concepts forms the 'socio-technical system psychodynamics' framework adopted by some of my colleagues and myself. It was developed by, and from the particular perspective of, professional social scientists taking consulting roles in organisations (Miller 1976a). And this brings us to the remaining elements of Figure 10.1.

As the figure shows, the conceptualisation of the consultancy role also reflects the influences of the psychoanalytic strand in the early development of The Tavistock Institute. Some practitioners saw organisational consultancy as a macro-version of psychoanalysis and the term 'sociotherapy' was sometimes used (Sofer 1961). Others of us disliked the connotations of illness and treatment but were influenced by the nature of the psychoanalytic relationship. What has emerged is commonly an ongoing collaboration in which the consultant and client work together in gaining a deeper understanding of the system and generating possible courses of action. The decision to act (or not) rests with the client; both jointly review the outcomes and, if appropriate, move to a next phase. It is an action research approach. There are two more specific influences. First, the transference is central to the analytic method. That is to say, the analyst becomes a screen onto which the patient projects underlying and perhaps unconscious feelings towards key figures in the patient's earlier life. In the analyst this evokes counter-transference: the analyst either has the experience of becoming the fantasised character in the patient's internal drama (a process of projective identification) or the projections resonate with some parallel dynamic in the analyst's own inner world. Correspondingly, the feelings evoked in the organisational consultant about the role one is being put into and the way one is being used provide data about underlying processes in the client system. The other influence is the recognition that, as with the analyst, it is an important function to provide for the client system a 'holding environment' (Winnicott 1965) by serving as a safe container who can accept and survive the anxieties and sometimes hostile projections coming from the client system.

These few pages have outlined the main elements of the conceptual framework that I take with me into the role of organisational consultant. For a somewhat expanded version see Miller (1993b: Chapter 1); but a much richer account is to be found in parts of the first volume of Trist and Murray's anthology of Tavistock early work (1990, 1993). The case outline that follows illustrates some of the practical applications.

CASE STUDY

What the consultant was bringing

As is often the case, I was bringing to this assignment not only a conceptual framework but some prior experience of the sector and context. Over the previous decade I had worked on a number of consultancy assignments in Mexico, mainly in the public sector. Examples included: organisation of the Federal Electricity Commission (CFE); inter-agency collaboration in national planning; re-design of a nation-wide rural development programme (Miller 1976a, 1993b, 1995a); and organisation of the National

Council for Science and Technology. Most directly relevant, however, was intermittent consultation to the National Water Planning Commission (CPNH) (Miller 1993b). From this, though I had only a superficial picture of the organisation for water supply and drainage in Mexico City, I had good knowledge of issues relating to water management in the country as a whole and of the somewhat complex set of agencies involved. The government's task of managing the country's hydrological systems requires regulation of extraction and discharge by user systems and I was particularly conscious that in some regions, including the Valley of Mexico, this boundary was blurred.

In the course of that work I had also become familiar with the Mexican political system, including relations between the federal and state governments and the shifting power relationships among secretaries of state *vis-à-vis* the President. The sexennial presidential elections produce a huge redeployment not only of ministers but of hundreds of other senior people in the ministries and agencies. I had myself benefited from this because sometimes the consultant follows them.

The initial negotiation

It was during another assignment in Mexico in June 1978 that a contact in CPNH introduced me to a fellow water engineer recently appointed director-general (DG) of Construction and Operations for water and drainage for the federal district of Mexico. We agreed that I would gather data and offer my observations and interpretations during an initial phase of two weeks of work.

> I learn that this service is one of the many functions of the department of the Federal District (DDF), which is headed by a 'Jefe' who is equivalent to a secretary of state and is a member of the cabinet. Up to now Construction and Operations have been separate directorates, quite different in their structures and cultures. The task of the DG, for which he is seeking consultancy, is to amalgamate them into a single organisation.
>
> To call it 'a service' is a misnomer, since meter-reading and collection of payments is the responsibility of DDF's Treasury department which, along with various other sections of DDF's bureaucracy, has regulatory and service roles in relation to Construction and Operations (C & O). Moreover C & O is responsible only for the primary distribution network: Construction is involved in the secondary networks but their operation and maintenance are in the hands of a number of 'delegaciones' that cover the federal district. These are local authorities run by elected members. However, some delegaciones are less self-sufficient and C & O also supplements their maintenance work. C & O serves the

Federal District, with a current population of 9 million, but Mexico City is expanding rapidly over the border into the state of Mexico, where another 4 million people live in the metropolitan area. Their water and drainage services are provided by local municipalities (similar to the delegaciones of the Federal District).

I am aware of the technical and economic problems of supplying water to Mexico City, which is 2,240 metres above sea-level in an enclosed basin where the aquifers are insufficient and already dangerously over-exploited. The DG amplifies. The current intake into the water supply system of the Federal District is 39m³/sec. Of this about 9m³sec are supplied in block through a Water Commission for the Valley of Mexico (CAVM), an agency of the ministry responsible for water resources. (CAVM also supplies about the same amount to that part of the Metropolitan Area that lies within the State of Mexico.) The remaining 30m³/sec come from the Federal District's 'own sources'. However, these 'own sources' include nearly 13m³/sec from the State of Mexico – from Alto Lerma and Chiconautla – under long-standing agreements. Alto Lerma is at present the only source outside the Valley and provides a quarter of the total intake; but massive new imports from other basins will soon be required. Pumping the water up is extremely costly and the tariffs charged to consumers fall far short of meeting even operating costs, let alone capital expenditure on updating and expanding the system.

Data collection and feedback

Probably like most consultants I use a combination of extended interviews and documentary material. Besides key role-holders in the client system, where relevant (and with the client's permission) I also meet external stakeholders and other informants. In this case these included representatives of CAVM, CPNH and two water engineering consultancy firms closely linked to C & O (which contracted out almost all its project engineering and construction). I also visited one of the delegaciones and met top executives and the head of its 'water office'. And as I became interested in the possibility of creating a more autonomous utility, I consulted a legal specialist in DDF on possible forms that this might take. Documentation included plans and policy statements, consultants' reports, organisational proposals and minutes of meetings.

Towards the end of the second week I was ready for an extended discussion with the DG to review and check out my understanding of the issues and to put forward initial propositions about a form of organisation. He endorsed my diagnosis and thought that my proposals, though radical, were interesting and worth pursuing. I undertook to prepare a working note and sent it to him soon after my return to London.

A working note

Use of the working note as a tool in consultancy arose from the action research stance of the early Tavistock Institute and the emphasis on the collaborative relationship between consultant and client (Miller 1995b). Unlike the expert's report, with recommendations or prescriptions, it is a more tentative interim account of the consultant's thinking. It often offers working hypotheses (akin to the psychoanalyst's interpretations to the patient) to try to explain why things are the way they are and proposals for possible alternatives. The working note thus provides an agenda for dialogue with and within the client system, leading towards a shared understanding. By being invited to apply their own expertise, those in the client system tend to feel freer to voice anxieties and resistances – better earlier than later. In this way the consultant, by not being defensive and not pretending to know all the answers, provides a model which may help to diffuse a culture of dialogue more widely within the system.

Part I of that first working note to C & O was entitled 'The Task and Boundaries of a Water and Drainage System: Existing Problems and Constraints' and began with a conceptual input:

A Water and Drainage Service can be thought of as a set of physical installations together with the organisational arrangements through which the installations are constructed, operated and maintained in relation to the requirements of the population being served. Insofar as the Service constitutes a system with clearly defined boundaries and is able to regulate transactions across those boundaries with its environment, then its management can be held accountable for performance of its task. Every such system is, of course, subject to constraints, which reduce or remove its ability to regulate some transactions with its environment: at these points the boundary becomes narrow or non-existent. As the number of constraints increases and thus the environment penetrates directly into the system, so fewer alternative courses of action are available: the enterprise is increasingly at the mercy of external forces and its viability is diminished. In these circumstances the Service is likely to be unreliable, inefficient and/or excessively expensive.

Here, therefore, I shall examine various boundary problems in the existing Service and show how these are constraining task performance at present; and then in Parts II and III, I shall propose a form of organisation in which at least some of these constraints can be eliminated.

The theme of the first section of Part I was the socio-political environment. It began with a quotation from a new plan for urban development in the Federal District: 'The capital of the country . . . has been made into the direct receptacle of the problems produced by the country's growth.' The working note went on to say:

As rapidly as the physical infrastructure and the socio-economic system
are expanded, there is always a huge marginalised population, not yet
incorporated, posing problems of poverty, disease, crime and a constant
threat of serious instability . . . Within the Capital, the Federal District's
Water and Drainage Service has been 'the direct receptacle' of many of
these problems. Whilst it can be criticised for uncontrolled losses, lack
of measurement (both of inflow and of users' consumption), haphazard
and unstandardised additions to the networks, absence of planned
maintenance etc., it is in fact remarkable that the Service has coped so
well as it has with the task of expanding the system and keeping it going.

(Tactically it is always wise to give credit for what the client *is* doing well!)

Apart from the sheer physical and technical problems of dealing with
such a high rate of growth, the Service has to contend with the fact that
water is not simply a commodity but also a psychological and socio-
political symbol. Failure to supply water (or failure to control flooding)
tends to be interpreted by the citizens as basic and tangible evidence of
a non-caring Government; it often arouses strong feelings of deprivation
which actually belong not simply to water as such but to other less
tangible deprivations – low income, hunger, over-crowding, ill-health
– for which the Government is held to blame. Correspondingly, the
Service tends to be the receptacle of more than the problems directly
concerned with water. Implicitly, the task that the Government,
through the DDF, has laid upon the Service is not merely to develop and
operate a water and drainage system but to prevent public discontent.
Fluctuations in the political value assigned to that implicit task are
obviously constraints on ordered development of the system . . . Water
is used to extinguish political fires as well as real ones.

Still on the socio-political environment, the note drew attention to huge
variations in the estimated population in the year 2000, to the lack of
integrated planning mechanisms and to such policy issues as the debate
over tariffs: should the federal government subsidise the city's water or
should users pay full costs? 'Insofar as the federal government and DDF
are uncertain or ambivalent about their policies they project difficulties
into the Service and fail to provide boundaries within which it can perform
a defined task and be held accountable.'

Part I of the working note explored three boundary issues. One was
lack of clarity about responsibility for regulation of the hydrological
system – control of extraction and discharges. The second related to the
boundary with the State of Mexico and the absence of an overall policy
for development of water resources. The third, already mentioned, was
the fragmentation of the activities of the Service among different units of
DDF. Such institutional constraints are not uncommon in other countries
too, but not all of them are unalterable.

Part II of the working note postulated that:

Some of the problems identified in Part I could be mitigated or solved by creating a single enterprise to undertake the water and drainage service for the Federal District. For the moment I will call this a 'Utility Company': alternative organisational forms are discussed below. With regard to water, the Utility Company would have the task of obtaining and receiving water, both from its own sources and from CAVM, operating and extending as necessary the treatment plants and primary and secondary networks, and supplying the users. The tariffs for users would be calculated on the basis of full economic costs, including: the price paid for bulk water supplies from CAVM; the cost of extraction from own sources; distribution costs; the servicing of the Utility Company's own capital investments; and administrative expenses including the costs of meter-reading and collection of payments. Graduations in the tariffs should be designed to promote conservation of water rather than to promote social justice. Similarly, the Utility Company would construct, maintain and operate the city's sewerage and drainage system. This again should be paid for by users – possibly through a drainage tax calculated as a percentage of the charge for water. (Obviously special charges would have to be levied in respect of industrial effluents.) In this way the Utility Company would be a self-financing enterprise. It would aim not to operate at a profit, but to cover its investments and, taking the good years with the bad, to break even.

Such a form of organisation would have a number of advantages:

1   It would facilitate the formulation and implementation of long-term plans and investment programmes, consistent with DDF's urban development plans and policies.
2   Investment proposals would be more clearly evaluated against economic criteria.
3   Exposure of the full economic costs of the City's water would encourage conservation both by users and within the system itself.
4   It would still be open to the Federal Government or DDF to subsidise water and/or drainage for the City as a whole or for particular locations or categories of users; but the amounts of subsidy would be explicit instead of being implicit or even uncalculated, as at present. (So far as possible, subsidies should operate on the principle of helping the user to afford to pay the economic cost, rather than paying the Utility Company to reduce its tariffs. For example, cheap rates for irrigation should be subsidised by the ministry responsible for agriculture and not by the company.)
5   By bringing together all the necessary facilities – financial, technical, administrative etc. – within its boundary, the Utility Company would

be in a position to develop a form of organisation, together with systems, procedures and also a culture of working, which would diminish bureaucratisation and contribute to effective and efficient operation.

6 Overall, the management of such an enterprise would have a more clearly defined task and thus be more readily accountable for performance.

I went on to propose a more radical alternative: that the 'utility company' should be jointly sponsored by DDF and the State of Mexico and cover the entire metropolitan area. In applying the socio-technical framework to large systems, the 'technical' dimension, as noted earlier, includes the economic. In this example I also included the financial, suggesting that investment capital for either version of the utility company could be raised through the national and international banking systems and possibly through floating Metropolitan Water Bonds.

In Part III, looking ahead, the working note presented a picture of increasing decentralisation for the delegaciones. These, within twenty years, might well become mini-cities, with an average population of a million or so. As such they would be capable of sustaining their own separate water utility companies, taking over all the functions of distribution and drainage. At that stage the Metropolitan-wide or DDF-wide utility company would become redundant: bulk water supplies would be routed directly to the delegaciones. Meanwhile the note recommended that plans for developing the infrastructure should ensure that boundaries of the distribution sub-systems should correspond to those administrative boundaries. In addition – pursuing one of the themes that I had brought to this consultancy – I made proposals for differentiating the government function of water management from that of the utility as a user system.

Part IV of the working note was entitled 'Initiating a Process of Institutional Development and Change':

In Parts II and III I have outlined a scenario for the organisation of water and drainage for the Metropolitan Area over the next twenty years. It may seem somewhat unusual to be recommending the formation of a significant new Metropolitan Utility Company and then, almost in the same breath, to be talking of dismantling it. However, if we are to cope effectively with the rates of growth and development that Mexico is facing, then we have to be able to build, re-build and discard institutions at a corresponding rate . . . in response to trends that are not now foreseen.

Whatever the future holds, the present moment appears to be especially favourable for setting in motion the process of institutional development and change. At least three factors are important here:

1 At the macro-political level there is an unusually positive relationship between the Jefe de DDF and the Governor of the State of Mexico, which can be built on.
2 At the micro-political level, the policy of expanding the role of the delegaciones and of encouraging more active citizen participation increases the chance that local services can be created and effectively run.
3 The recently formed C & O, with its infusion of much new technical skill, provides an excellent nucleus around which to construct the new enterprise for the Metropolitan Area.

Three immediate steps that need to be taken are:

1 Preparation of a memorandum outlining these proposals by C & O to the Jefe de DDF.
2 Agreement between DDF and the State of Mexico to pursue the exploration (without committing themselves in advance to the outcome).
3 Establishment of a joint working party to recommend more specifically on the task, jurisdiction, financing and legal form of the proposed enterprise.

I would recommend that this working party concerns itself only with those decisions that are essential to get the enterprise launched. For example, it will be necessary for the new enterprise to become the 'proprietor' of all waters coming into the Metropolitan Area, whether from DDF's 'own sources' or from CAVM. On the other hand, some difficult decisions will have to be made about whether or not to equalise charges to local systems and tariffs to users throughout the Metropolitan Area; but initially the enterprise will take over whatever currently exists, and such decisions can be deferred until after it begins to operate.

As I have indicated earlier, even if the State of Mexico refuses to participate, the model of the Utility Company is well worth applying to the Federal District alone. In that case it will be important at least to promote joint planning mechanisms, both for water and drainage and for other aspects of metropolitan planning.

In the immediate future it will be desirable for C & O to maintain an internal organisation that is flexible and adaptive, and also to ensure that its actions will be consistent with and supportive of the direction of change that has been outlined. For example, the territorial boundaries of the delegaciones need to be taken into account in the design of networks, and it may also be valuable over the next year to amplify the Water Plan to include water plans for each delegación, developed in collaboration with its representatives.

In conclusion, I would re-emphasise that this working note should not be interpreted as presenting a firm set of recommendations. It outlines a scenario that appears to be appropriate on the basis of the evidence that I have; but the propositions need to be scrutinised and amplified. I nevertheless hope that C & O, in collaboration with other relevant bodies, will be able to use them as a starting point in the process of creating the new organisational forms that are required.

I wondered at the time, and still ask myself today, how far, in going beyond my brief and producing such a grand plan, I was unconsciously responding in an omnipotent way to the dependency that the client was investing in me. All his problems solved in one 16-page working note! Was I being too directive? Was I allowing space for dialogue? Also, was it too much to swallow? Quasi-privatisation of a public service felt much more radical in 1978 than it does in the 1990s. My answer is that I intuitively felt it to be the right solution – it was the logical product of applying my built-in conceptual framework to the knowledge I had of that system in that environment – and it would have been professionally wrong not to offer it.

It also illustrates what I believe is an important function of the organisational consultant: I was providing containment by showing the client not only that his problems were not insoluble but that they could be reframed in a creative way. Moreover, it is often important, when, as in this case, we are dealing with a merger of two somewhat incompatible units, to provide some overarching visualisation of the future that they will both have a part in creating. In relating to the consultant as a new third party representing that possible future, they have a new channel for some of the energy and affect invested in their rivalrous pair relationship, thereby relieving the chief executive – here the DG – of some of their negative transference onto him.

The working note, in English and Spanish, had been distributed to the C & O people I had interviewed at the end of September 1978. Two months later the message came back that the Jefe of DDF had approved the utility company proposal for the Federal District but not the joint venture with the State of Mexico. This might come later but he did not want that to delay implementation, for which he set the date of January 1980 – just a year ahead. I had agreed with the DG to reserve two weeks in January for a possible Phase 2. This promised to be an intensive fortnight.

I saw myself as having two tasks. One was to work on a form of organisation for C & O's current activities – essentially the task for which I had originally been hired. The other was to put in train a process and a set of transitional structures for creating the new enterprise. Each was to be the subject of a working note.

Organisational arrangements for current activities

This can be seen as an example of applying the conceptual framework to organisational design. I defined the aim of the working note as 'to encourage critical analysis of alternative forms of organisation and selection of the organisation most appropriate to the task to be performed'.

It focused first on the existing organisation, which retained the inherited differentiation between Construction and Operations, except that Construction had been subdivided into two divisions: Construction proper and a new 'Technical Division' responsible for planning, studies and projects, with some infusion of new engineers.

> The assumption underlying this form of organisation is that the central process of C & O is:

$$\text{Planning} \rightarrow \text{Projects} \rightarrow \text{Construction} \rightarrow \text{Operations}$$

> Correspondingly it is implied that the key internal boundaries are between Projects and Construction and between Construction and Operations. Every project requires co-ordination across these boundaries.

There was general recognition that this co-ordination was not happening and vertical communication was also poor. Failure to use Operations experience in selection and design of projects resulted in unforeseen snags in construction.

> There is a lack of conception of the system as a whole except in the person of the DG. Many technical decisions therefore escalate to his level.

The note mentioned other problems and continued:

> Some of these difficulties may be attributable to the absence of a client for the projects undertaken. In most other settings, construction is commissioned by and carried out for a client, who has a reasonably clear idea about the nature of the project he wants and how it fits into his existing system. Even though he may delegate most of the engineering responsibilities to consultants, he is usually monitoring their activities and is concerned with costs and timing, so that the client role provides an important focus and discipline for the engineers engaged in designing the project and supervising construction. On the face of it, it would seem reasonable to expect Operations to take this role. In practice, however, Operations is seldom involved in the initiation of projects and is usually invited to participate only when the planning and projects groups have done their preliminary work. In effect, therefore, the client role for the projects is invested in the Director General – which accounts for the amount of technical decision-making in which he is involved.
>
> So long as technical expertise is concentrated in the project engineers and consultants, Operations is unlikely to acquire a conceptualisation of the system that would enable it to take on an effective client role as an initiator of projects. And if those who actually run the water and

drainage systems are kept in a relatively lower status and are constantly having to take charge of installations that they have had little say in designing, then we can expect their commitment to their tasks of operation and maintenance to remain relatively low.

To sum up: In the existing organisation, every project involves, or should involve, the participation and co-ordination of all three divisions – a formidable quantity of co-ordination; no one of these three is specifically accountable for seeing a project through from beginning to end; and the one division – Operations – that might be expected to take a focal and integrative role as client is in practice the least qualified to do so.

The working note then proposed an alternative organisational model:

In the present organisation, as we have seen, the first order of differentiation is into types of activity – Planning and Projects, Construction, Operations – within these the second order of differentiation is for the most part into types of installation. Thus the principal units in Operations are: Water Supply, Distribution, Drainage, Treatment Plants, and Connections and Meters. There is a similar differentiation in Projects.

An organisational alternative would be to base the first order of differentiation on the main boundaries that occur within the two systems – water and drainage – for which C & O is responsible. The accompanying diagram (Figure 10.2) gives a simplified picture of these systems and shows where organisational boundaries might be drawn.

What this form of organisation implies is that each of the units would be responsible, technically and financially, both for the operation and for the development of the sub-system concerned. Each would have the capabilities for keeping the sub-system under review, both internally and in relation to neighbouring sub-systems, and for originating projects. Thus in many respects it would operate as a semi-autonomous sub-enterprise. Among the advantages of this form of organisation are: that operating staff would be working within a clearer and more dynamic conception of their sub-system; that project staff would be better able to draw directly on operating experience; and that many issues that now escalate to the Director General for decision would be settled at the level of the unit.

In order to fulfil the client role described earlier, each unit would require a small permanent nucleus of planners and project engineers. However, this could not be self-sufficient. Accordingly it would hire the specialist skills required either from outside consulting firms or from a pool of engineers within the enterprise.

What I was offering in Figure 10.2 was a typical example of using an open system model to identify core intakes and outputs together with the internal conversion processes required for performance of the primary task of the enterprise. These define the technical sub-systems and their

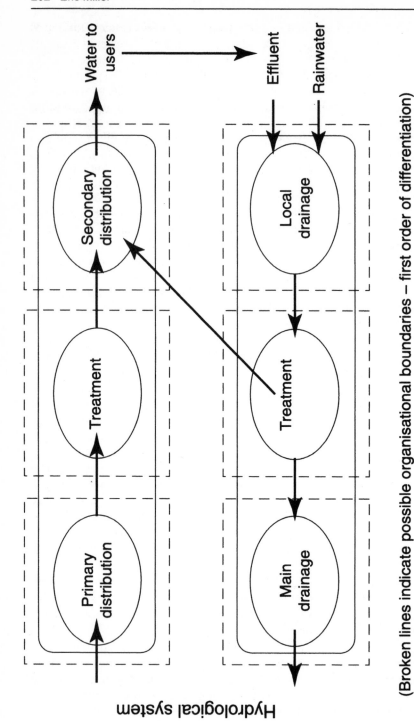

(Broken lines indicate possible organisational boundaries – first order of differentiation)

Figure 10.2 Schematic diagram of the water supply and drainage systems

boundaries, which are likely to be appropriate organisational boundaries (Miller 1959; Miller and Rice 1967). Or to put it another way, if those boundaries do not coincide, problems over accountability are inevitable.

The organisational boundaries suggested in the diagram are not sacrosanct. The Treatment unit, for example, brings together two quite independent sub-systems, each with quite different boundaries to be managed. Thus the systemic arguments for keeping them separate have to be weighed against the technological similarities which make it convenient to put them together. Similarly, Primary Distribution and Main Drainage are shown as separate sub-systems, but the high civil engineering component in both might be seen as one argument for combining them.

Much the same applies to the proposed unit for Secondary Distribution and Local Drainage. Here, however, there is a further set of considerations. The plan for the organisational development of the Utility Company requires that the delegaciones become independently capable of operating and developing their local systems for water supply and drainage. Not all delegaciones are yet able to operate the local systems; none is capable of developing them. It is essential that the form of organisation for the Utility Company is consistent with its task of bringing about this transition. Thus I would envisage within this unit a territorial differentiation into a number of 'Local Network Development Groups', each responsible for working with two or three adjoining delegaciones. Their task would have a strong consultancy and training component in the first instance. Later, as the delegaciones acquired greater self-sufficiency, these groups would nevertheless continue to exist in modified form, partly as technical monitors and partly as the means through which the delegaciones could obtain access to the specialist resources of the Utility Company. The Local Network Development Groups would have an important task of boundary management in relation to other sub-systems, particularly if, as proposed in the previous working note, the boundaries of the local networks are to be progressively modified so as to correspond to delegación boundaries. The Groups would have one other important function, which is not provided for in the present organisation. The systemic boundaries between Primary Distribution, Treatment, Secondary Distribution etc. are relatively clear-cut. Territorially, however, they are overlapping. Not uncommonly at present, extensions or modifications to one sub-system are planned without consideration for other installations in the same territory, and adjustments then have to be extemporised. The territorial differentiation proposed here should mean that each group would be familiar with all the installations in its territory, and not merely with the local networks themselves. It should therefore automatically be involved in other sub-systems' plans for installations within that territory.

In the working note the organisational model was elaborated, with a discussion for example of the centralised regulatory and service functions required. If, as in both the first working note and this one, the consultant is offering the client a new and perhaps radical way of looking at the system, it is reassuring to indicate what to do next. It relates the future back to the present. Here are extracts from 'Next Steps' in this example:

> This working note has produced only an outline of an alternative organisational model. More detailed work is needed in order to decide exactly how existing units would best fit into the proposed configuration.

(This is followed with examples of issues needing further consideration.)

> Initially, this more detailed exploration can be started by the working group which is to be set up to prepare for the transition to the utility company.

(This is a reference to the content of the following working note which was simultaneously under discussion with the DG.)

> However, it is desirable that this process of organisational design should involve others, starting with the present Subdirectors [heads of divisions]. (I assume that the Subdirectors and others can safely be told that, although their precise positions in the new organisation cannot yet be known, their future level and salary will not be lower than at present.) This will help to identify and solve possible difficulties in advance and also to procure greater commitment to the reorganisation than if it were simply imposed from above. At the same time, it is not necessary for all details to be worked out before the reorganisation is implemented.
>
> Similarly, implementation does not have to wait for the formal transition from C & O to the utility company. Indeed, there would be advantages in implementing these changes well in advance, so as to give time for the reorganisation to settle down before taking on the additional responsibilities and complexities of the new enterprise.

As may be inferred from the sentence in brackets about the subdirectors, my immediate client for this note was the DG only. It was for him to decide on wider distribution – which he did. Eventually my proposed model was judged to be too radical: senior engineers could not accept the possibility of being under an Operations person. Nevertheless there were positive outcomes. Relevant Operations managers became more involved and more influential in project design and construction; and a version of the proposed local network development groups was implemented.

THE PROCESS OF DESIGNING AND BUILDING THE NEW ENTERPRISE

It was neither possible nor indeed desirable for me to have any detailed involvement in this next phase. I saw my main task as trying to ensure that appropriate transitional institutional arrangements were put in place. I felt an understandable excitement that my proposal was going to be implemented; but I was also anxious that it might go wrong. I had past experience of major reorganisation and institution-building in large systems, so I know some of the pitfalls and how they might be circumvented. Experience had also taught me that whilst one must be cautious about pressures from the client system, not always unconscious, to put the consultant in a directive role, there are times when such a role is appropriate. This was one of them.

For the task of designing the new enterprise the DG got authorisation from the Jefe of DDF to set up a multi-disciplinary working party. This needed the Jefe's authority because the enterprise would be absorbing some DDF functions, including regulatory mechanisms, in addition to construction and operation. Presumably he would also have to approve the terms of reference. I saw these as critical. Consequently the first part of my next working note was a draft statement of the terms of reference, followed by a presentation of key organisational design issues that it needed to address. (Headings included: the legal form of the enterprise; financing; organisational structure; relations with employees and unions; and inter-institutional implications.) Part II of the note discussed institution building, and because of its more general relevance it is reproduced here in full:

Even though the new enterprise may not be legally inaugurated until January 1980, it will be necessary long before this to start designating people for new positions. This applies in particular to the totally or substantially new departments and sections that have to be set up – notably financial control and accounting, purchasing, and industrial relations. Procedures have to be designed and subordinate staff recruited and trained. A considerable amount of training will be involved and will need to be planned in advance.

The Working Party will have to phase this process, acting on the principle that so far as possible people should participate in designing the organisations and systems that they will subsequently operate. On this assumption, the first appointment should be the Director General of the enterprise: he will have to be named by the Jefe de DDF in the very near future. At that point, it will be important to clarify in what areas the Jefe delegates authority to the Director General Designate to make 'institution design' decisions, and in what areas decisions are reserved to the Jefe.

Once appointments are made, even if the incumbents are available only part-time, institution design begins to merge into institution building, and institution building into the actual operation of the new enterprise. In some respects, this merging of the processes is no bad thing: in this way people become involved and committed. Experience elsewhere, however, suggests that it is desirable to keep the processes conceptually distinct. Design must be conceived systemically. That is to say, proposals in one sector – e.g. financial control – have to be tested for their compatibility with others. If design is pursued unilaterally in one area and moves to implementation, there is a risk of inconsistencies. For example, if managers are to be held financially as well as technically responsible for particular water or drainage sub-systems, then those organisational boundaries need to be respected in the system of management accounting and perhaps also in procedures for appointment of staff and purchasing materials. It will therefore be an important task of the Working Party to secure consistency and integration in design while the number of people involved in design is rapidly growing. One way of doing this will be through convening meetings that mobilise managers and specialists in their design roles (as distinct from their future operational roles), so that the emerging designs can be tested against each other and against hypothetical events. (For example: Who intervenes and how if a labour dispute in the water department of one of the delegaciones jeopardises the local water supply?) In this way, new systems are not only pre-tested but sometimes creatively developed, and moreover the mutual learning that occurs during this process will help working relationships when people move into their operational roles.

The process of institution-building includes not only the allocation of people to roles and the installation of new systems but also the inculcation of philosophies and values. People when brought together inevitably and unconsciously form a social system and develop a culture, and the emergent values and behavioural patterns are not always what the institutional leaders might have wished. C & O, as a newly created organisation, is itself in a transitional phase, in which the amalgamation of the two previous divisions and the infusion of new staff has led to the co-existence of several different cultures which are still not synthesised. (The terms 'bureaucratic', 'technical', 'entrepreneurial' and 'professional' give a flavour of the differences but are over-simplistic.) The transition towards a financially self-sufficient enterprise requires the conscious inculcation of a new set of values. Some people, for example, may find it difficult to appreciate the concept of 'enterprise', which they may associate with pursuit of profit for its own sake rather than being a device for making sure that money and other resources are used as effectively as possible. It is also an excellent opportunity to re-think the philosophy and style of management. (This is not the simple matter of choosing between authoritarian and participative styles. The systemic organisational model introduced in Working Note No. 2 defines management as a boundary function, concerned with matching the internal activities of the system with the opportunities and constraints existing in the external environment. This leads to a *negotiating* style of management: it involves negotiation with other systems of the same level and negotiation with sub- and supra-systems.)

Formation of a new enterprise is an exciting moment. The fact that very many employees will see themselves as doing exactly the same work in January 1980 as in December 1979 makes it all the more important to publicise, both internally and externally, the new philosophies and values. However, it is not through rhetoric that new values are inculcated but only through behaviour that expresses these values.

Institution design

At that point my consultancy assignment with C & O had been completed. As the working note implies, if I were to have any ongoing involvement at all it would be as a consultant to the working party. And that is what transpired. The person appointed as the full-time chairman of the working party was the water engineer who had introduced me to C & O. The choice was influenced by the fact that he had effectively acted as an internal consultant for my external consultancy with the Water Planning Commission so he was well versed in my thinking and committed to my proposal. My consultancy became intermittent, once or twice with the working party as a whole, but mostly with him. All reports came to me and I commented from a distance, spent days with him during visits to Mexico on other assignments, and once met half-way for an intensive three-day session in New York.

It was three months before appointments to the working party were completed and it was ready to start work – the feet-dragging largely attributable to resistance within DDF. The voluminous preliminary report, when it emerged in August 1979 (followed two months later by a shorter version for wider distribution), was a thorough piece of work, covering all the recommended topics. For example, it included a full financial analysis, with long-term projections, to test the viability of self-financing.

By then it was apparent that the target of January 1980 could not be met and implementation was deferred for a year. There was still much to do. A separate committee (with some overlap of membership) was appointed to decide on the organisational structure. (The eventual outcome was a compromise: it maintained the boundary between projects/construction and operations within a tight matrix structure. Its report quoted extensively from Miller's working notes even though his proposals were not adopted in full!) Five working groups were appointed to study specific issues.

Institution building

A key step in this transitional phase was the formation in November 1979 of a 'committee for the transfer of functions', initially presided over by the Jefe of DDF himself. Plans for implementation progressed. The first key role-holders were nominated in March 1980. At the same time programmes were set up for pilot implementation in two delegaciones. Arrangements for transfer of functions were completed in September, and by January 1981 all the main elements of the new enterprise were in place.

Consolidation

My consultant role had become increasingly sporadic, but it did not disappear entirely. In an organisational transformation of this kind, the new conception can be clearly stated (in the 1990s probably through a mission statement) and people can occupy their new positions, but this of itself does not automatically bring about the appropriate change in values and culture and a sense of identification with the new enterprise – a shared sense of 'we'. To acquire an identity as a consultant, as distinct from a label, I need a client. Similarly the organisational 'we' is fragile unless there is external recognition and confirmation.

During the 18 months following implementation two significant actions were taken to consolidate the identity of the new enterprise. The first started as a tentative idea for an international conference on large urban water systems which was immediately seized upon and elaborated by the Jefe into a major event. He sent an emissary to issue personal invitations to the top people in the water systems of all major cities round the world. Their travel and other expenses would be covered in full. They were provided with a format to pre-circulate descriptions of their systems (including Figure 10.2 as a basis for plotting the organisation). The representatives, who came from more than 30 cities, were given ambassadorial treatment. It fell to me to design the 5-day programme, which the President of Mexico opened. The programme included small group sessions as well as plenaries, all with simultaneous translation in 5 languages The small groups of 10 to 12 met in closed sessions to encourage frank discussion and this worked (though as facilitator of one of them I had initial anxieties about having Moscow, Peking and Los Angeles round the same table!) A large contingent from the new Mexican enterprise attended the plenaries. All participants seemed to value the conference, but what was especially important for the Mexicans was realisation that their new organisation was envied by many of the others.

The second and quite deliberate act of consolidation was a book. A few years earlier, when I was involved in redesigning the new national programme of rural development I had, with the encouragement of the secretary of state concerned, produced a book about it (in Spanish), which was widely read and was later reprinted (Miller 1976a). The 1982 book entitled *The Water System of the Federal District: a Public Service in Transition* (English translation of the title) was a collaborative effort by some 40 engineers and managers of the new enterprise. We all met in an initial conference to design the content and to allocate authors, and a few months later there was a second conference to review the drafts. The outcome was a comprehensive account of the current water and drainage and service including the organisational model (Aguilar Amilpa, Garduño Velasco and Miller 1982), but the process was as important as the product.

CONCLUDING COMMENT

In the case study I have tried to show a number of applications of the conceptual framework of systems psychodynamics in Part I, though not everything is relevant every time. On this occasion, for example, Bion's theory of basic assumption groups was not much drawn upon. Over the last fifteen years I have continued to learn, both from ongoing consultancy experience and also as a core faculty member of The Tavistock Institute's Advanced Organisational Consultation programme. That experience confirms that the framework, though it does not pretend to be all-embracing, is nevertheless the basis of a robust theoretical and practical tool-kit. For me, two lessons stand out. One is the importance of trying to hold on to the whole range of dimensions of a system – technical, economic, financial, legal, political (macro and micro), social, psychological – without being captured by one end or the other of this spectrum. The second is recognition of one's educational and at times mentoring functions in equipping the client system to become independent of the consultant in managing the processes of change. Withdrawal is not always easy. The client may make mistakes that could have been avoided; dependency is beguiling and, by prolonging the consultancy, perhaps more lucrative. But a well managed ending, though not without difficulties, leaves both parties satisfied with their work together.

Nor is it always a permanent 'goodbye'. In Mexico's next sexennial shake-up the new president installed the DG as director general of the Federal Electricity Commission, so I found myself consulting to an old client system under his new leadership.

Water brought me back to Mexico again in 1988, this time in developing and implementing the major restructuring of the whole water sector on the basis of a model first developed with the Water Planning Commission in 1975. It involved a clear separation between the water management task, through regional water authorities, and independent, self-financing user systems, of which the Federal District 'water utility' was an early example. There were two aspects in which that utility had not lived up to the original proposal. First, it had not become fully independent of DDF; and second, the idea of raising tariffs to cover costs was politically too controversial. The national restructuring coupled with the economic policies of the new government finally made it possible to tackle the issue of subsidies and resume the move towards a self-financing enterprise.

SUMMARY OF GUIDELINES EMERGING FROM THIS CASE

- Acquire a sufficient understanding of the technological, economic, legal and political dimensions and of how they impact on the task and organisation.
- During data collection, where possible interview external people who may have relevant perspectives.
- Be alert to underlying (perhaps unconscious) factors that may shape the way in which the organisation carries out its task.
- Use working notes as a non-threatening device to feed back findings and hypotheses and to generate dialogue both with and within the client system.
- Give credit for positive aspects of the current system that should be valued and preserved, rather than focusing only on deficiencies.
- Operate in a way that provides containment for the anxieties generated by the prospect of change: for example, through re-framing the client's problems and also through being prepared to accept negative projections.
- Use an open system framework to generate one or more possible organisational models for comparison with existing structures, and in particular pay attention to discrepancies between organisational boundaries and boundaries of technical sub-systems.
- Design temporary institutional structures for the transitional phases.
- Try to find devices to consolidate the identity of the emerging new organisation.

NOTES

1   Nearly forty years later Jaques claimed that he had been wrong, arguing that such unconscious dynamics were a product of ineffective organisational design (Jaques 1995). Others, including myself, continue to find the hypothesis persuasive (Amado 1995). However, see note 2.
2   This might seem to support the recantation by Jaques. However, the possibility that the interference of unconscious processes can be reduced by no means implies that they could disappear.

REFERENCES AND FURTHER READING

Aguilar Amilpa, E., Garduño Velasco, H. and Miller, E. J. (1982) 'Algunas tendencias en el manejo de sistemas hidráulicos en grandes urbes', in G. Guerrero

Villalobos, A. Moreno Fernandez and H. Garduño Velasco (eds) *El Sistema Hidráulico del Distrito Federal: Un Servicio Publico en Transición*, Mexico: Departamento del Distrito Federal, 16.1–16.18.

Amado, G. (1995). 'Why psychoanalytical knowledge helps us to understand organisations: a discussion with Elliot Jaques', *Human Relations*, 48: 351–57.

Bertalanffy, L. von (1950a) 'The theory of open systems in physics and biology', *Science*, 3: 23–9.

—— (1950b) 'An outline of general system theory', *British Journal of the Philosophy of Science*, 1: 134–65.

Bion, W. R. (1948–51). 'Experiences in groups, I–VII', *Human Relations*, 1–4.

—— (1961) *Experiences in Groups and Other Papers*, London: Tavistock Publications.

Emery, F. E. and Trist E. L. (1960) 'Socio-technical systems', in C. W. Churchman and M. Verhulst (eds) *Management Sciences, Models and Techniques*, Oxford: Pergamon, 2: 83–97.

Jaques, E. (1951) *The Changing Culture of a Factory*, London: Tavistock Publications.

—— (1955) 'Social systems as a defence against persecutory and depressive anxiety', in M. Klein, P. Heimann and R. E. Money-Kyrl (eds) *New Directions in Psychoanalysis*, London: Tavistock Publications, 478–98.

—— (1995) 'Why the psychoanalytical approach to understanding organisations is dysfunctional'; 'Reply to Dr Gilles Amado', *Human Relations* 48: 343–9; 359–65.

Klein, M. (1946) 'Notes on some schizoid mechanisms', in M. Klein *et al.* (eds) *Developments in Psychoanalysis*, London: Hogarth Press, 292–320.

—— (1952) 'Some theoretical conclusions regarding the emotional life of the infant', in M. Klein, P. Heimann, S. Isaacs and J. Riviere (eds) *Developments in Psychoanalysis*, London: Hogarth Press 198–237.

—— (1959) 'Our adult world and its roots in infancy', *Human Relations*, 12: 291–303. Also in M. Klein, *Our Adult World and Other Essays* (1963) London: Heinemann, 1–22.

Lewin, K. (1936) *Principles in Topological Psychology*, New York: McGraw-Hill.

—— (1946) 'Action research and minority problems', *Journal of Social Issues*, 2: 34–46.

—— (1947) 'Frontiers in group dynamics: I. Concept, method and reality in social sciences; social equilibria and social change', *Human Relations*, 1: 5–41.

—— (1950) *Field Theory in Social Science*, New York: Harper Bros.

Mayo, E. (1933) *The Human Problems of an Industrial Civilization*, New York: Macmillan; London: Routledge & Kegan Paul.

Menzies, I. E. P. (1960) 'A case-study in the functioning of social systems as a defence against anxiety', *Human Relations*, 13: 95–121. Reprinted as Tavistock pamphlet no. 3, The Tavistock Institute (1961) and in Menzies Lyth (1988) 43–85.

Menzies Lyth, I. (1988) *Containing Anxiety in Institutions*. London: Free Association Books.

Miller, E. J. (1959) 'Technology, territory and time: the internal differentiation of complex production systems', *Human Relations*, 12: 243–72.

—— (1975) 'Socio-technical systems in weaving, 1953–1970: a follow-up study', *Human Relations*, 28: 349–86.

—— (1976a) *Desarrollo Integral del Medio Rural: Un Experimento en Mexico*. Mexico, DF: Fondo de Cultura Económica, 1–18.

—— (1976b) 'Role perspectives and the understanding of organizational behaviour', in E. J. Miller (ed.) *Task and Organization*, Chichester: Wiley, 1–18.

—— (1976c) 'The open-system approach to organizational analysis, with special reference to the work of A. K. Rice' in G. Hofstede and M. Sami Kassem (eds)

European Contributions to Organization Theory, Assen/Amsterdam: Van Gorcum, 43–61.

—— (1993a) 'The human dynamic', in R. Stacey (ed.) *Strategic Thinking and the Management of Change: International Perspectives on Organizational Dynamics*, London: Kogan Page, 98–116.

—— (1993b) *From Dependency to Autonomy: Studies in Organization and Change*, London: Free Association Books.

—— (1995a) 'Dialogue with the client system: use of the "working note" in organisational consultancy', *Journal of Managerial Psychology*, 10(6): 27–30.

—— (1995b) *Integrated Rural Development: a Mexican Experiment*, 'From the archives': occasional paper no. 1, The Tavistock Institute.

Miller, E. J. and Rice, A. K. (1967) *Systems of Organization: Task and Sentient Systems and their Boundary Control*, London: Tavistock Publications.

Rice, A. K. (1958) *Productivity and Social Organization: the Ahmedabad Experiment*, London: Tavistock Publications. Reprinted, New York and London: Garland Publishing (1987).

—— (1963) *The Enterprise and its Environment*, London: Tavistock Publications.

Roethlisberger, F. J. and Dickson, W. J. (1939) *Management and the Worker*, Cambridge, Mass: Harvard University Press.

Sofer, C. (1961) *The Organization From Within: a Comparative Study of Social Institutions Based on a Sociotherapeutic Approach*, London: Tavistock Publications.

Trist, E. L. and Bamforth, K. W. (1951) 'Some social and psychological consequences of the longwall method of coal-getting', *Human Relations*, 4: 3–38.

Trist, E. L., Higgin, G. W., Murray, H. and Pollock, A. B. (1963) *Organizational Choice: Capabilities of Groups at the Coal Face under Changing Technologies*, London: Tavistock Publications.

Trist, E. L. and Murray, H. (eds) (1990) *The Social Engagement of Social Science: a Tavistock Anthology*, vol. 1, *The Socio-Psychological Perspective*, Philadelphia, PA: University of Pennsylvania Press; London: Free Association Books.

Trist, E. L. and Murray H. (1993) *The Social Engagement of Social Science: a Tavistock Anthology, vol. 2, The Socio-Technical Perspective*, Philadelphia, PA: University of Pennsylvania Press.

Winnicott, D. W. (1965). *The Maturational Process and the Facilitating Environment*, New York: International Universities Press.

Chapter 11

Consulting to organisational implications of technical change

Richard Holti

Market pressures mean that many corporations now see new information and communication technologies as a key to more efficient forms of organisation, based on decentralised operational control. The benefits on offer are in terms of some combination of increased responsiveness and reduced cost. Whilst recent versions of 'business process re-engineering' claim to provide an integrated approach to 'change management', the reality of most programmes of technical and organisational change is that there are a number of distinct change initiatives, led by people with different occupational backgrounds, identities, and 'change' techniques.

This chapter re-evaluates some of the original insights of those who worked at The Tavistock Institute in the 1950s and 1960s, concerning the analysis and redesign of what they decided to call 'socio-technical systems', and offers some directions for developing an understanding of the issues associated with interactions between technical and organisational changes. I argue that there is no explicit and unifying overall methodology for integrating technical and social change. Integrating different aspects of change is about paying attention simultaneously to a number of different levels or aspects of organisational life, which tend to be the concerns of distinct 'change' occupations – whether managers or consultants. The divide between social and technical spheres is only part of the story. In this chapter, I explore the usefulness of thinking in terms of four levels of organisational life: the political and economic, the logistical and cognitive, the cultural or interpretative, and the psychodynamic.

This conceptualisation of the nature of socio-technical systems stems from an attempt to integrate the original spirit of the socio-technical framework of The Tavistock Institute pioneers with an understanding of the growth over the last 40 or so years of social science frameworks relevant to understanding and consulting to organisational changes. What is needed is a framework which can guide a consultant or action researcher to pay attention to a number of different levels of organisation, deploying a range of different diagnostic and intervention techniques in relation to one another.

The chapter is in three main sections. The first sets out a general perspective on the current state of what may broadly be called the socio-technical tradition, and some directions for its future development. The second part illustrates these generalities through their application in a recent Tavistock Institute action research project. A brief conclusion draws together some implications for consultancy practice.

PERSPECTIVES ON THE DEVELOPMENT OF THE SOCIO-TECHNICAL TRADITION

A few central socio-technical systems (STS) insights can be traced back to the writings of Trist, Bamforth and Emery during the 1950s and early 1960s (Trist and Bamforth 1951; Trist 1982). These may be summarised as follows: a work organisation can be conceived of in terms of the separate dynamics and requirements of its 'technical sub-system' and its 'social sub-system'. Both have a role in achieving performance of an overall organisational task, and the requirements of one constrain the other without fully determining possibilities. In principle, it is possible to come to an accommodation or 'joint optimisation' of the two, such that both overall task performance requirements (the technical) and the social–psychological needs of workers (the social) are catered for. These social–psychological requirements include the need for some form of autonomy at the level of individual jobs, and, where appropriate, workgroups.

The concepts and practical recipes for analysing and redesigning work organisations that claim to utilise these principles have multiplied over the intervening years. Although authoritative summaries have been produced at various points (see for example Klein 1976; Cherns 1976; Cherns 1987; Pasmore 1988), both the theory and practice of socio-technical systems show a great deal of diversity. Examples include:

- the rather mechanistic redesign recipes of the Modern Dutch STS tradition (see for example de Sitter *et al.* 1990), based on cybernetic ideas;
- the normative approaches to establishing 'high commitment', in what used to be called a unitarist framework of industrial relations, character-istic of 'STS' as practised within many US manufacturing multinationals (see for example Hanna 1988);
- the more politicised emphases on creating democracy within workplaces through dialogue between different stakeholders and groupings, charac-teristic of Scandinavian workplace reform (see for example Gustavsen 1992);
- an approach to analysing tensions in organisational roles and relation-ships as a prelude to redesigning them, in terms of task-related and sentient relationships, found in an important stream of Tavistock Institute work during the 1960s and 1970s (Miller and Rice 1967).

There are of course other approaches to analysing and redesigning work organisations which draw on certain similar insights, although arrived at from different sources. Currently, most significant amongst these are various approaches to the design of production systems pursued by systems engineers, and ideas of 'business process improvement' or 'business process re-engineering'. Both use concepts of analysing work organisations as processes of transformation of inputs into outputs, and then designing or redesigning the technical and organisational arrangements used to achieve these transformations to optimise certain parameters.

The emphasis in both of these traditions is however much more on achieving performance objectives for a process as a whole, rather than on delivering satisfying working conditions or maximising the use of human judgement. Both do at the same time tend to draw on rhetorics of putting stakeholders in charge of their processes, and mobilising commitment. Depending on the extent to which this is so, the actual practice of business process redesign can look very like that of the high performance work system version of STS applied within US multinationals.

Returning to the development of the socio-technical tradition, in more recent times Land and Hirschheim (1983), Mumford (1983) and Eason (1987) have for example, made important contributions to developing approaches to the design and implementation of computer systems within work organisations, which explicitly draw on the classic Tavistock socio-technical work. Within the world of 'soft' operations research, Checkland (1981) and Jackson and Keyes (1984) have worked on further aspects of analysing work systems and designing social and technical arrangements.

REFORMULATING THE SOCIO-TECHNICAL APPROACH

A recognition of this diversity and interworking of several streams of theory and practice is part of what underlies the following summary of the socio-technical stream of applied social science. The summary is also something which I find appropriate to the kind of work that my colleagues and I at The Tavistock Institute are currently engaged in. It contains a number of important insights or assumptions, some of which are very much in line with the insights and assumptions of classic socio-technical work, although perhaps formulated rather differently. It also has some aspects which mark a break with tradition. Together, they form an 'enabling' conception of socio-technical work, general and adaptable enough to deal with the range and complexity of issues that have to be faced currently in designing or redesigning work organisations.

The analysis and redesign of work organisations may be guided by a few basic insights, which come directly from the early Tavistock work:

- The organisational arrangements, social relations and techniques, including machinery, used to transform objects or information affect one another and generally need to be understood in the context of one another, but do not determine one another.
- In analysing the functioning and contradictions of work organisations, greater insight can usually be achieved by taking more aspects than is customary of the 'psycho-social whole' into consideration, by conducting and inter-relating analyses at different levels.
- Design options for social and technical arrangements which decentralise decision-making in the sense of moving it away from the apex of management hierarchies and which minimise supervision through the direct control of activities have advantages from a number of viewpoints. They can provide satisfying work, minimise some aspects of alienation and conflict, as well as encourage learning and innovation on the part of workers, within areas for which they have authority to act.

There are two further assumptions underlying this conception of socio-technical theory and practice. These additional assumptions are important influences in making the overall conception more general, broadening the scope of phenomena that can come under consideration beyond those encompassed by the analytical frameworks espoused by many socio-technical writers. The first assumption represents the most important break with much of the socio-technical tradition, in that it questions the use of some concepts derived from general systems theory, introduced by Emery at an early stage in the development of the field, and fairly ubiquitous points of reference ever since. The second assumption is an attempt to provide a basis for reconstructing the field for the late 1990s, still drawing on some of the most general insights of The Tavistock Institute pioneers, without being limited to the particular middle-range concepts they used to flesh out these insights.

The nature of conflict

Much socio-technical writing implies that conflict within work organisations stems from a mismatch between the demands of the social system and those of the technical system, stemming from their independent dynamics. According to this view, conflict can be minimised by adapting one to the other, such that certain basic requirements of the social system can be satisfied. Such a formulation however makes it very difficult to bring to view several aspects of power and conflict. The assumption I introduce here is that it is important to recognise conflicts of social and economic interests within the social system at the level of the enterprise, and the way they are shaped by relations and institutions outside. As a great deal of work in the labour process tradition has shown, the existence of these conflicts may be demonstrated in the way that technical systems are designed and implemented. However, they can also be expressed in terms of conflict over the terms of the employment relation, over issues of pay, grading, opportunities for advancement and job security, for example.

All of these are issues which concern things other than the way that work is done in the present. The simple redesign of technical arrangements and work organisation is unlikely to come to grips with conflicts over such issues. In general, the existence of overall organisational goals or uncontested primary tasks cannot be taken for granted, and conflicts may be located in sites other than the failure of production systems to meet social–psychological needs.

The variety of phenomena making up the 'psycho-social whole'

The real inclusion of power and conflict within the analysis leads one to be sceptical about the general utility of the idea of joint optimisation of the social and technical systems, which has featured so heavily in much socio-technical prescriptive writing. It is however possible to reinterpret one of the earliest and most general features of the tradition to provide a direction for its future. I am here referring to the insight implied in the second element of the enabling summary above, which concerns the importance of considering a work organisation as a psycho-social whole.

Trist, Bamforth and Emery drew heavily on general systems theory, and to a more limited extent on psychoanalysis, to provide an overall understanding of organisational processes, in the 1950s and 1960s. This understanding was productive for deriving frameworks for analysing contradictions between principles of technical design, and goals of increasing job satisfaction and overall organisational effectiveness. I have already questioned whether this biologically derived general systems theory is adequate for conceptualising the varied forms of conflict that are part of the fabric of work organisations. However, it is possible to defend the more general assumption that developing an understanding of the different levels or types of psychological, social, economic and political processes involved in an organisation, and their inter-relations, will be fruitful for the various stakeholders involved. This deeper type of understanding of the psycho-social whole can provide a basis for working out what scope there is for collaborative reform of how their organisation functions.

The implication is that a range of concepts needs to be drawn on and combined in socio-technical work today, according to the nature of the contradictions and conflicts that require illumination. Those developing practical approaches to analysing and redesigning work organisations need to be in dialogue with the various branches of social science currently shedding light on the dynamics of work organisations. As new phenomena emerge within work organisations, interacting with broader processes of cultural, political and technological development, new conceptual and methodological frameworks come into existence for studying them. Socio-technical thinkers and practitioners of the 1990s have a much broader range of social science concepts to draw on and integrate than the pioneers of the 1950s and 1960s.

Current thinking within The Tavistock Institute suggests that the various frameworks to be drawn upon can be located at four different conceptual levels. The development of this meta-framework of socio-technical analysis is very much work in progress, and the four levels are offered here with only a very brief exposition. Much of our current work is concerned with developing ways of using and inter-relating concepts at these different levels.

1 The political and economic

Here we are concerned with the conscious struggles for resources, influence and control that occur as members of an organisation set about furthering what they see as legitimate personal, group and organisational objectives. In the way these struggles are conducted, interpretative frameworks and psychodynamic processes may play a significant part. Cultural assumptions, in particular, have a strong role in shaping how individuals and groups perceive their objectives. Political processes do however require a level of analysis that is distinct from the cultural and psycho-dynamic, in that they are concerned with the ways that individuals and groups mobilise and utilise various sources of power to achieve these objectives. The issue for the redesign of technical and organisational arrangements is to recognise that political processes and economic conflicts are present and to make sure that they can be worked through explicitly, rather than denied.

2 The logistical and cognitive

This level of analysis concerns the constraints placed on organisation by the finite capacity of individuals and groups to process information, and the configurations of systems of planning, execution and control which may be more or less effective in addressing the information-processing demands of a particular organisational task. Typical issues considered at this level of analysis are the ways in which existing divisions of labour may lead to over-complex procedures for taking corrective action when errors are detected, and may prevent important information from being acted upon, because the employees who have access to the information are not expected to take part in decision-making.

3 The cultural

This level concerns the interpretative frameworks, the sets of assumptions, values and strategies for going about their working lives, that people learn when they join an organisation and become involved in its life. Such frameworks are the lenses people use to construct a meaningful image of their situation, and a sense of who they are in it. Analysis at this level often concerns how the way an organisation functions is bound up with the sense of self and view of organisational life present within its different constituent groups. This kind of analysis can bring to visibility contradictions that arise when senior managers set in motion responses to what they see as new environmental pressures, disrupting the conditions which have nourished established occupational identities. Thus, this level can bind together the two preceding ones.

4 The psychodynamic

This level of systems analysis concerns the unconscious processes which shape the way that individuals and groups within an organisation experience their relationships to one another. In particular, work on these dynamics has used the concepts of 'projective process' and 'splitting' to illuminate the way that different groups or individuals may 'carry' conflicting aspects of the pressures impinging on an organisation, so that they are each protected from facing dilemmas and contractions, blaming others for the hostile ideas they represent. The implication of this sort of analysis may be the need to establish more secure conditions within which individuals and groups can develop an understanding of how their perceptions are shaped by 'splitting', providing space for the development of more integrated views of organisational life. In addition, there may be scope for new structural arrangements which disrupt established patterns of splitting.

We now turn to a description of some aspects of a recent action research project conducted by researchers from The Tavistock Institute, in collaboration with managers and workers at a UK chemical company. The purpose is to illustrate the way that analyses at all four levels needed to be drawn upon, to identify issues and suggest alternatives for proceeding in the redesign of social and technical arrangements.

CASE STUDY

The chemical company is a UK subsidiary of a US multinational. The company now has two factories, producing two different types of bulk material. One plant was built in the late 1960s, when this particular company was established; the other was built in the late 1980s. Its construction formed the immediate context for work with The Tavistock Institute. Both types of material being produced are well established products with mature but competitive markets. In the mid-1980s, the parent corporation was seeking to protect and gradually expand its market share in both product markets through competing on the basis of the superior quality of its products, whilst matching competitors' prices. In terms of the older plant in the UK operation, this meant seeking improvements in quality, reducing the level of substandard output that had to be reprocessed, with the ultimate goal of achieving a 'preferred' ranking from its customers, who were located throughout Europe, Africa and Asia. For the new plant, the overall strategy was to establish a standard of production from the outset that was seen as preferred by customers, with minimum defective output. This strategy was considered realistic due to the significant technical improvements and control systems built into the new plant's technology.

In this context, in 1986 the new site was selected by the corporate vice-president for a European initiative in 'new work systems' or 'teamwork'. This followed a series of organisational change initiatives within US plants, designed to achieve greater workforce participation and commitment, particularly in decisions affecting product quality. Most recently, in two or three American plants, the vice-president had launched somewhat controversial initiatives to introduce 'semi-autonomous' work teams, or 'new work systems', as the most direct way to 'empower' workers in taking control of their own decisions on production and quality control. The vice-president persuaded the UK managers to recruit the workforce for the new plant to work in semi-autonomous teams from the outset, without pro-duction supervisors.

With its two plants on the one site in the UK the company had over 300 employees, 200 of which were on hourly rates and organised in a single trade union. The site had a history of stable and co-operative industrial relations, and low labour turnover. The company was a near top payer in a region of high unemployment in northern England.

In 1987, The Tavistock Institute was engaged to assist the UK manage-ment team with the following tasks:

- to design and implement a teamwork system, without supervisors, in the new plant;
- to minimise disruption to the existing plant associated with starting up the new plant;
- to lay the foundations for a 'new style of management' throughout the UK company.

At the outset, staff experts from the corporate centre introduced UK managers to the principles of 'semi-autonomous teams', 'participation', and 'empowerment'. Managers expected to introduce teamwork through a 'step-wise socio-technical design' process, to which they had been introduced by consultants in the USA. This offered a mechanistic way of analysing and redesigning work organisation at the shop-floor level, emphasising issues at the logistical and cognitive level at the expense of the other three of our levels of analysis.

The Tavistock Institute action researchers instead advocated a more exploratory approach to organisational change, based on principles of collaborative action research. The change process was managed through a number of rounds, each consisting of a few major initiatives, each round lasting between six months and one year. At the beginning of each round, senior managers and Institute researchers together identified initiatives required to move the organisation in the direction desired by senior managers. A representative infrastructure was then set up for each initiative, in which Tavistock Institute staff and chemical company personnel could study and come to a joint understanding of issues that needed to be tackled, and begin to implement changes that would address them, within terms of reference set by senior managers.

What follows is a brief overview of the issues that needed to be tackled in one part of this large-scale change project. This concerns the design of a new type of group-based work organisation for the existing plant. Under each of the four headings of the framework of the previous section, I indicate the diagnostic analysis that the action researchers arrived at and the range of intervention approaches used to address these issues.

Political and economic issues: the distribution of benefits

Chronologically, the first issues that needed to be tackled in this part of the overall programme of change were at the political and economic level. Data gathered from individual and group interviews with workers and managers in the existing plant, once their new colleagues were being trained to use teamwork for the start-up on the new plant, indicated that teamwork would only be acceptable in the old plant if issues of collective bargaining and reward for the additional responsibilities involved in teamwork were recognised. The issues were twofold. Operators and craftsmen in the existing plant saw teamwork as involving greater job flexibility as well as greater responsibility for the day-to-day allocation, control and administration of work. They expected this to be recognised in terms of higher rates of pay, derived from the economic benefits of such teamwork to the company. There was also a complex set of issues in terms of equality of opportunity. Workers on the existing plant who had gained higher grading and rates of pay through length of service wanted some continuation of this privilege, whilst the majority of workers on the existing plant wanted the same opportunities for pay progression through teamwork as those available on the new plant. In terms of the language used on the two plants, on the new plant workers demanded 'pay for working unsupervised'. On the old plant, the call was for 'pay for teamworking', before the workers would consider co-operating with a new work system.

The implication of this was that a redesign of work organisation on the existing plant would not stand any chance of acceptance without a parallel reshaping of collective-bargaining arrangements, based on a new payment structure. The origin of the conception of 'payment for self-regulation' which lay at the heart of the new payment structure that was in fact created has been described elsewhere (Neumann and Holti 1990). The point here is that socio-technical redesign of work organisation was intimately bound up with a negotiation of how the benefits of teamworking would be recognised, and how this would affect different groups within the workforce.

The vessel for working through these issues was a participative redesign of payment structures, through a design team with representatives from management, the trade union, and workers from both plants. They negotiated with each other to come to a common set of principles for reward, leading to the definition of a payment structure, the main feature of which was tying the level of reward of a work team to its collective competence along a number of dimensions of self-regulation. This then provided the basis for collective bargaining between management and union over the monetary value to be assigned to working teamwork. The fact that this re-design of payment systems and collective bargaining had been initiated were necessary conditions for those engaged in a similar participative redesign of work organisation to feel that it was legitimate for them to proceed with this activity.

Logistical and cognitive issues: design of roles, boundaries and information systems

The logistical and cognitive level in this case concerned the redesign of the division of labour in production operations, so that they could be performed and controlled by semi-autonomous teams. This was under-taken by a representative design team of managers and shop-floor workers, on the principle that those directly involved in working on a production process are best placed to understand how the division of labour can be redefined to emphasise greater shop-floor control and discretion. The analysis and redesign process used was recognisable as a classic socio-technical change project, using a 'step-wise' methodology, first codified by Tavistock Institute staff in their work with Shell during the 1960s, and documented by Hill (1971). The methodology consists of dividing an over-all production or operating process into unit operations, then defining areas to be staffed and controlled by work teams, each responsible for a meaningful set of unit operations. Rather than having individual jobs defined in terms of a detached division of labour, jobs are redesigned as far as possible as 'whole tasks', each with responsibilities for monitoring and controlling variances within the overall team task. There is an assumption that team members will learn several jobs within a team area, and so be able to rotate through them. This leads to greater flexibility in providing holiday and sickness cover and in dealing with emergencies, as well as encouraging greater appreciation of the overall team task, increasing workers' ability to solve problems and make improvements.

As Neumann (1991) points out, this step-wise method for analysing and redesigning production operations has, particularly in the USA, been taken up by some consultants as the definition of 'socio-technical' design *per se*. This case illustrates that issues of the division of labour, and associated mechanisms of co-ordination and control, were however only one aspect of a complex and multi-level change process. It was also only one of a number of interventions concerning roles and the flow of information. Shortly after implementation of the new job designs, a separate initiative driven from corporate headquarters saw the introduction of a computerised information system which gathered information on the performance of the part of the process being managed by a shift team, providing performance reports to team members as well as to management. The socio-technical design work had identified a number of 'key variances' that needed to be controlled by each team. The action researchers took care to help the client understand the emerging links between the design of the new work system and the new information system. It rapidly proved that these key variances could be fed directly into the specifications of the team's information system, so that the information system could be used to monitor them over time.

Cultural issues: conceptions of managerial roles and status

The cultural level was manifest in a variety of ways during the course of this project. However, one aspect in particular pervaded the programme of change, concerning the future of management and supervisory roles. In a variety of contexts, middle managers and first-line supervisors expressed a mixture of enthusiasm, doubt and outright opposition to the new organisational principles. Part of this resistance can be understood at the political and economic level. The new style of management was intended to increase the authority and capability of production workers, and curb direct managerial involvement in operational matters. This implied a greater emphasis on managers' technical competence and supporting role, as opposed to their direct authority. Managers and supervisors feared that rewards would still be tied mainly to hierarchical position, and that their opportunities for financial advancement would suffer. However, resistance also stemmed from an associated framework of ideas through which managers and supervisors had learned to order their experience of work as well as their aspirations for the future. This framework emphasised the importance of promotion to positions responsible for direct control of production or maintenance workers.

Some senior managers within the company and Tavistock Institute staff spent a great deal of energy launching initiatives to explore the ways of thinking that lay behind middle-management resistance, to find methods for opening-out the frameworks through which these managers experienced their working lives. Initiatives included the establishment of a monthly 'open forum' meeting for middle and senior managers and technical staff, in which debates about the future of their roles, and the nature of their enthusiasm and resistance to the new principles of organisation could be aired. However, senior managers and Tavistock Institute staff also recognised that the sort of cultural change envisaged would need to be linked to changes in reward systems and career structures. A participative redesign of payment structures for salaried staff was launched.

Psychodynamic issues: providing 'containment' for anxiety

Some aspects of how employees within the organisation reacted to the change suggested the need for analysis at an unconscious level. One illustration was the antipathy to the new work-system design on the existing plant by a small group of operators who staffed the boiler house, which generated steam and other gases vital to the production process. The members of this group had all been working in that particular job for well over ten years, in many cases for twenty. The job involved monitoring dials on boilers, often by one worker on his own in a room totally isolated from the life of the plant, with the knowledge that, if there was any kind of failure, their prompt action was vital to the continuity of production. However, there could be weeks or months without anything out of the ordinary happening.

These boiler men adopted a thoroughly ambiguous stance towards teamwork. At first, at least some of them expressed enthusiasm for the idea of joining a wider production team, so that they could escape their 'prison' and have the opportunity to learn and work in other positions. However, this rapidly gave way to vehemence in opposing the new work system. The men cited the impossibility of having the time to train others to learn the boiler-house jobs, and they chose instead to repeat again and again a demand that management assign more full-time workers to the boiler house, so that there was sufficient cover for each worker to take breaks outside, and there were more hands with which to respond to emergencies. Some of what was being expressed can be understood as a fundamental terror of taking on new responsibilities outside the familiar boiler house 'prison'; however other data suggested something more.

Workers in other parts of the plant took to citing the injustice of what the design team was expecting of the boiler men, apparently avoiding their own anxieties as to whether they could handle the wider responsibilities for which they expected to be paid more. The boiler men became the focus for undifferentiated feelings of anxiety about whether members of the workforce were capable of taking on what, at a conscious level, they sought.

The implication of this was the need for guarantees and special provisions for those workers, particularly older ones, who 'wouldn't move'. The design team for the pay structure arrived at a system where a team would not be severely disadvantaged, at least at first, if one or two members did not learn additional jobs. Higher levels of team development were expected after a few years, and these would require more comprehensive cross-training. This was one amongst several features of the plan for implementing a team structure that provided some sort of reassurance that not everybody would have to switch immediately to a new way of working. There would be considerable persistence of familiar elements, and space for people to adjust to the new direction.

GUIDELINES FOR CONSULTING

The case above illustrates two important guidelines for the theory and practice of consulting to complex technical and organisational changes. First, consultants need to take account of a number of different levels of organisational life, each of which tends to be characterised by distinct sets of concepts for diagnosing organisational issues and recipes or techniques for intervening. One of these, which I have called the logistical and cognitive level, includes an analysis of organisational tasks and technologies that support them, and this generally needs to be set in the context of three different social aspects of the organisation – the political and economic, the cultural and the psychodynamic. Second, in terms of consulting practice, the key is to find ways of understanding the relationships in time between a number of discrete interventions needed to tackle issues in these different spheres, rather than to look for one overarching framework to guide diagnosis and intervention.

The purpose of this chapter has been to make a case for both continuity and innovation in the future development of the field of socio-technical consulting and action research. The elements of continuity are, first, that it is possible to organise both the social and technical aspects of work on the basis of considerable individual and group autonomy, and second, that the achievement of this requires consideration of a work organisation as a 'psycho-social whole'. The elements of innovation are that a wider range of social-science perspectives need to be brought to bear on achieving this integrated type of understanding. In particular, an understanding of the cultural, political and economic aspects of organisations needs to be added to the logistical and social-psychological emphases of earlier socio-technical work. The need to recognise different frameworks and the need to work with their interdependence is perhaps the central challenge for those working from either the theoretician or practitioner side of the application of social science to organisational consulting.

ACKNOWLEDGEMENTS

Whilst this chapter is a personal view, and moreover, work in progress, many of the ideas in it have emerged from discussions with colleagues inside and outside of The Tavistock Institute. Lisl Klein (now at the Bayswater Institute), Frank Heller, Dione Hills, Eric Miller, and Elliot Stern have all helped me understand important points, whilst the credit goes to Fergus Murray at UMIST School of Management for pointing out the basic distinctions between several of the levels of analysis set out in the 'enabling summary' of the socio-technical approach. The action research work described here was led by Jean Neumann, and much of what is written here stems from her thinking. None of the above bear the slightest responsibility for the article's shortcomings. Nor should it be taken as representing their views.

REFERENCES AND FURTHER READING

Checkland, P. B. (1981) *Systems Thinking, Systems Practice*, Chichester: Wiley.
Cherns, A. B. (1976) 'The principles of socio-technical design', *Human Relations*, 29(8): 783–92.
—— (1987) 'The principles of socio-technical design revisited', *Human Relations*, 40(3): 153–61.
de Sitter, L. U. den Hertog, J. F. and van Eijnatten, F. M. (1990) 'Simple organisations, complex jobs: the Dutch socio-technical approach', paper presented at the annual conference of the American Academy of Management, San Francisco, 12–15 August.
Eason, K. D. (1987) 'Methods of planning the electronic workplace', *Behaviour and Information Technology*, 6(3): 229–38.
Gustavsen, B. (1992) *Dialogue and Development*, Assen: van Gorcum.
Hanna, D. (1988) *Designing Organisations For High Performance*, Reading, Massachusetts: Addison-Wesley.
Hill, C. P. (1971) *Towards a New Philosophy of Management*, London/Kent: Gower Press/Tonbridge.
Jackson, M. C. and Keyes, P. (1984) *Towards a System of Systems Methodologies*, Journal of the Operational Research Society, 33: 473–86.
Klein, L. (1976) *New Forms Of Work Organisation*, Cambridge, MA: Cambridge University Press.
Land, F. and Hirschheim, R. A. (1983) 'Participative systems design: rationale, tools and techniques', *Journal of Applied Systems Analysis*, 10: 91–107.
Miller, E. J. and Rice, A. K. (1967) *Systems Of Organisation: the Control of Task and Sentient Boundaries*, London: Tavistock Publications.
Mumford, E. (1983) '*Designing Human Systems for New Technology*, Manchester: Manchester Business School.
Neumann, J. E. (1991) 'Why people don't participate when given the chance', *Industrial Relations*, 601: 6–8.

Neumann, J. E. and Holti, R. (1990) 'A case for measuring and rewarding self-regulation in group-based job design', London: Tavistock, paper presented at the conference on Man and Work on the Threshold of the Third Millennium, Bratislava, January.

Neumann, J. E., Holti, R. and Standing, H. (1995) *Change Everything at Once!*, Didcott: Management Books 2000.

Pasmore, W. A. (1988) *Designing Effective Organisations: the Socio-Technical Systems Perspective*, New York: Wiley.

Trist, E. L. (1982) 'The evolution of socio-technical systems. A conceptual framework and an action research program', in A. H. van den Ven, and W. F. Joyce (eds) *Perspectives on Organisation Design and Behaviour*, New York: Wiley, 19–75.

Trist, E. L. and Bamforth, K. W. (1951) 'Some social and psychological consequences of the long wall method of goal-getting', *Human Relations*, 4(1): 3–38.

Chapter 12

Assisting work restructuring in complex and volatile situations

Enid Mumford

The focus of this chapter is on organisational design in situations which are complex and volatile. An important objective for the design of work organisation will be the creation of greater stability through securing more effective control over problems which cause major disturbance. This should have the result of both increasing efficiency and improving the job satisfaction and quality of working life of employees. The chapter will show how, when work structures change, other factors in the situation also have to be altered. These will include wage payment systems, methods of supervision, decision-taking procedures and trade union behaviour.

The first task for the consultant is deciding the nature of the problem that he or she is being asked to solve. Is this primarily organisational or do other factors have a greater importance? Most problems will have an organisational component which affects diagnosis or solution to some extent although the influence of this will vary with the situation. The consultant needs to establish how important organisational issues such as the design of jobs and work flows are and this requires separating symptoms from causes. Managers may present the problem to the consultant as, for example, a training or a leadership difficulty when the underlying causes are, in fact, poor work organisation. This is the situation in the coal mining case discussed in this chapter where management views the problem as bad industrial relations and does not recognise that it is the organisation of work that is creating the industrial relations difficulties.

SELECTING A DESIGN APPROACH

One of the first decisions for a consultant is what approach to use to obtain a good understanding of the presenting problem and to assist the formulation of a solution. Many will have their own approaches but others may find that it is useful to examine available tools and methods that can assist analysis and redesign. This chapter suggests that the socio-technical approach will provide a helpful, people focused philosophy and a set of useful design tools. There are however approaches that the new consultant, in particular, may want to be aware of. Today, in addition to socio-technical design there are 'total quality' and 'process re-engineering' (Mumford and Beekman 1994). It is worth asking how similar, or different, these are from each other (see Table 12.1). There is a view that the three approaches are complementary and that if they could be brought together a very powerful system for improving organisational performance would result.

Socio-technical design was developed in the late 1940s by The Tavistock Institute in England (Trist and Murray 1993). Total quality emerged from the ideas of an American statistician, Dr W. Edwards Deming (Deming 1982). Both The Tavistock Institute group and Deming seem to have shared similar views on how organisations and people could be helped to function more effectively. Process re-engineering is a more recent phenomenon and has been developed and publicised by Michael Hammer, James Champy and Tom Davenport (Hammer and Champy 1993; Davenport 1992). They originally saw it as incorporating many of the ideas and principles of both total quality and socio-technical design although they now believe their ideas have been driven out by the urge of US managers to downsize and reduce their labour forces. The following is an attempt to highlight some of the similarities and differences of the three approaches (Lytle 1992).

The consultant must recognise that the method of analysis he or she chooses will greatly affect the nature of the data that is collected. The method must therefore be appropriate for the problem. The case for socio-technical design is strengthened by the fact that it addresses social issues and all change will have an impact on people.

THE SOCIO-TECHNICAL APPROACH

The method selected here to address complex problems is socio-technical design. Socio-technical design is the product of a group of social scientists who came together to form The Tavistock Institute of Human Relations in London in 1946 (Trist and Murray 1993). Many of the group had collaborated in wartime projects concerned with the mental health of repatriated prisoners and most had been members of the Tavistock Clinic. This has always been concerned with mental health and individual development. The members of the new Tavistock Institute of Human Relations decided that their role was to work with small groups in industry, helping them to become more aware of the psychological factors that hindered the successful completion of the group's task. They believed that the work-group must be of a size to allow close personal relationships, that it must have a capacity for co-operation in completing its primary task and that it must be able to derive satisfaction from the successful accomplishment of this task (Trist 1981).

The Tavistock Institute researchers began their work by looking at morale and health problems in collieries in the Durham coalfield. Their

Table 12.1 A comparison of BPR, TW and STS

	Business process re-engineering	Total quality	Socio-technical systems design
Philosophy	Revolutionary change.	Continuous improvement.	To optimise the contributions of people and technology.
Primary objectives	BPR seeks to improve performance by removing old functional boundaries, improving speed and quality. It uses information technology as an important facilitator.	Total quality has as its primary objective the satisfaction of the customer. It tries to create work processes that produce products that meet customer needs.	STS is trying to create a high performance organisation and a high quality work environment. It makes changes to processes to attain business and human goals.
Stimulus for change	With BPR this is usually all the environment e.g. increased business competition.	TQ's primary focus is on customer requirements.	STS pays attention to factors operating in environment, customers, competition and community.
Work processes	Information is improved through IT. Change focuses on improving co-ordination and obtaining relevant information from the environment. The emphasis is on improving 'competitive edge' through major change.	Improvement of the work process to secure higher quality. The emphasis is on continuous process improvement.	Solutions are social, organisational and technical with the aim of optimisation of all three. The emphasis is on organisational renewal.

Table 12.1 continued . . .

Organisational structures	A new structure will be created as a result of examining processes and establishing what each must achieve. Change may be based on engineering values. BPR should be designed to create commitment and pride but may not be. Work is based on multi-skilled teams.	The structure remains bureaucratic. The focus is not on total systems design but on the internal customer/supplier relationship. Jobs and roles include quality responsibilities. Management ask for a commitment to quality. Normal supervisory roles are maintained.	The structure will be flexible with decision taken where problems arise. Boundary problems will be addressed. The organisation is designed to elicit commitment and pride. Improved quality of working life is a design outcome. Jobs are designed for multi-skilling.
Norms	Acceptance of major change.	Participation on quality. Innovation. Teamwork. Discipline. Excellence.	Participation on most work issues. Teamwork. Commitment. Flexibility.
Values	Competitive advantage.	High quality.	Effective use of people and machines.

Source: Lytle 1992

ideas then spread to Scandinavia and were used by many firms including Norsk Hydro in Norway and Volvo in Sweden. Other European countries became interested and the message also travelled across the world to India and the United States. In many countries both management and the trade unions were interested in the approach. A book published by the Swedish Employers' Confederation in 1975 provides examples of five hundred successful socio-technical design projects. Swedish managers were convinced that work reform through a combination of industrial democracy and more challenging jobs could increase productivity and profitability. It could also lead to a higher level of personal commitment at all levels, a more attractive and human work environment, the opportunity to participate in a flexible work structure and to develop personally. All of these should assist any company to achieve its goals (Jenkins 1975).

From the early days of its development the guiding principles of socio-technical design have always been that effective organisations require skilled and motivated workers able to accept responsibility, a humanistic use of technology that assists rather than controls the employee and work structures that stimulate and reinforce efficiency, learning and effective problem solving. In order to achieve these objectives consultants following The Tavistock Institute approach will pay a great deal of attention to the external environment in which the firm is operating and to the relationships between different parts of the targeted system.

In order to facilitate socio-technical design The Tavistock Institute group developed a set of guidelines and principles to assist themselves and other consultants or managers concerned with improving the design of work situations. These are shown below. This approach requires a consultant to work closely with the users of the system that is to be considered for redesign. It is they, not the consultant, who will decide on what changes to make. The role of the consultant is to help them analyse their own needs and problems, evaluate alternative solutions and arrive at design decisions (Trist 1981).

Step one: initial scanning

The consultant should first get an understanding of the pre-change situation by making a description of the existing work system and its internal and external environments. He or she should try to determine where the most serious problems are located and where the emphasis of the analysis should be placed.

Step two: identification of unit operations

Next, the consultant should identify the main stages of the work process: sets of activities which help move the product into its finished state yet which are relatively self-contained. Usually there will be some kind of discontinuity between each stage – for example, the introduction of a new set of procedures, a new input or an elapse of time.

Step three: identification of variances

The consultant should next look in more detail at the problems or variances. A variance is defined as a weak link in the system where it is difficult to achieve required or desired norms or standards. A variance is considered 'key' if it affects the quantity or quality of output, or operating or social costs. Variances should be carefully documented. For example, showing:

- where the variance occurs and why;
- where it is first observed;
- where and how it is corrected;
- who does this;
- what they have to do to correct it;
- what information they need to correct it;
- what other resources are required.

Step four: analysis of the social system

The social system should next be examined and documented. This will cover the work relationships associated with the system and include:

- a brief review of the organisational structure: who works with whom;
- a description of the relationships required between workers for the optimal production of the product;
- a note on the extent of work flexibility: the knowledge each worker has of the jobs of others;
- a description of pay relationships – the nature of the pay system, differentials, bonuses etc.;
- a description of the workers' psychological needs;
- the extent to which the present work structure and roles meets these needs.

Step five: the maintenance and supply systems

An assessment should be made of how the system of support and maintenance in operation impacts on, and affects, the targeted system. The same should be done for the system that supplies materials and services to the change area.

Step six: the corporate environment

Information should be obtained on how development plans may affect the future operation of the department.

Step seven: proposals for change

The consultant should gather together all this information and after discussions with the different interest groups, should arrive at an agreed action programme. Proposals for action must contribute both to the improvement of the work system, including its technology, and to the improvement of the social system. The latter requires strategies directed at improving job satisfaction and the quality of the work environment.

In many situations the Tavistock concept of self-managing groups will be found to be a solution that successfully achieves both work and social objectives, although the degree of self-management permitted will depend on the views of management. In most situations a degree of self-management will increase motivation, and assist the better control of work problems, quality improvement and the achievement of production targets.

CASE STUDY

The case study chosen to illustrate the socio-technical approach is not new. The project was undertaken in the North West coal field in the late 1950s and early 1960s. Readers may now ask 'why write this old research up again in the 1990s when it was carried out in the 1960s?' There are a number of reasons for doing this. First, we can still learn a great deal from old projects. Many of the problems that were experienced then are little different from those of today. Second, the North West study was never written up from a socio-technical perspective as the principal interest of the research unit was industrial relations, not organisational design. Third, it seems to illustrate many of today's problems. The work environment is extremely complex and difficult to manage. It bears no relationship to the tight, bureaucratic industrial structures found in mass production factories. In this respect it is similar to the volatile environments increasingly found in industries today. Car manufacture may prove to be a relevant modern example of this trend. Commentators are now saying that the days of 'just-in-time' production processes are numbered. These are cheap and efficient but they have the disadvantage of producing a standardised car. The argument is that the successful car manufacturer of the future will have to provide its customers with a large variety of models tailored to fit individual needs. Only by doing this will it be able to compete and survive (Baker 1996). John Baker suggests that a company of this kind will have to be 'agile'. The successful management of complexity and volatility will be a necessity and appropriate organisational structures will need to be developed to handle this.

Most students and researchers are aware of The Tavistock Institute's experiments in the North East coal field in the late 1940s and early 1950s which produced the first socio-technical organisational design principles (Trist and Bamforth 1951). They may be less aware that the Coal Board approached the Tavistock again in the late 1950s asking for a second study. The Tavistock Institute did not agree to do this as they wished their research to be independent of management.

The Coal Board then approached a research group in the Social Science Department at Liverpool University asking for a study which focused on industrial relations (Scott *et al.* 1963). It wanted to discover why certain pits were extremely strike prone, while other pits in the same area were relatively free of strikes. The author was a member of the Liverpool research team. We accepted the project and this led to three of us spending three years working in the North West coal field. Two pits were selected for study in the Wigan UK area. One, called Chanters was, in Coal Board terms, the 'virtuous pit', the other, called Maypole was the 'wicked' pit. I was given Maypole to investigate and my two male colleagues were given Chanters. This led to one of the most interesting, enjoyable and intellectually rewarding research experiences of my career. It also led to my spending almost a year underground and becoming intimate with the long wall method of coal mining.

Maypole is an old, deep coal mine with poor, unstable underground conditions. Organisational problems there are made difficult to solve by the volatility and complexity of the work environment. Working conditions can change in minutes from stability and safety to extreme danger with rapid decisions having to be made. The men underground require intelligence, flexibility and the ability to take fast, appropriate action. At the same time they have to fulfil their primary work objective of mining coal and transporting it from the coal faces to the surface.

In this chapter the socio-technical analysis described earlier will be used to examine the different factors causing this volatility, the impact these had on work practices and, in turn, on industrial relations and the miners' attitudes to their work. Although a socio-technical reorganisation of work was never tried at Maypole, for the colliery closed when its many problems made its coal too expensive for the market, the contribution a socio-technical approach could have made will be examined in this case study. Here is how a consultant might proceed.

Step one: initial scanning – the coal mine and its environment

This first step is essentially getting a feel for the consultancy situation and the problems that have to be addressed. The Maypole environment includes the local community where the miners live and its culture, attitudes and beliefs. It also includes the pit itself, its work practices and its history.

Maypole is located in a village called Abram, near Wigan, and most of the miners live in this village. There is little local industry other than the pit and despite the claims of fathers that 'no son of mine shall work down the pit', most sons do in fact follow in their fathers' footsteps. But in the 1950s and 1960s it is not a bad occupation to have. Work is reasonably secure, earnings are good, hours of work are short in today's terms and for miners with ambition the National Coal Board has an excellent training programme which allows young men to work their way up to management positions through taking a day a week off and attending technical college. The greatest disadvantage of underground work is the possibility of lung disease through constantly breathing in coal dust contaminated air.

The local community does not regard Maypole colliery as a lucky pit. It has a bad history. In the early part of the century there was a major underground explosion and all of the miners were killed with the exception of two who managed to escape through old workings to a neighbouring pit. This episode is known locally as the Maypole disaster and it leads to many local miners doing their best to avoid working there. Another problem is that a neighbouring colliery, Wigan Junction, has recently closed and the miners transferred to Maypole. According to Maypole management these men are very militant and unlikely to have a calming effect on the colliery's volatile industrial relations climate.

The underground environment in the North West coal field presents many management problems. Maypole colliery, although referred to as 'the pit' is, in fact, two pits and in both seams of coal are narrow, contaminated with bands of stone, and difficult to work. They are also deep and at the beginning and end of each shift moving cages descend and ascend taking men perhaps half a mile underground and back up to the surface. These cages are also used for bringing coal from the pit bottom to the pit top. Once underground, because the pits are old and a great deal of coal has been removed, the miners have to travel a considerable distance to reach the faces they are currently working. Some collieries have underground transport but Maypole does not and the journey has to be made on foot. This means that the men do not start work until up to an hour after the official time. Similarly work stops early in order to allow the men to get back to the pit bottom for the period when the cage is taking men and not coal to the surface. This is known as 'man winding time'.

Working conditions, although always warm are usually cramped and uncomfortable with men mostly working in a kneeling position because of the low height of the seam of coal, and occasionally having to work lying on their backs. In addition to these poor conditions there are constant unpredictable and hazardous events. These include falls of roof, water being found in the coal seam and problems with methane gas – the cause of the earlier disaster. The miners not only have to cope with their routine work, they have also to be constantly dealing with these demanding occurrences. Needless to say, this unstable environment leads to many accidents and Maypole is the colliery with the worst accident record in the North West region. If we examine the history of Maypole we find that, despite poor working conditions, the social structure of work in pre-mechanised times was quite good. The men worked in small family groups using a 'pillar and stall' approach that is still used in some US mines. Each group had a section of the coal face for which they were responsible. The tools for extracting coal were picks and shovels and the roof was held up by wooden pit props. Tubs were pulled manually to the pit bottom for transfer to the surface. In Victorian times this had led to women and children being used for haulage because they were small. Legislation eventually outlawed their employment although historians tell us that the banning of women was not for health and safety reasons but because the Victorians would not tolerate men and women working together in the dark. It could lead to immoral behaviour. A major factor leading to improvement in working conditions was not technology but the use of pit ponies underground. Pit ponies meant that roadways leading to coal faces had to be well made and high enough for a pony to walk along. Maypole did not have pit ponies although it did have canaries which were taken underground to give warning of gas.

During this early period all the coal mines were privately owned. It was not until 1946 that they became nationalised and the National Coal Board took over. Unfortunately nationalisation was a let down for the miners. They had looked forward to it in the belief that everything would change. They would lose the exploitive private coal owners and become the owners of the pits themselves. In the event, nothing really happened. The owners did go but the managers who had worked for the coal owners still remained. They could not be dispensed with as the newly nationalised industry had no one else with the knowledge to run the pits.

Nationalisation brought with it an official system of joint consultation as this was a condition of the reorganisation. The miners too had the advantage of now belonging to a single trade union, the National Union of Mineworkers. This was formed in 1944 from the Mine Workers Federation of Great Britain, a federation of virtually independent district unions.

By the end of the Second World War a new technical system was revolutionising coal mining production. This was called the long wall method and was, to some extent, an adaptation of the moving assembly line that was now dominating mass production industry. The long wall method introduced a cyclical production system in which a different activity took place on each shift.

Step two: the production system – identification of unit operations.

Step two requires the consultant to create a description of the principal activities that make up the production system. This is done by identifying what are called 'unit operations'. These are the major transformations, or changes that take place in the product as it moves through the production process. These changes may be caused by manual activities or by machines including computers. One unit operation can usually be separated from another by looking for a discontinuity of time, material, change of state or change of activity (Trist 1981). Unless the organisational changes made are very revolutionary, as for example, with some kinds of business process re-engineering, or the nature of the primary production task changes considerably, these unit operations will still have to be completed irrespective of any new organisation of work or introduction of new technology.

The first unit operation includes breaking up the coal, transferring it to conveyor belts and making the roof safe. On the morning shift, from 6 am to 2 pm, the coal face is drilled at intervals along its length by a shot firer who is also a grade two deputy. The shot firer then places explosive in the holes that have been made and fires these, a process that breaks the coal up into small pieces. The morning shift miners, who are called fillers in North West mines, then shovel the coal onto moving conveyor belts. These transport it to the pit bottom where it is transferred into trucks and sent up to the surface. The fillers also have to ensure that the roof is stable by placing new pit props along the line of the advancing face. The technical innovation for this stage of the process is the moving conveyor belt and metal pit props although some of the faces at Maypole still use wooden ones.

The second unit operation involves moving the conveyor belts forward. On the afternoon shift, which lasts from 2 pm to 10 pm a second group of miners called conveyor movers are in charge. With the removal of the morning coal the face has now advanced several feet forward and their job is to take the conveyor belts to pieces and reassemble them at the new face line.

The third unit operation is packing the worked face. On the evening shift, from 10 pm to 6 am, a group of young miners holding their first face job come underground. They are called packers and it is their responsibility to remove the pit props furthest away from the worked face and allow the roof to fall in. This fills the gap left as the face advances. To enable the roof to fall in a controlled manner the packers build packs of stone at intervals along the previously worked face. These support the descending roof and ensure that too much subsidence does not damage buildings on the surface. One other activity on this shift is carried out by a highly skilled miner called a cutter who operates a coal cutting machine. This has a four foot six inch jib that goes into the bottom of the new face and removes a slice of coal. This provides a space for the broken coal to fall into when it is shot fired on the morning shift. The new technology here is the use of a coal cutting machine.

This is the level of technology at Maypole at the time I was there although, as technology became more advanced, roof supports and conveyor belts that could be automatically moved forward became available and coal cutting machines became cutter loaders able to automatically cut and load the coal onto the conveyor belts. These innovations eventually changed the organisation of work and removed the three shift cycle of activities.

There are two other groups working underground carrying out other significant operations. One is a highly skilled group of tunnellers, called rippers, who are responsible for driving the new roadways necessary to keep up with the advancing face. These work in small, integrated teams. The second is a group of men who look after the haulage and ensure that it keeps moving. These are usually older men who can no longer meet the heavy demands of face work and need a less demanding occupation.

Underground supervision consists of an under manager responsible for the running of the pit, two overmen who are assistant managers, and a group of deputies, acting as foremen, who have to ensure high production and a safe work environment. At Maypole these two responsibilities are usually incompatible. In addition there is a checkweighman whose role is to make sure the miners are correctly paid for the amount of coal they produce. There is also a group of skilled maintenance men who are located on the surface and only come underground when they are required.

Step three: production problems – the analysis of variances

An analysis of variances is one of the most useful socio-technical tools. This identifies and highlights the major problems that are preventing the work system operating at high efficiency. A variance is a part of the system where a weakness occurs and required or desired work standards are not being achieved. Many of these weaknesses will be due to unsatisfactory forms of work organisation. Some will be a consequence of inadequate information.

Variances can be of two kinds. There are 'key' variances or variance areas where problems cannot be eliminated altogether but they can be brought under more effective control. Most of the variances in the Maypole colliery are of this kind. There are also 'operational' variances. These are due to bad working practices and can usually be eliminated altogether. The introduction of new computer-based information systems can often make a contribution to their reduction.

The long wall cyclical method of mining is an excellent idea in theory and can work satisfactorily in pits were working conditions are stable.

Unfortunately Maypole is not one of these. The Maypole reality is that water or dirt and stones, or difficult roof conditions will occur. The miners have to deal with these and this means that the fillers on the morning shift frequently cannot finish shovelling all the coal onto the moving conveyor belts before the end of their shift. They will then leave the face, the conveyor movers will arrive for the next shift and find that they cannot start working on the belts as there is still coal on the face. They have to complete the fillers' job before they can commence their own. This means that at the end of their shift they will leave with the conveyor belts only partially assembled. The packers will then arrive and find that they have to finish assembling the belts before they can start their packing activity. This transfer of work from one group to another can continue until the week end when the cycle will be restored to normal.

Face problems are exacerbated by the poor state of the roadways leading from the pit bottom to the working faces. This makes the transportation of necessary materials slower and more difficult than it should be. Fillers on the morning shift are often unable to adequately support the roof as they transfer coal to the conveyor belts. This is because the haulage has not been able to deliver the required number of pit props. These problems add to the dangers of underground work and also slow down the production process.

It can be seen that the most damaging variances occur at the interface between one shift and another, and one occupational group of miners and another. The variance matrix (Figure 12.1) shows how a problem that occurs early on in the production process, for example the bringing of supplies of pit props to the coal face, can amplify all the subsequent variances.

Figure 12.1 shows how insufficient pit props and tools lead to the roof being inadequately supported on the morning shift. This causes avoidable small falls of roof with stone falling on the conveyor belts and breaking these. The fillers have to repair these and this means that the filling operation is not completed on the morning shift. When the conveyor belt movers arrive they have to place the remaining coal on the belts before they can start moving the belts forward. This, in turn causes them to do a rushed job and the belt moving operation is not finished before the packers arrive. The packers have to finish this with the result that packing is done badly because some of the packers are now not available for their normal job. This results in valuable pit props being lost when the roof of the worked face is brought down. Insufficient pit props can also affect the rippers' roadway extending operations and falls of roof can also occur there. This example shows how an efficient and timely face supplies system could make a considerable contribution to problem reduction.

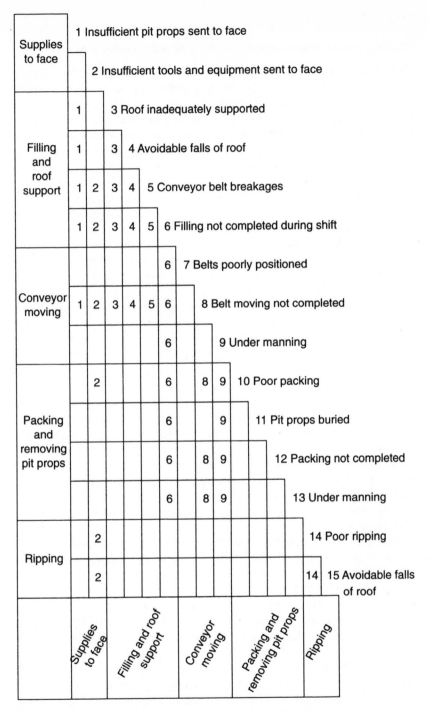

Figure 12.1 A variance matrix showing the effect of inadequate supplies reaching the working faces

Step four: social relationships – analysis of the social system

This social analysis must first identify and examine the overall climate of social relationships. Do people work happily and co-operatively together or is there stress, tension and aggression? Next, the consultant should examine group and individual relationships more closely. Who needs to work with whom, why is this the case and how successful in efficiency and morale terms are these relationships. Relationships between management and workers must also be studied. Are there conflicts of interest which place supervision under pressure? For example, the requirement for pit deputies to take responsibility for both safety and production output.

The transfer of work from one group to another causes intense hostility amongst the face workers. A major reason for this is the fact that each occupational group receives a different level of financial reward. The fillers are the highest paid of the face workers, the conveyor movers come next and the packers are the lowest paid. Each group bitterly resents having to do the work of the previous group, and for less money. This hostility often takes a retaliatory form. For example, the conveyor movers can deliberately leave some of the bolts on the belts undone when they finish their shift. This means that when the fillers put coal on the belts the next morning the belts will fall apart. This causes the fillers to retaliate against the conveyor movers and the result is a general increase in conflict. Similar provocative actions are taken by the other groups.

Relationships between the different occupational groups are not made easier by the fact that Maypole has a permanent shift system. Fillers always work the morning shift, conveyor movers the afternoon shift and packers the night shift: they rarely meet each other in the work situation. One group hears and sees another as a set of tramping boots and moving black figures passing by in the underground roadways on the way to the coal faces. Some, of course, will be neighbours but the fact that they are on different shifts means that they will rarely be together in the pubs or Miners Institute.

While relationships between the different occupational groups are not good, relationships between the men and the management are even worse. This is first because many of the managers have worked for the old hated coal owners, and second because they continually pressure the men for higher output. Many of the men respond by giving a low degree of commitment to the colliery and staying away from work on Fridays. Thursday is the day they are paid. Many men are also absent on a Monday as the faces are more difficult to work after the week end break. Management appear to have few sanctions to apply against this continual, regular absenteeism. Similarly, the trade union does not get a great deal of support. The local NUM hierarchy tends to respond to the grievances of the most powerful underground groups but to ignore the problems of those with less power and less pay.

Industrial relations problems cover both official, union supported, disputes and unofficial 'wild cat' strikes in which strikes take place without the union being consulted or taking part. It is important for the consultant to obtain a good understanding of the structure of industrial relations and to establish good relations with the trade union. Maypole has a full time trade union official representing the National Union of Mineworkers. His office is at the colliery although he is not often found underground. The National Coal Board and the National Union of Mineworkers has an agreed conciliation machinery for settling disputes at district and national level. Colliery managers are responsible for the operation of this scheme at local level. They have been given a six step procedure to follow when disputes occur. At Maypole most of the disputes are short and unofficial and so the disputes machinery rarely becomes operational.

The reason I was asked to study Maypole was because it has one of the worst strike records in the Wigan area. Most of these are unofficial strikes over earnings with men on different faces coming out on strike at different times. It is rare for the whole colliery to be on strike at the same time. The reason for these strikes is almost always pay. Because of the uncertain and volatile face conditions the earnings of face groups can vary dramatically from week to week for reasons entirely outside the men's control. Although there is a compensation system to allow adjustments to be made the men rarely agree with management's decisions.

Pay disputes are encouraged by the wage payment system in operation. When a new face is opened a face agreement is made which takes account of the length of the face and the amount of coal to be produced. Unfortunately, this agreement does not take account of changing face conditions as these will not be known until production is underway. Water, rock, poor roof conditions all affect output and the wages of the men working there.

Strikes are mostly located in the face workgroups and the strategies used by the men to achieve success vary from one occupational group to another and are usually related to the power of the group. Fillers are the most strike prone as their earnings are the most affected by adverse face conditions. The men on each face can place pressure on management by stopping work as a group. Conveyor movers react in the same way, although the fact that they are moving belts, not shovelling coal means that they have less industrial muscle to apply. Packers rarely strike. They are too young to know much about industrial relations, and they have no experience of organising themselves. Rippers are also a relatively strike free group. They work in small tightly knit groups and their importance to the running of the pit means that management will listen to and rectify their grievances. Haulage workers also rarely go out on strike. They are not affected by changing face conditions and their earnings, although low, are stable. They are also older men unfit for face work through age or ill health.

Step five: the maintenance and supply systems

The maintenance system is the arrangement for servicing and repairing underground machinery. Maypole has little planned, preventive maintenance. The miners wait until a machine breaks down before summoning the maintenance crew. This causes problems. Skilled maintenance staff such as electricians are located on the surface and only descend underground when sent for. This leads to considerable delays before an electrical or mechanical fault is repaired.

Supply systems are the methods for moving equipment to the working faces. The poor state of the underground roadways means that the transportation of supplies, such as pit props, is slow and difficult. It can take a day for urgently needed material to move from the pit bottom to the coal face.

Step six: the corporate environment

This is the external colliery administrative environment with the principal influence being the Area Coal Board and its managers. There is continual area management pressure for more production and a strategy which is described by the collieries as 'coal at any price'. Because Maypole is such a difficult pit to work, in order to respond to these demands for more coal, both safety and maintenance are neglected by men and management.

The consulting problem is clearly not an easy one. First, the consultant must acquire a good understanding of how Maypole operates and the values, attitudes and behaviour patterns of the people who work there. Second, the consultant must decide, in collaboration with all interested groups, if work restructuring can contribute to an organisational solution of the needs and problems. If it is agreed that this is the case and work arrangements should be redesigned then the implications of such a change for the wage payment structure, the industrial relations conciliation procedure and other related activities must be carefully worked out. Strategies for the introduction of change must also be discussed and agreed. The consultant's task and challenge is to see if a socio-technical approach can make a contribution to a viable solution.

Step seven: proposals for change

Socio-technical design is a democratic process and so it is necessary to begin by creating a design group and a steering committee. As any proposed solution needs to be tried out experimentally before being introduced on a wider basis it is suggested that at Maypole the design group consists of the men from one face. This will be the face where any reorganisation is first implemented. The design group will need to include representatives from fillers, rippers, and packers, and to have a deputy as a member. It will also need to consult representatives from the cutters, rippers and haulage workers during its deliberations. The steering group should include the colliery trade union official, a deputy, the pit under manager, the colliery manager and the colliery nurse.

The mission of the project will follow the socio-technical tradition and will be to improve efficiency, reduce the number of accidents, eliminate strikes and provide a more satisfying work environment for the miners. Attention will be paid to identifying the critical success factors associated with the achievement of these objectives. In addition to the reorganisation of work, these will include factors such as the improvement of roadways to assist the movement of materials, the rethinking of the methods of wage payment and an examination of the colliery consultative system and the grievance procedure.

A good starting point for the design group discussions is an identification of problems, or variances, which have to be removed or reduced in impact before the mission can be achieved. The definition of a variance is a system, or part of a system, which tends to deviate from some required or desired norm or standard. Variance matrices can show how a variance located at the start of a process can travel through the system affecting many things that come after. The variance matrix shown earlier provides an example of how haulage problems can lead to too few supplies arriving at a face. This in turn affects all subsequent activities and could result in serious injury or loss of life.

The analysis of variances shows that a major source of problems is the fact that each occupational group of face workers has to make good the unfinished work of the previous group and is doing this for less pay than the group responsible for the activity. There are also constraints. Face conditions cannot be improved because they are largely related to the quality of the seam of coal that is being worked and the long wall technology cannot be altered. Can the problem be solved through the reorganisation of work? The earlier Tavistock Institute coal mining project suggests that this is possible. A solution may come from following the important socio-technical guideline of making each group responsible for solving its own problems.

This can be assisted by creating teams of face workers and making each team responsible for every activity on a section of the coal face. This would lead to a more flexible deployment of available labour. A team of nine, if they are all multi-skilled and able to carry out the filling, conveyor moving and packing activities, could take complete responsibility for a section of the coal face, say 30 yards. They could then organise themselves as the conditions require. If the face is likely to be difficult on the morning shift, then four men could come in instead of three thus ensuring that the filling operation is completed in the time available. Similarly if the packing operation is straightforward then only two may be required. This solution would require all the men in each team to be trained in all the face operations and for them all to be paid the same amount. This payment could have a productivity element in it. While the forward advance of a coal face is related to the four foot six inch blade of the cutter jib and all teams must advance the same amount if the face is to stay level, efficient teams can take a wider span of face than other groups.

This new structure must be tried out on experimental face before being more widely installed but it appears to have a number of advantages. These are:

- It will enable efficient teams to increase their output of coal and their earnings.
- It provides flexibility so that more or less men in the team can be deployed to meet good or bad face conditions.
- It removes the conflict between the different occupational groups as all men are now multi-skilled and paid the same rate. It also reduces stress.
- It reduces the conflict with management as each team can take many of its own decisions.

Other changes that would be required with this solution are as follows:

- a new training programme with each team being prepared to learn new skills and accept trainees;
- a different wage payment system based on groups not individuals; given the volatile underground conditions and the nature of disputes, any incentive component must be carefully designed and approved of by the miners;
- a willingness by men and management to try the new approach;
- trade union willingness to accept the new approach.

Difficulties that would have to be overcome are as follows:

- The present system provides a job hierarchy with an upward movement from packer to conveyor mover to filler. Some men may be reluctant to lose this and the phased increase in earnings it provides.
- The proposed structure greatly improves vertical flexibility and integration as each team now handles its own. But it may reduce horizontal integration as work will become team focused. Rivalries between the teams may develop.
- It does nothing to solve the safety and supplies problems. These require a change in management priorities and less emphasis on output alone.
- It gives the trade union a new bargaining responsibility. It is used to bargaining for separate occupational groups. It must now look after the interests of multi-skilled groups.

An important message here is that new solutions may remove old variances but they invariably bring with them new problems. New structures may improve efficiency, stability and job satisfaction to some extent and if they do this they are very well worth while. They are unlikely to make major differences to all of these unless they are very revolutionary. Despite this qualification, if all interested groups agree, they should still be tried. At Maypole conflict could have been reduced, output increased and quality of working life improved by the changes suggested above. Interestingly, the revolutionary change that was to totally alter the future organisation of work was more new technology. Machines were developed which moved up and down the face cutting and loading coal automatically. At the same time the conveyor belts were moved forward by machine. This removed the need for cyclical work and resulted in small multiskilled teams of miners following behind the cutter loader on each shift to ensure everything worked effectively.

A second message is that changes such as those suggested above are doomed to failure unless they are wanted by employees, management and the trade union. All three groups must assist their introduction. The early Tavistock Institute project failed because the trade union was not involved, did not like the results of the restructuring and withdrew its co-operation.

GUIDELINES FOR CONSULTANTS

Participation or direction

Most consultants will want to use a participative approach and involve all groups directly affected by design decisions. The question is how to do this and how far to go with participation. The answer depends very much on the situation, what people want, and what is possible. If a new organisation structure is going to cause people to lose their jobs then the author believes that any real user participation is virtually impossible. Employees cannot be asked to make their colleagues redundant.

My experience is that in many situations a high level of participation is possible and leads to a sense of user ownership and enthusiasm for the new system, provided that the replacement system delivers what has been promised and does not create any victims. No amount of enthusiasm will survive if the system, and this is usually its technical component, turns out to be unsatisfactory or a mistake. This question of participation is discussed in detail by the author in other publications (Mumford 1995, 1996).

Monitoring and evaluation

What is planned and intended and what happens in practice are often two very different things. The wise consultant will ensure that a system for closely monitoring the efficiency and human effects of the new system is introduced. Further changes can then be made to iron out deficiencies that had not been anticipated when the system was designed. Once the system has been in operation for some time a comprehensive evaluation needs to be made of how well it is meeting the organisational, technical and social objectives that were originally set for it. A further check needs to be made to establish how valid these objectives still are. Monitoring and evaluation are valuable in assisting the learning process of how to manage change effectively. Learning is the route to success both for a consultant and as a company or an industry grappling, like our coal mine, with the problems of a difficult, complex and volatile environment.

Other possible guidelines

An important conclusion for consultants is, first, that in most situations the restructuring of work is not enough. Any changes in work organisation will affect wage payment systems, industrial relations behaviour and management attitudes. The design task must encompass these. Second, new procedures have to be acceptable to users and accepted by them. The importance of participation in the socio-technical approach usually ensures this. Because workers have played a major role in the design task they see the change as their responsibility and they are committed to it. But flexible team work may be less acceptable where the initiative has come solely from management. This has proved to be the case in the British Post Office and in many American business process re-engineering projects.

Another important point is that while the management of a complex and volatile environment can be greatly facilitated by flexible structures, success also requires employee knowledge, responsibility and the ability to take appropriate action. Where there is an excess of complexity and little commitment to its control workers may respond, as in Maypole, by avoiding the situation and being absent from work. This greatly increases the stress of managers who now have to cope with the problems stemming from this complexity with inadequate resources.

A cybernetic principle developed by Professor Ross Ashby is relevant here. He maintains that only variety can control variety. By this he means that simple solutions are unlikely to work in complex environments. Any change must have enough variety and flexibility within it to cope with the complexity it is addressing (Ashby 1956).

Socio-technical design works well. It provides an excellent and comprehensive diagnosis for problems and needs. This is an essential requirement in complex and volatile environments where it is not always easy to separate cause from effect. Its emphasis on participation means that the knowledge and requirements of the users of the system contribute to design solutions.

In the past socio-technical design has been applied within the boundaries of departments and functions. It now needs to be extended to cover companies, even industries. Eric Trist has provided some excellent advice on what is required. He argues that the socio-technical knowledge base is unevenly distributed. It has focused on the remodelling of departments and new plants. It now should be directed at the transformation of entire work establishments, even industries. It also needs to address macro-social processes and advanced technology (Trist 1981). These are important challenges for the future.

REFERENCES AND FURTHER READING

Ashby, W. Ross (1956) *An Introduction to Cybernetics*, London: Chapman and Hall.

Baker, J. (1996) 'Less lean but considerably more agile', *Financial Times*, 10 May.

Davenport, T. (1992) *Process Innovation: Reengineering Work Through Information Technology*, Cambridge, MA: Harvard Business School Press.

Deming, W. E. (1982) *Quality, Productivity and Competitive position*, Massachusetts: MIT.

Hammer, M. and Champy, J. (1993) *Reengineering the Corporation*, New York: Harper.

Jenkins, D. (ed) (1975) *Job Reform in Sweden*, Swedish Employers' Federation.

Lytle, W. O. (1992) *A Comparison of the Socio-technical Systems and the Total Quality Approaches to Organisational Change*, W. O. Lytle and Associates.

Mumford, E. (1995) *Effective Systems Design and Requirements Analysis: the ETHICS Method*, London: Macmillan.

—— (1996) *Systems Design: Ethical Tools for Ethical Change*, London: Macmillan.

Mumford, E. and Beekman, G.-J. (1994) *Tools for Change and Progress: a Socio-technical Approach to Business Process Reengineering*, London: CSG Publications.

Scott, W., Mumford, E., McGivering I. and Kirkby, J. (1963) *Coal and Conflict*, Liverpool: Liverpool University Press.

Trist, E. L. (1981) *The Evolution of Socio-technical Systems*, Toronto: Ontario Quality of Working Life Centre.

Trist, E. L. and Bamforth, K. W. (1951) 'Some social and psychological consequences of the longwall method of coal getting', *Human Relations*, 4: 3–38.

Trist, E. L., Higgin, G. W., Murray, H. and Pollock, A. B. (1963) *Organisational Choice*, London: Tavistock Publications.

Trist, E. L. and Murray, H. (1993) *The Social Engagement of Social Science, Vol. 11, The Socio-technical Perspective*, Philadelphia: University of Pennsylvania Press.

Chapter 13

Aligning strategy, culture and leadership

William E. Schneider

The line of reasoning taken in this chapter – i.e., that focus, integration, alignment, balance, and completeness are critical to an organisation's success – began with this consultant's experience consulting with a wide range of organisations over the last twenty years. The first problem that appeared prevalent was the alarming extent to which organisations would try to adopt 'one-size-fits-all' remedies dreamed up by others and over-applied to the universe of organisations. In many, many cases, this consultant's experience and the experience of the client organisation was that the remedy quickly became part of the problem and that, lo and behold, one size did *not* fit all. Many of the management and organisational development approaches proposed to prospective client organisations encourage, directly or indirectly, people to look *outside* themselves and their organisations for direction, formulas, and lessons for success. People are encouraged to adopt the practices of the 'excellent' companies, the Japanese, the 'innovators', or the 'changers', those who are the most intense, and those who emphasise 'transcendence' and purpose. While these proposals may have considerable value, they are often unwittingly pulling their prospective clients off centre by insisting that conclusions reached from observing the practices of one kind of organisation or group of organisations must apply to all organisations. This is surely an over-generalisation or a kind of organisational benchmarking writ large.

In addition, this consultant has also found that organisations traditionally emphasise the determination of a strategy for gaining distinctive competitive advantage in their marketplace, but few explicitly address the cultural and leadership path required to realise such a strategy. Culture has everything to do with *implementation* and leadership has everything to do with *mobilising people*. Unless culture and leadership are given equal attention to strategy, the probability that the organisation will be held back or taken off course increases geometrically. And, unless culture and leadership operate in a consistent and congruent manner with strategy, the organisation will work, to one degree or another, at cross-purposes with itself. The most successful organisations, especially over the long term, are those organisations that have a clear strategy, a culture that congruently implements the strategy, and a leadership approach that consistently mobilises people to understand and accomplish the strategy and understand and build and live out the culture that most effectively fits the strategy. The essence of a highly successful organisation 'comes in the translation of its core ideology and its own unique drive for progress into the very fabric of the organisation – into goals, tactics, policies, processes, norms, management behaviours, building layouts, pay systems, accounting systems, job design, – into *everything* that the organisation does' (Collins and Porras 1994: 201).

The more all of the elements of an organisation work together in concert with the organisation's core strategy, the greater the probability that that organisation will prosper.

ORGANISATIONAL EFFECTIVENESS = 'BALANCED INTEGRITY'

Effective organisations exhibit 'balanced integrity'. Integrity means to be complete, whole, or unified. Balanced means to be in a state of equilibrium. Effective organisations are:

- focused, integrated, aligned;
- continually working at maintaining a state of dynamic equilibrium;
- continually working to bring in whatever is missing in order to be more and more complete.

Organisational development must start from the nature and inherent strengths of the organisation in question. The *system* has to be the constant. Unless the organisation is dying or unless it was hopelessly mis-conceived from the beginning, honouring the nature and inherent strengths of the organisation is critical to the success of any intervention within that organisation. This is true for TQM, business process re-engineering, quality circles, empowerment programmes, restructuring programmes, downsizing programmes, visioning programmes, excellence programmes, strategy programmes, or any other programme. Each organisation's cultural nature and unique mix of cultural strengths and weaknesses frames the essential basis for what that organisation can become. Organisational success and the essential paradigm for getting there lie within.

Any one organisation's success and prosperity:

- starts from self knowledge;
- comes from the inside out;
- springs from insight, not imitation;
- comes from building on that organisation's strengths.

Because organisations are self-organising systems, they naturally form a core culture or a core paradigm for how to go about accomplishing success. One cannot force-feed a generalised principle, practice, or programme into any one core culture and expect it to work unless it is congruent with the core culture of the organisation. Any intervention within an organisation must be *system-focused*, not *component-focused*. It cannot be blanketly grafted onto any system, regardless of the inherent nature of that system. At a minimum, the principles of that intervention must be adapted to fit at least four distinct core cultures – which will be discussed shortly.

The three fundamental pillars of organisational functioning are: *strategy, culture, and leadership*. Any intervention in the organisation must integrate with all three of these key pillars. In addition, the more aligned these three fundamentals are, the more effective the organisation and the more easily any specific intervention will be accepted. Conversely, the less aligned these three factors are, the harder any specific intervention will be.

Organisational culture is so important because it provides consistency for an organisation and its people. It provides order and structure for activity; tells people what activities are in bounds and what are out of bounds. Over time, culture establishes communication patterns – the kind of language people use with one another and the assumptions upon which they consistently operate.

Culture establishes membership criteria, who is included and who is excluded. It establishes the conditions for judging internal effectiveness and sets the expectations and priorities and conditions for reward and punishment. It determines the nature and use of power within an organisation and installs the process for how decisions get made. Culture establishes management practices.

Culture is very, very important because it either enables or limits the accomplishment of strategy. Many organisations have learned the hard way that new strategies that make sense from a financial, product, or marketing viewpoint cannot be implemented because they are too far out of line with the organisation's existing assumptions. The new strategies do not fit within the cultural paradigm. While leaders must formulate strategy first, if their culture and their subsequent leadership practices do not reinforce that strategy, they either will have a terribly difficult time accomplishing their strategy or they won't get there at all.

Recent research by Collins and Porras (1994) and by Kotter and Heskett (1992) speaks directly to these issues.

Collins and Porras surveyed 700-plus CEOs and asked them to define a 'visionary company' and to then, name their top three such companies. From the survey results, Collins and Porras came up with 18 visionary companies and 18 comparison (same industry) companies. They, then, compared the visionary companies as a group with the comparison companies as a group to see what differentiated the one group from the other.

To see if these 18 visionary companies actually outperformed (economically) the 18 comparison and the general market, Collins and Porras looked at three 'funds' of stocks: visionary company fund; comparison fund; and a general market stock fund. They presumed equal US$1 investments in each fund – starting on 1 January, 1926. They tracked actual stock performance for each of these three funds from 1 January, 1926 to 31 December, 1990. If you reinvested all dividends and made appropriate adjustments for when the companies became available on the Stock Exchange (they held companies at general market rates until they appeared on the market), that $1 in the general market fund would have grown to $415 on December 31, 1990. The $1 invested in the group of comparison companies would have grown to $955 – more than twice the general market. The $1 in the visionary companies stock fund would have grown to $6,356 – over six times the comparison fund and over fifteen times the general market.

Collins and Porras next engaged in a lengthy and extremely thorough research effort to determine what exactly differentiated the visionary companies from the comparison companies. They discovered that the visionary companies (and not the comparison companies):

- had leaders who focused on building the organisation *per se*, not who focused on doing the 'business' of the organisation;
- built core ideologies;
- they did not identify profits as the goal;
- preserved the core *and* stimulated progress;
- set big hairy audacious goals;
- built and preserved cult-like cultures;
- experimented a great deal and kept what worked;
- grew management from within;
- kept working to do things better.

Very importantly, Collins and Porras concluded:

The essence of a visionary company comes in the translation of its core ideology and its own unique drive for progress into the very fabric of the organisation – into goals, strategies, tactics, policies, processes, cultural practices, management behaviour, building layouts, pay systems, accounting systems, job design – into *everything* that the company does. A visionary company creates a total environment that envelops employees, bombarding them with a set of signals so consistent and mutually reinforcing that it's virtually impossible to misunderstand the company's ideology and ambitions ... What just might be the most important point to take away from this book ... is the central concept of *alignment*. By 'alignment' we mean simply that all the elements of a company work together in concert within the context of the company's core ideology and the type of progress it aims to achieve.

Collins and Porras's work is powerful independent research that points in the same direction as what this consultant is saying in this chapter and in what he says in his own book (Schneider 1994). Collins and Porras are, in essence, saying that 'balanced integrity' is the most important differentiator between visionary companies and comparison companies.

Kotter and Heskett's research is equally confirming and equally compelling. Kotter and Heskett, two Harvard Business School professors, investigated the connection, if any, between corporate culture and economic performance. They chose 207 firms from 22 different US industries to research. The administered a survey to determine cultural strength, they interviewed 75 experienced and highly regarded industry analysts, and they calculated measures of economic performance between 1977 and 1988. In addition, they conducted in-depth analyses of firms that were: culturally strong and less effective; culturally strong and more effective.

First of all, they discovered some important facts about corporate cultures themselves. All companies have corporate cultures. Some cultures are much stronger than others. 'Strong' and *effective* cultures are cultures that:

• fit with the company's business strategy;
• are adaptive, but preserve core values;
• work to satisfy the legitimate interests of stockholders, customers, and employees – all three, all the time.

Culture's influence appears to be '*more powerful than anything else,*' including strategy, structure, leadership, financial analysis and management systems. As far as the connection between corporate culture and economic performance, Kotter and Heskett discovered that corporate cultures that are strong and effective have a *significant impact* on a firm's long-term economic performance. Over an 11-year period, strong and effective culture companies vs. less effective companies increased revenues by an average of 682 per cent vs. 166 per cent; expanded workforces by 282 per cent vs. 36 per cent; grew stock prices by 901 per cent vs. 74 per cent; improved net incomes by 756 per cent vs. 1 per cent. 'Corporate culture will probably be an even more important factor in determining the success or failure of firms in the next decade', the authors conclude.

In this consultant's view, corporate culture is more powerful than anything else primarily in the sense that it has everything to do with *implementation*. An organisation can have the best strategy in the world, but if the organisation's culture does not align with that strategy and leadership practices, the organisation will not get there. But, *all three* are important: *strategy, culture, and leadership.* Any attempt to develop the organisation must address all three factors. This chapter will highlight *culture* because it has been so neglected. Importantly, however, this consultant would like to re-emphasise that the connection between *strategy, culture, and leadership* is what must be kept uppermost in any intervention.

WHAT CULTURE IS AND WHY IT IS SO IMPORTANT

Culture is defined as: *The way we do things around here in order to succeed.*

Culture has to do with an organisation's way to success. Every business, church, school, symphony orchestra, etc. seeks its own brand of prosperity, its brand of success. Every organisation formulates and implements its own essential way to get there. The essential way, or fundamental method of operation, chosen by an organisation establishes and quickly becomes equivalent to the culture of that organisation.

As mentioned earlier, culture has everything to do with implementation. It is the company's MO or method of operation. If an organisation has been around a while and is reasonably successful, the probability is high that that organisation has developed a *core culture*. A core culture is the central or innermost part of a company's culture, the nucleus of the culture.

There is no such thing, however, as a pure core culture embedded within any one organisation. This is particularly the case when it comes to larger organisations. Every organisation of any size has sub-cultures that are different from the core culture. It is very important, however, that different sub-cultures *operate in service to the larger core culture* and not vice versa. Unless this principle is adhered to, the organisation will become fragmented, unintegrated, and mis-aligned.

Importantly, for any endeavour that entails intervening within the organisation, the four core cultures serve as *organising frameworks for development and planned change.* Any intervention will be all the more effective the more it adapts to the core cultural nature of the organisation within which it is being applied. The intervention will work best when it is implemented in an *incremental* way designed to *improve the existing business system* or *core culture.* Culture is intimately tied to *leadership.* How the leaders of an organisation believe things should be done drives the kind of culture that is established.

THE FOUR CORE CULTURES

This author's research indicates that there are four core cultures: control, collaboration, competence and cultivation. Leaders form one of these four core cultures, consciously or unconsciously, from their own personal history and nature, from their own socialisation experiences, and from their *perception* of what it takes to succeed in their marketplace. As far as socialisation and personal history and nature are concerned, each of the four core cultures emerges from the following:

- *Control:* military system; power motive.
- *Collaboration:* family and/or athletic team system; affiliation motive.
- *Competence:* university system; achievement motive.
- *Cultivation:* religious system(s); growth, or self-actualisation, motive.

There is a strong connection between *strategy, culture, and leadership.* The fundamental connections are as shown in Figure 13.1.

The four 'epistemologies' are listed that correspond to each of the four core cultures. By 'epistemology' I mean the primary or central way that each core culture *knows, understands, and makes decisions.* This notion of epistemology for each core culture is particularly important for any kind of intervention. The more that an intervention adapts to the epistemology appropriate to the core culture in question, the more probable that that intervention will take hold and significantly impact the organisation. Of course, this is true for all the other core characteristics of each of the core cultures as well.

Culture	Strategy	Leadership	Epistemology
Control	Market share dominance Commodity Commodity-like High distribution intensive Life & death	Authoritative Directive Conservative Cautious Definitive Commanding	Organisational systematism
Collaboration	Synergistic customer relationship High customisation Total solution for one customer Incremental, step- by-step, relationship with customer	Team builder First among equals Coach Participative Integrator Trust builder	Experiential knowing
Competence	Superiority Excellence Create market niche Constant innovation to stay ahead Typically, carriage trade markets	Standard setter Conceptual visionary Taskmaster Assertive Convincing persuader Challenger of others	Conceptual systematism
Cultivation	Growth of customer Fuller realisation of potential Enrichment of customer Raise the human spirit Further realisation of ideals, values, higher-order purposes	Catalyst Cultivator Harvester Commitment builder Steward Appeal to higher-level vision	Evaluational knowing

Figure 13.1 Strategy, culture and leadership connections

The four core epistemologies mean the following:

- *Control:* Organisational systematism means that the fundamental issue in a control culture is to preserve, grow, and ensure the well-being and success of the *organisation per se*. The organisation as a system comes first. Accordingly, the design and framework for information and knowledge in the control culture is built essentially around the goals of the organisation, and the extent to which those goals are met.
- *Collaboration:* Experiential knowing means that the fundamental issue in a collaboration culture is the connection between people's experience and reality. The organisation moves ahead through the collective experience of people from inside and outside the organisation. Collaboration culture people know something when collective experience has been fully utilised.
- *Competence:* Conceptual systematism means that the fundamental issue in a competence culture is the realisation of conceptual goals, particularly superior, distinctive conceptual goals. The framework for information and knowledge is built essentially around the conceptual system goals of the organisation and the extent to which those goals are met.
- *Cultivation:* Evaluational knowing means that the fundamental issue in the cultivation culture is the connection between the values and ideals of the organisation and the extent to which those values and ideals are being operationalised. The key emphasis in this culture is the connection between what is espoused and what is put into operation.

In this consultant's (1994) book, *The Reengineering Alternative: a Plan for Making Your Current Culture Work*, these four core cultures are fully elaborated and compared with one another. Examples of actual companies that typify each of the four core cultures are as shown in Table 13.1.

Table 13.1 Company examples

Control	Collaboration	Competence	Cultivation
Wm. Wrigley Jr	Delta Airlines	Bell Labs	Celestial Seasonings
Kellogg	Goldman–Sachs	Cray Research	Herman Miller
P&G	Dana Corporation	ADP	Esprit de Corp
General Dynamics	Motorola	Citicorp	3M
Exxon	Southwest Airlines	Four Seasons Hotels	W. L. Gore
Marriott Hotels	CRS Sirrine	Intel	Shorebank Corp.

An important corroborating work that has recently been published is the work of Treacy and Wiersema at CSC Index in Boston. Their (1995) work is titled *The Discipline of Market Leaders: Choose Your Customers, Narrow Your Focus, Dominate Your Market*. Treacy and Wiersema studied over 80 companies and came up with the following research results.

- No company can succeed today by trying to be all things to all people. It must instead find the unique value that it alone can deliver to a chosen market.
- There are *value propositions*. A 'value proposition' is the implicit promise a company makes to customers to deliver a particular combination of values – price, quality, performance, selection, convenience, and so on.
- Every company must build a *value-driven operating model*. This is that combination of operating processes, management systems, business structure, and culture that gives a company the capacity to deliver on its value proposition. It is the systems, machinery, and environment or culture for delivering value. If the value proposition is the end, the value-driven operating model is the means. (This consultant's overall concept for 'value-driven operating model' is *core culture*).

The *value disciplines* are the three desirable ways in which companies can combine operating models and value propositions to be the best in their markets. 'Value disciplines' are so called because each discipline produces a different kind of customer value. It is critical that a company concentrate on only *one* value discipline. Choosing one discipline to master does not mean that a company abandons the other two, only that it picks a dimension of value on which to stake its market reputation. Research demonstrates that it is *ineffective* to try to drive all three value disciplines from within the same company. One must be the core discipline; the other two become 'threshold' disciplines, meaning that they must meet a threshold level of effectiveness. (Here, Treacy and Wiersema are taking the exact same position re: business strategy that this presenter takes re: culture – i.e., to be effective, an organisation must develop a focused, core culture; it can allow for other kinds of sub-cultures, but it must preserve and prioritise its core culture).

Treacy and Wiersema's research points to the presence of three *value disciplines*:

- *Operational excellence*: Companies that pursue this are not primarily product or service innovators, nor do they cultivate deep, one-to-one relationships with their customers. Instead, operationally excellent companies provide middle-of-the-market products at the best price with the least inconvenience. Their proposition to customers is simple: low price and hassle-free service. Wal-Mart epitomises this kind of company, with its no-frills approach to mass-market retailing.
- *Product leadership*: Practitioners in this discipline concentrate on offering products that push performance boundaries. Their proposition to customers is an offer of the best product, period. Moreover, product leaders don't build their positions with just one innovation; they continue to innovate year after year, product cycle after product cycle.

Intel, the product leader in computer chips, is an example of a 'product leadership' company.

- *Customer intimacy*: Adherents to this discipline focus on delivering not what the market wants but what specific customers want. Customer-intimate companies do not pursue one-time transactions; they cultivate relationships. They specialise in satisfying unique needs, by virtue of their close relationship with – and intimate knowledge of – the customer. Their proposition to the customer: We have the best solution for you – and we provide all the support you need to achieve optimum results and/or value from whatever products you buy. Airborne Express is an example of a 'customer intimacy' company.

In effect, Treacy and Wiersema have come up with the exact three core strategies that this consultant discusses in his work. Operational excellence corresponds with the control culture. Product leadership corresponds with the competence culture. Customer intimacy corresponds with the collaboration culture. Given the likely companies included in their research study, the fact that they did not come up with a business strategy that fits with the cultivation is predictable.

THE GENESIS OF ORGANISATIONAL CULTURE

When looked at together, the four core cultures reveal an even more fundamental underlying pattern that, upon investigation, speaks to where these four cultures came from. This underlying pattern is illustrated by two basic axes that, when combined with one another along two separate axes, yield a four-element table. Each section in this four-element table represents one of the four core cultures.

The vertical axis considers what an organisation *pays attention to*, or the *content* of the culture. The horizontal axis considers *how an organisation makes decisions or forms judgements*, or the *process* of the culture. The content axis is bounded by *actuality* and *possibility*; the process axis is bounded by *impersonal* and *personal*. Please see Figure 13.2.

Collaboration and control are actuality cultures, cultivation and competence are possibility cultures. Collaboration and cultivation are personal cultures; and control and competence are impersonal cultures. Each core culture is a unique blend of one content element and one process element. Control is an *actuality-impersonal* culture; competence is a *possibility-impersonal* culture; cultivation is a *possibility-personal* culture; and collaboration is an *actuality-personal* culture.

Organisational content: what the organisation pays attention to

At the most fundamental level, every organisation focuses either on what is actual or what is possible. Actuality has to do with what is; possibility

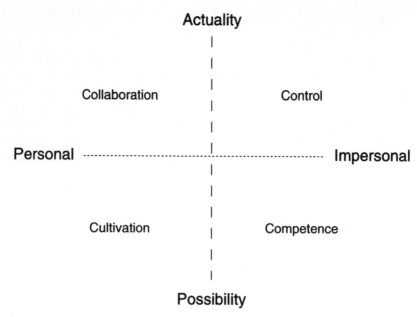

Figure 13.2 Organisational content and process

has to do with what might be. The content of an actuality culture has to do with concrete, tangible reality; facts; what has occurred in the past and is occurring in the present; actual experience and actual occurrence; practicality; utility; what can be seen, heard, touched, weighed, or measured. The content of a possibility culture has to do with insights; imagined alternatives; what might occur in the future; ideals; beliefs; aspirations; inspirations; novelty; innovations; creative options; theoretical concepts or frameworks; underlying meanings or relationships.

Organisational process: how the organisation decides

The other fundamental dimension that underlies organisational culture is how the organisation forms judgements. Every organisation emphasises either impersonal analysis or personal/interpersonal involvement. Impersonal analysis entails the use of detached reasoning. Personal and interpersonal involvement entails the use of people actively judging, deciding, and acting.

The process of an impersonal culture is: detached; system, policy, and procedure oriented; formula oriented; scientific; objective; principle and law oriented; formal; emotionless; prescriptive. The process of a personal culture is: people driven; organic; evolutionary; dynamic; participative; subjective; informal; open-ended; important-to-people oriented; emotional.

These two dimensions are very important dimensions to be aware of when working with each of these four core cultures. Again, an intervention will work much more effectively if the content and process of the organisation are carefully taken into account before and during implementation.

TWO EXAMPLES OF ACTUAL CONSULTING APPLICATIONS OF THIS MODEL

Client A

The client was a $265 million waste-to-energy company with four plants on the east coast of the US. We met with the senior executives of this company and established (with them) their business strategy. We also asked them to tell us the following: key measures of productivity; key historical influences; critical success factors of the business; perceived strengths and weaknesses; existing and historical economic performance; and the extent to which their strategy is working or not working.

We, then, conducted an extensive assessment of the executive group's (and each individual's) leadership practices. Next, we administered our proprietary 96-item *Organisational Culture Survey (OCS)* to all of top management and a stratified sample of the rest of the organisation. We compiled the results of all of the above and developed a beginning description of the strengths of the organisation, the key developmental needs of the organisation, and a proposed step-by-step plan for addressing those developmental needs.

We met with senior executives to go over all the results and to make a decision to go ahead or to not go ahead. Senior management decided to go ahead. We, then, developed a detailed implementation plan with the client and, then, began implementing the plan with them. Along the way, we continually measured progress with our client. Where required, we corrected and/or changed the plan because of new learnings.

The above-referenced diagnostics provided our client with the following important information about their organisation. Top management was perceiving the rest of the company as a core collaboration culture, but the rest of the company saw the company to be much more mixed and unintegrated. How the company approached its customers was being contradicted day in and day out by internal cultural behaviours. The strong control sub-culture in the company's plants needed to be both understood and preserved. The plants with the most control culture at the core were also the most successful plants. The plant that was more mixed and the plant that was competence at the core were much less successful. Compensation practices in the company were unclear and, in some respects, working against the company's business strategy.

The company's collaboration culture at the top of the organisation was too disconnected with the plant sub-cultures. Senior management was collaborating within their own team at the top of the organisation, but were not inculcating such below them. Generally, the company was low in integration, alignment, and focus. This was due primarily to the company's youth and the acquisition of two plants built and run by other business organisations. In addition, the leaders of the company were behaving, to some extent, in a manner incongruent with the strategy and culture of the company.

Given the above findings, the client made the following changes. They put plant managers on the executive committee of the company. They redesigned and implemented a performance management system that emphasised key competencies that reinforced a collaboration culture and that pinpointed the values and mission of the company. At our behest, they brought in a strategy consulting firm and recast the company's business strategy in a manner that reflected synergy and partnership with local communities where their plants are located.

They decided to develop a profile of the company's ideal customer and, then, go out and find and recruit such customers. They clarified the distinction between collaboration behaviour at the core of the company and control behaviour at the plant level – particularly where variability is not possible and where issues are more high risk. They changed the company's compensation system to reflect reward for collaboration culture performance. They also recast the company's mission and values to reflect the importance of the collaboration culture perspective and paradigm. They instituted a systematic auditing and development process designed to drive the building of a core collaboration culture.

They designed and implemented a selection system built to select in people who are a good fit with top performers and with the core collaboration culture. This system included the addition of a team selection method to the system. Team selection is a natural fit with a collaboration core culture. They implemented a collaboration culture-building training programme. They implemented a leadership and management training programme that reflected how leadership and management operate within a collaboration culture. They designed and implemented a succession planning system that is congruent with a collaboration core culture. They also designed and implemented a customised executive development programme that reinforced a collaboration core culture.

The selection system alone has already saved the company $1,000,000 in reduced turnover and other costs. The company's revenues have grown 61 per cent between 1993 and 1996. Company profitability has grown 12 per cent between 1994 and 1995. Plant managers are much more involved in the company's core collaborative process. Teamwork within the company has significantly improved. The company's strategy, culture and leadership are much more aligned. Employees are much clearer about expectations of them and about the company's mission, values, and way of doing things.

The company's approach with customers is much more aligned with internal operating behaviours. Leaders and managers are much clearer about what is expected of them and are leading and managing more effectively. The company's compensation system is much more aligned with the strategy and culture of the company. Working relationships between home office and the plants has significantly improved. The selection system and process is much more aligned with the strategy and culture of the company.

Client B

FJK Consulting, Inc. is a $15 million multi-service management consulting firm headquartered in the Southeast USA. The firm has five separate offices located in five different parts of the United States. The five senior managers of this consulting firm stated that they were having difficulty working together as a senior management team. They also reported that the firm was having considerable difficulty getting people to co-ordinate with one another. We engaged in the same process described above regarding Client A.

Our diagnostic work with this client yielded the following results. The firm was a very strong competence culture (with a loading of 57.9 per cent on our survey). The firm was operating in a severe out-of-balance manner regarding most of the firm's key operational practices. The firm's actual behaviour regarding strategy implementation was not integrated with the natural and automatic business strategy congruent with a competence core culture. The OCS results, particularly, helped to pinpoint exactly where the strengths of the firm were and where the firm was operating in an out-of-balance manner.

The following recommendations were made to FJK's senior managers. The firm should fully address the firm's framework for doing business. They should, specifically, refocus the firm's strategy toward striving for superiority within its market. This is the congruent strategy for a competence culture. They should institute a strong focus on the long term. They should operate much more fully on what diagnosed customer needs dictate rather than on what individual FJK consultants can do. They should also reorganise the firm so that each office in the firm has all the firm's specialties housed within it. In addition, they should recast the role of the senior management group, significantly increase general management behaviours within the senior management team, develop standards for such, meet more often as a senior management team, and develop a different process for this senior management team that changes decision-making, resolving conflict, and team functioning. We provided a plan for implementing these recommendations to senior management.

One year later, FJK's senior managers reported that they were functioning much more effectively as a senior management group. They implemented the recommendations and reported that the firm's co-ordination had significantly improved, customers were much more satisfied with the firm's treatment of them, and the firm had its best economic year ever.

A QUICK SUMMARY OF APPLICATION GUIDELINES

The consultant and his colleagues have now applied this framework, system and process with over 30 organisations. They recount the following:

- Taking the system focus, not a component focus, allows for a much more impactful intervention.
- Identifying and building on an organisation's strengths is an important and constant emphasis to take.
- Any intervention must be customised to the client's unique nature and business.
- Honouring the uniqueness of each client is very important. This is half science and half art. Each client is its own, unique mosaic.
- The approach must continually address the *framework(s)* being applied; it must be *systematic* (i.e., planned and stepped out); and it must emphasise a *collaborative process* that treats the client as a true partner.
- *Strategy* is the decider – meaning that all roads of difference lead back to the organisation's strategy. What it takes for the organisation to gain distinctive competitive advantage in its marketplace is the guidepost for the resolution of all differences.
- The relationship between strategy, culture and leadership is multiplicative, not linear. All three must be kept in mind, all the time. This is a spiral process, not a linear process.
- All organisations have *core or lead* cultures and sub- or subsidiary cultures. The key is that the sub-cultures must function in service to the core or lead culture.
- All systems have four primary characteristics. These characteristics must be kept in mind, all the time, and worked with one another in the 'right' spiral manner. These four primary characteristics are: maintain, relate, renew and transcend.
- Applying the *principles* of the other three cultures to the core or lead culture helps an organisation develop more completeness. Applying the *principle* of the opposite culture helps an organisation develop more balance.
- It is very important to honour the readiness and stage of development of the client organisation. We must build from where the client is in its own development.
- The intended acts on the innate. What people want and desire affects their objectivity when asked to look at how things actually are within their organisation. It is important to continually keep this in mind.

REFERENCES AND FURTHER READING

Bennis, W. and Nanus, B. (1985) *Leaders: the strategies for Taking Charge*, New York: Harper & Row.

Clifford, D. K. and Cavanaugh, R. E. (1985) *The Winning Performance: How America's High-Growth Midsize Companies Succeed*, New York: Bantam Books.

Collins, J. C. and Porras, J. I. (1994) *Built to Last: Successful Habits of Visionary Companies*, New York: HarperCollins.

Deal, T. E. and Kennedy, A. A. (1982) *Corporate Cultures: the Rites and Rituals of Corporate Life*, Reading, MA: Addison-Wesley.

Denison, D. R. (1990) *Corporate Culture and Organisational Effectiveness*, New York: Wiley.

Drucker, P. F. (1980) *Managing in Turbulent Times*, New York: Harper & Row.

Fayol, H. (1949) *General and Industrial Administration*, New York: Pitman.

Garsombke, D. J. (1988) 'Organisation culture dons the mantle of militarism', *Organisational Dynamics*, summer: 46.

Harmon, F. G. and Jacobs, G. (1985) *The Vital Difference: Unleashing the Powers of Sustained Corporate Success*, New York: AMACOM.

Harrigan, K. R. (1985) *Strategies for Joint Ventures*, Lexington, MA: Lexington Books.

Harrison, R. (1972) 'Understanding your organisation's character', *Harvard Business Review*, May–June: 119–28.

Hirsch, S. and Kummerow, J. (1989) *Lifetypes*, New York: Warner Books.

Horton, T. R. (1986). *What Works for Me: 16 CEOS Talk about Their Careers and Commitments*, New York: Random House.

Jung, C. (1923) *Psychological Types*, London: Routledge & Kegan Paul.

Kirp, D. and Rice, D. S. (1988) 'Fast-forward: styles of California management', *Harvard Business Review*, January–February: 80.

Kluckhohn, F. R. and Strodbeck, F. L. (1961) *Variations in Value Orientations*, New York: Harper & Row.

Kotter, J. P. and Heskett, J. L. (1992) *Corporate Culture and Performance*, New York: The Free Press.

Kuhn, T. S. (1970) *The Structure of Scientific Revolutions*, Chicago: University of Chicago Press.

Levering, R. and Moskowitz, M. (1993) *The 100 Best Companies to Work for in America*, New York: Currency/Doubleday.

Levering, R., Moskowitz, M. and Katz, M. (1984) *The 100 Best Companies to Work for in America*, Reading, MA: Addison-Wesley.

Maddi, S. R. (1968) *Personality Theories: a Comparative Analysis*, Homewood, IL: Dorsey Press.

Maslow, A. H. (1954) *Motivation and Personality*, New York: Harper.

—— (1968) *Toward a Psychology of Being*, Princeton, NJ: Van Nostrand.

McClelland, D. C. (1961) *The Achieving Society*, Princeton, NJ: Van Nostrand.

—— (1975) *Power: the Inner Experience*, New York: Irvington.

McClelland, D. C. and Winters, D. G. (1969) *Motivating Economic Achievement*, New York: Free Press.

Myers, I. B. (1987) *Introduction to Type*, Palo Alto, CA: Consulting Psychologists Press.

Myers, I. B. and Myers, P. B. (1980) *Gifts Differing*, Palo Alto, CA: Consulting Psychologists Press.

Nichols, N. A. (1992) 'Profits with a purpose: an interview with Tom Chapman', *Harvard Business Review*, November–December: 94.

O'Boyle, T. F. and Russell, M. (1984) 'Troubled marriage: steel giants' merger brings headaches, J & L and Republic fined', *Wall Street Journal*, 30 November.

O'Toole, J. (1985) *Vanguard Management: Redesigning the Corporate Future*, Garden City, NY: Doubleday

Ouchi, W. G. (1981) *Theory Z*, Reading, MA: Addison-Wesley.

Peters, T. J. (1987) *Thriving on Chaos: a Handbook for a Management Revolution*, New York: Knopf.

Peters, T. J. and Waterman, R. H., Jr (1982) *In Search of Excellence: Lessons from America's Best Run Companies*, New York: Harper & Row.

Peters, T. J. and Austin, N. A. (1985) *Passion for Excellence: the Leadership Difference*, New York: Random House.

Pritchett, P. (1985) *After the Merger: Managing the Shockwaves*, Homewood, IL: Irwin.

Quinn, R. E., Faerman, S. R., Thompson, M. P., and McGrath, M.R. (1990) *Becoming a Master Manager: a Competency Framework*, New York: Wiley.

Schein, E. H. (1985) *Organizational Culture and Leadership*, San Francisco: Jossey-Bass.

Schneider, W. E. (1994) *The Reengineering Alternative: a Plan for Making Your Current Culture Work*, Burr Ridge, IL: Irwin.

Shils, E. (1975) *Center and Periphery: Essays in Macrosociology*, Chicago: University of Chicago Press.

Treacy, M. and Wiersema, F. (1995) *The Discipline of Market Leaders: Choose Your Customers, Narrow Your Focus, Dominate Your Market*, Reading, MA: Addison-Wesley.

Webber, A. M. (1991) 'Crime and management: an interview with NYC police commissioner Lee P. Brown', *Harvard Business Review*, May–June, 117.

Weber, M. (1947) *The Theory of Social and Economic Organization*, New York: Oxford University Press.

Welles, E. O. (1992) 'Captain Marvel', *Inc. Magazine*, January: 44–7.

Wells, K., and Hymowitz, C. (1985) 'Takeover trauma: Gulf's managers find merger into Chevron forces many changes', *Wall Street Journal*, 5 December.

Wilkins, A. L. (1989) *Developing Corporate Character: How to Successfully Change an Organization without Destroying It*, San Francisco: Jossey-Bass.

Chapter 14

Developing organisational communication

Jon White and Helena Memory

Understanding patterns of communication within and between organisations, and other groups important to them, provides another means of acting upon organisations and their functioning. Communication in organisations occurs through the information that gets transmitted and received, through the managerial behaviour that is exhibited and through the corporate policies and systems that are instituted. This chapter considers how communication is interlinked with other aspects of organisational life. Methods of working with, or of changing, patterns of communication to support specific goals within organisations are illustrated through case descriptions.

THE BACKGROUND TO THIS AREA OF CONSULTANCY

In recent years, a number of consultancies have been established in the United Kingdom which describe themselves as communication management consultancies. In their own terms, they have grown beyond their origins in public relations and corporate communications. They now find that the territory they have marked out is regarded with interest by more conventional management consultancies, who are in some cases moving into the area themselves. The Management Consultancies Association's annual report for 1995 noted a substantial increase in the amount of work being done by members in communication, which is still seen, by the association as closely allied to marketing activities.

Communication management consultancies focus on problems in organisational communication. They search for solutions which will improve organisational effectiveness, communication itself and influence the motivation organisation members feel for their roles and place in the organisation.

Communication consultancy holds out the promise of improving overall management performance by inviting managers and organisations to consider the content and processes they use to inform people, and the alignment of the messages they convey through their behaviour and the policies and procedures they introduce. These latter two speak louder than the words. In doing this, they can prompt managers to reconsider their objectives – are they sufficiently clear? – and their assumptions. By examining what they wish to communicate, managers can develop a clearer sense of what they wish to do.

There are many typical organisational situations that have communication implications where specific consulting expertise in communication can provide an appropriate intervention. Frequently these situations are expressed as management concerns that employees appear not to understand what is expected of them and why. They feel that a lack of understanding of organisational objectives on the part of significant groups may be impeding the organisation's progress, perhaps towards achieving needed organisational change or winning trust, or towards success in the marketplace.

In times of major change in particular, such as during a merger, organisation restructuring, introduction of new operating methods etc. managers and employees may appear to be unclear about the organisational context in which they are operating and its implications for them. Employees feel that they are working to business objectives which are at variance to those set out at management levels.

Employees can express dissatisfaction with their opportunities to contribute ideas, or with the extent to which they feel that they are listened to and their views acknowledged and responded to. In turn, managers feel that communication needs improvement in order to bring about change in employee motivation and job satisfaction.

Communication problems are quite naturally linked to other problems. These may relate to the need to bring about organisational change, understandable staff resistance to change, and to overall management style and experience. Communication problems are generally vague and ill-defined, and may not demand a solution until some crisis point is reached, through – for example – the build-up of commercial pressure, or a result of conflict between groups, such as unionised employees and management. Communication management consultants are currently concerned that communication should be on the general management agenda, so that communication is managed routinely, in the way that an organisation's financial affairs are managed routinely, rather than taken for granted until difficulties arise as a result of its neglect.

Because communication problems are less defined than other problems which may present themselves, consultants, managers and others confronted with them may be uncertain as to how to proceed to deal with them. This difficulty is compounded. Other management problems, arising for example from the management of people or as a result of changes in the market for the organisation's goods and services, are problems which have been marked out for previous examination and there are certain principles which can be drawn on. In communication, the practices have been left unstudied and only now is the communication element of the overall management task and its importance being recognised.

Communication management consultants have traditionally brought insights from public relations, corporate communication and marketing practice to more general communication problems. Now they are beginning to make more use of the principles and findings from psychodynamics, and organisational psychology, and are developing and recording experience in dealing with client problems. The next section of this chapter will give a theoretical framework and discuss some of the methodologies available to and used by communication management consultants as they work with clients to solve communication problems.

A THEORETICAL FRAMEWORK

To be an effective communication consultant it is important to be clear with the client about what 'communication' encompasses. Traditionally, organisations have viewed communication as simple information transmission. Therefore, they have focused primarily on the channels of communication. Managements have been keen to ensure that certain messages about the organisation and its expectations of employees have been transmitted *via* a wide range of media including newsletters, videos, noticeboards, posters and more recently, e-mail and other electronic channels. This communication which *informs*, falls at the bottom of the communication hierarchy (see Figure 14.1) because it is the least powerful form of communication in terms of its impact on employee attitudes and behaviours. In spite of this, it is the type of communication to which organisations allocate most resource and it is often not as effective as it might be because the different types of information – *operational, strategic and corporate* – are treated in the same way when each requires a different approach. The largest category – operational, is task-related information that people require for day-to-day problem-solving and decision-making. It needs to flow fast and unimpeded between individuals and teams and encompass the objectives and service standards employees need to meet plus details of performance being achieved. Conversely, strategic information is far more emotive in that it relates to the direction of the business and therefore to change, and thus has significant implications for employees which can only be well understood through discussion. Corporate information relates to the corporate environment and is what most employee communication programmes focus on – information about corporate results, investment, new contracts, pay and benefits – the kinds of information that encourage employees to feel they belong to an organisation.

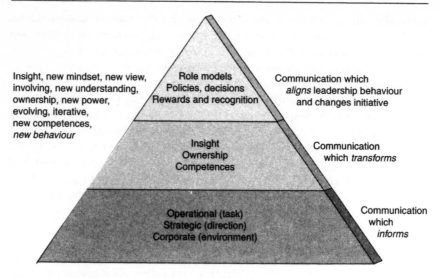

Insight, new mindset, new view, involving, new understanding, ownership, new power, evolving, iterative, new competences, *new behaviour*

Role models
Policies, decisions
Rewards and recognition

Communication which *aligns* leadership behaviour and changes initiative

Insight
Ownership
Competences

Communication which *transforms*

Operational (task)
Strategic (direction)
Corporate (environment)

Communication which *informs*

Figure 14.1 Hierarchy of internal communications
Source: Hedron Consulting Ltd

The next level in the hierarchy – communication which *transforms* – is about communication that gives employees, and particularly managers, the necessary understanding, motivation and skills to deliver the new behaviours that are desired of them. Communication that is based on 'telling' does not achieve this. Investment is required in communication processes that involve people in such a way that they gain insight for themselves about what is required of them and develop a sense of ownership for meeting that requirement in a way that may be different from what they have done before. These are communication processes that provide a safe environment in which people can take risks, try different ways of communicating with one another, allow for genuine two-way dialogue and provide opportunities for people to learn and develop new communication skills and to support one another while doing so.

The most powerful level in the hierarchy is communication which *aligns* leadership behaviour and change initiative. Here it is the examples set by leadership at all levels in the organisation, coupled with the messages from the 'silent communicators' – policies and decisions, reward and recognition – that communicate. If what people observe in these communicators does not align with what they are told, then communication in the organisation will not be effective in supporting the desired changes.

Taking the view that an organisation can be regarded as a more or less open system, dependent on its environment and involved in a continuing effort to develop a degree of autonomy or freedom from dependence or restriction provides a useful perspective. Communication is part of the process of negotiation of autonomy. Drawing on a systems perspective, it becomes of interest to examine processes at work within the organisation and between the organisation and its environment.

The organisation is seen as existing within, and dependent upon a network of relationships with important groups, some of which are part of the organisation itself. Necessary support for the organisation and its objectives are negotiated and re-negotiated with these groups, through communication.

THE STUDY OF ORGANISATIONAL COMMUNICATION

If this then forms part of the theory behind organisational communication, what is it that consultants operating in this field need to pay attention to? There are particular aspects of organisation behaviour, and the behaviour of the network, about which communication consultants will collect data. Theses might include a look at the vocal and silent communication channels, the missing links, the inconsistencies and the conflicts. It might also include investigation of the barriers to information flow, assimilation and understanding, and attitude and behavioural change, the three usually desired outcomes of communication activity. Of particular relevance are:

Characteristics of groups

Many groups will be easy to identify. The status of employees, shareholders, relevant members of government departments and so on is unambiguous. Less obviously identifiable are those groups whose interest in the organisation will be uncovered by close examination of organisation objectives and research among the general public. They might include employees who would be candidates for redundancy as a result of intentions to reduce the size of the workforce. Their common interest may not be known to them until the organisation announces its intentions. Among the general public, similar groups may exist. Market research may uncover groups of people who, unknown to each other, may share similar interests in a product which a company intends to introduce. Group structure can be studied, and within groups opinion leaders and patterns of communication can be identified.

Communication links and channels

As groups are identified, questions can be asked about the presence or absence of communication links and communication channels used, for communication between the organisation and important groups, and for communication between groups. For example, a chemical company might decide that, because of local community concern about the operation of one of its plants, it needs to establish a community consultation committee, which brings representatives of the local community and company together on a regular basis to discuss environmental matters. The same chemical company may be aware that pressure groups opposed to the company are using the Internet to communicate with each other and with potential supporters.

Information flows

The fact that communication links exist and that a channel for communication has been chosen does not mean that information will flow unimpeded from senders to receivers, or be understood when it is received. A variety of techniques can be used to examine the extent to which information is getting through a channel, qualities of the information itself, its reception, and how well it is understood and acted upon. These range from communication audits, through content analysis, to research which gathers and analyses feedback.

Barriers to information flow

Barriers to information flow may be discovered in an analysis of organisation structure, formal and informal, in studies of staff receptivity towards information, and in studies of the credibility, skills and motivations of originators of information.

Directions of information flow

Information flow may be top–down, bottom–up, lateral, one-way, two-way and multi-directional. Flow may become a matter of management or employee concern. Management may be concerned to know whether or not information is flowing from the top to the bottom of their organisations, and may use techniques such as cascade briefing to try to ensure top–down communication. They may also be concerned that they are receiving adequate feedback on employee or public concerns, and will look to improve flows of information back to them, perhaps through suggestions schemes or through employee or public opinion research.

Barriers to attitude and behaviour change

The desired outcome of communication activities is frequently a change in attitudes, perception or behaviour. There are many aspects of communication in an organisation that can influence these, over and above straight information channels and flows. Examples of such influencers include role model behaviour of leaders at all levels, corporate decisions and policies, organisation culture, performance management and appraisal systems, reward and recognition, recruitment and promotion policies, skills development activities. It is important that these 'silent communicators' are aligned with the verbal/written messages that are communicated.

CONSULTING METHODS

The next part of this chapter will outline how these methods can be used and some cases which show the results that can be achieved. In many organisations, the person with functional responsibility for communication takes on the role of an internal consultant, advising the organisation's management group on ways of improving communication within the organisation.

This consultancy may use a variety of techniques. In some cases, the consultant may work closely alongside individuals and groups inside the organisation, often to help them to identify solutions. In other cases, the relationship may be more distant and recommendations will be designed by the consultant for implementation by others. In all cases, the use of research is key to effective diagnosis.

Research

While its nature and type will vary, research among employees and often among external groups too, will help to determine precise objectives, define problems and provide a basis for advice to senior management. At its most simple, this research often starts with information transmission tracking studies such as readership surveys of internal publications, post-publication focus groups to gather response to publication contents and post-presentation research after management presentations to employee groups. This enables the internal communication department to adapt and develop the traditional channels of communication and ensure that they are being as efficacious as possible.

Research might then move to studies of the messages being conveyed and their relative degree of impact, *via* the behaviours management exhibit when communicating and the internal and external policies that are implemented. This enables the consultant to point out to decision makers at all levels where conflicting messages are occurring, where formal channel-based communication is being undermined and why possibly information being transmitted is not understood, not believed or just not acted upon.

Basic skills of consultancy practice, such as interviewing, collection of information in face-to-face meetings, and content analysis of relevant documents are important in communication consulting.

Research studies on the opinions of important outside groups, such as customers, the media and financial analysts also provide valuable diagnostic data for the consultant. These types of studies enable the consultant to relate more closely the achievement of business objectives to communication processes being promoted in the organisation.

In summary, research techniques of use in studying communication problems will include:

- depth interviews;
- focus groups;
- content analysis;
- surveys;
- analyses of communication processes – vocal and silent – links, flows and obstacles;
- participant and non-participant observation;
- culture surveys.

The communication audit

A widely used type of survey, which may include any of the techniques above, has been described as a broad scale, loosely structured survey technique which involves questions to management, employees and groups important to an organisation. These questions are aimed at establishing the extent to which organisation objectives are understood and the characteristics of communication between the organisation and these groups. The audit may discover discrepancies in understanding, and can form the basis for efforts to improve communication.

Gap analysis

Communication problems may raise questions about organisation design, staff training, general management preparedness to communicate, and underlying organisational performance. There is little point in an organisation claiming strong performance when experience of the organisation and what it has to offer contradicts or will not support claims made.

A technique which embodies this observation uses a form of gap analysis to enable communication management consultants to ask questions about communication and performance. Managers and communication consultants working together might consider: how do they believe the public or other important groups perceive the organisation (actual perception) and its performance (actual performance)? How would they, the managers, like to set their desired level of performance (desired performance) and how would they like the organisation to be perceived (ideal perception)?

Ranging these assessments along a line from poor to good, managers might find that actual performance falls short of desired performance, but that actual perception lags behind actual performance. This would suggest that managers have work to do to bring the organisation up to desired levels of performance. In the meantime, more effort might need to be made to communicate details of current performance.

Figure 14.2 illustrates how these points can be ranged along a line, from poor to good. Their precise location could be fixed following a review of organisation objectives and performance, and research information relating to public perceptions.

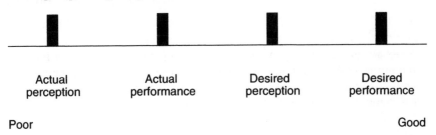

| Actual
perception | Actual
performance | Desired
perception | Desired
performance |

Poor   Good

Figure 14.2 Gap analysis

Armed with information about perceptions of performance, the communication management consultant can ask questions about performance itself. Performance itself will communicate. An organisation may claim to be customer focused, but then through performance show that the customer is not the main focus of staff activities. A constant interest in communication management consultancy is inconsistency, between what is said and what is done.

A process approach

Adopting a process approach to developing new communication methods in the organisation is not a widely used method, and too many consultants internal and external still employ a recommendations-based approach. This is despite the fact that time and again such recommendations fail to be implemented. A process approach develops the crucial personal insight of the various parties communicating or being communicated with. This is the cornerstone for success of any communication improvement programme.

Of increasing importance is the advocacy of positioning communication as an integral part of the change process within the organisation. In practice this requires that communication be treated as a key management lever in the planning, design and implementation of any change programme and be as well resourced and supported by senior managers as other functions.

Sadly it is still true to say that the majority of change programmes leave consideration of communication until well into the design phase. This is so, even though research shows that the majority of change programmes fail to

276 Jon White and Helena Memory

deliver precisely because they fail to take account of the people dimension, particularly communication. By drawing on the perspectives and services of external consultants and academics, communication practitioners can gain access to best practice and benchmark their own communication with that in other organisations, which often serves to reinforce and give credibility to their advice. These also illustrate the perspective and methods available to the communication management consultant.

CASE STUDIES

There are many different types of presenting situations that will face the communication consultant. The case studies in this section show how the theories and methods outlined above have been applied to a number of typical organisation situations.

The public to private sector transition

This is the case of the public sector organisation which has had to prepare itself for a more commercial style of operation in recent years, and for eventual privatisation and movement into the private sector. Research carried out at the beginning of concerted effort to bring about change found that significant groups, such as the organisation's own staff, and groups outside whose favourable commentary and support would be needed as the organisation tried to change, did not understand the need for change and did not believe the organisation could change. Many members of staff, committed to values and styles of working which had grown up over years in the public sector ethos, were strongly opposed to change.

The senior management group recognised that communication would play a major part in bringing about needed change. The research carried out over previous years as part of attempts to improve the organisation's overall efficiency had found that staff believed communication to be poor, and they felt themselves ill-informed about the organisation and its objectives. To improve communication, the senior management group brought in a new director of corporate communications with a mandate to improve this picture, and support the organisation in its drive towards commercialism and eventual privatisation.

Application of some of the techniques available to the communication management consultant outlined earlier in the chapter have led to improvements in organisation communication, to the extent that staff now understand the messages presented to them. While they still do not like the requirement for change, they are less resistant to it. The research carried out to gather information on employee concerns, and to assess their reaction to the content of publications addressing their concerns, has led to improvements in the relevance of those publications. Management performance and credibility in presentations to staff have also improved as a result of the feedback gathered through research after each meeting.

The organisation is now close to achieving its goals, having prepared to function as a strong, commercial entity, and having persuaded its staff to accept the inevitability of change. They are still uncomfortable with some of the uncertainties of change, but are now willing to recognise the opportunities that may accompany a move to the private sector.

Presentation difficulties for a multi-national's staff

In recent months, a multinational company has found itself subjected to powerful criticism and opposition as a result of decisions taken which have an environmental impact, and as a result of its operations in countries in which they are collaborating with governments with poor human rights records. Staff making routine, uncontroversial public presentations to student and other groups have found that they are facing public criticism, conflict and disruption in public meetings. They need preparation for this communication task, but are uncertain about how to prepare for managing and communicating with difficult groups.

A communication consultant analysed records of meetings at which the difficulties had arisen, interviewed all staff with experience of disrupted meetings, and observed company representatives at a student meeting, facing the difficulties encountered in earlier meetings. A training workshop with a group of staff most affected by the incidents reviewed experience of managers and politicians in dealing with difficult groups, and provided opportunities to identify and practise responses to likely questions. The workshop increased the level of confidence of staff involved, and helped them to decide on specific steps that they could take in future to develop their communication skills.

The fragmenting insurance company

As the result of recommendations made by a mainstream management consultancy, a large insurance company reorganised into strategic business units, which would be closer to their customers and responsible, with considerable freedom from central control for their own business performance. Each unit began to exercise their freedom, and to communicate on their own behalf with government, the media and the financial community. This strategy quickly led to embarrassment, as several parts of the same company approached the same groups. More seriously, the financial community began to raise questions about overall management control at the company.

At the centre, senior managers were concerned about the management of communication by the company as a whole and about how the separate business units could be encouraged to communicate consistently with important groups. In the business units, some of the problems of fragmentation were seen by business unit heads as an inevitable consequence of the reorganisation. To realise the benefits of the reorganisation, they felt that some of these problems would have to be tolerated.

A consultant, brought in by the central management group, carried out a series of interviews with central staff and with the business unit heads, to make recommendations regarding the management of communication. The consultant's findings were that:

- the centre had been left without a clear role;
- the reorganisation called the identity of the organisation into question; and
- the strategic planning committee of central senior management and business unit heads would have to agree on the role of communication and their part in effective communication.

Professional assistance to central communication staff enabled the organisation to gradually bring communication back under control. The case illustrates that questions about communication management can quickly raise further questions about organisational politics – who has the power, position and resources to speak for the organisation, and who should speak for the organisation? Communication problems may be presenting problems. Actual problems may turn on questions of management style, and personalities. Who has the power to give direction to the organisation?

Overcoming trade union opposition

A nationwide retailer wanted to phase in more flexible working procedures as a result of increasing competition, changing demands from its customers and the availability of new technology. Traditionally communication with the majority of its employees was through the recognised union channels. However, the company felt that its requirements for more flexible working were more likely to be met successfully if managers could be involved more directly in communicating the changes, and the implications of them, directly with their own staff.

In discussion with a consultant the company came to recognise that any attempt to communicate directly would be viewed by the unions as an attempt to undermine their position with employees. An alternative way forward was to involve union representatives, along with managers and shopfloor workers, in designing how new communication systems might work.

Facilitated by the consultant, an action team representing all levels and functions of manager, employee and union representative, designed an approach to face-to-face communication that recognised the communication needs of both the company and its employees. It enabled the organisation to invest its resources in communication activities, and training and development programmes, that responded to those needs. That achieved higher levels of credibility in the organisation because it was known that employees had been consulted and involved in the design. The involvement of the shop floor employees and trade union representatives in the process also helped to improve the industrial relations environment in the company and to build greater trust and respect between managers and employees.

Single issue communication in a utility

A recently privatised utility had been experiencing an unacceptably high level of accidents amongst its workforce, in spite of increasing levels of investment in health and safety procedures. The consultant helped the organisation to recognise that continuing to 'tell' employees to conform to procedures was unlikely to make any impact. It was decided instead to embark upon a series of interactive communication events that would involve employees themselves in setting the company's future agenda for health and safety matters.

A series of workshops, involving a total of several thousand employees, enabled them to identify the key issues relating to health and safety and the barriers that existed that could prevent these issues from being addressed effectively. Action plans were drawn up by employees themselves that prioritised areas for improvement. These plans, which included training, were then implemented by those employees, with support and resources from the company. The workshops were designed by a joint client/consultant team, with the consultant coaching managers to facilitate the sessions.

Changing employment contracts in the public sector

As outsourcing, cost-cutting and a more commercial approach to its funding became necessary this public sector organisation found it necessary to consider moving away from long-term, full-time 'jobs-for-life' to short-term, part-time contracts with more employees working from home.

It anticipated that this trend would increase over the next decade, with many employees also working for other organisations who required similar skills. The organisation was concerned to ensure that all of the people upon whom its output depended would be able to identify with the core values and standards of the organisation and that it would be able to communicate effectively with them all.

Due to these changing working practices and the rapid developments in communication technology, the organisation realised that the communication messages and processes of the next decade would need to be very different to its existing ones. Before investing in new technology-based communication systems it used a consultant to undertake a review of what the changing needs of employees would be in the future in order to make appropriate investment choices.

As patterns of employment and the 'psychological contract' between organisations and their employees change, so too must the issues and channels implicated in communication adapt. A key role for today's communication consultant is to help organisations anticipate, plan and prepare for future changing relationships with key stakeholder groups like employees.

Supporting organisational values in a functional department

The human resources function in a large financial services company wanted to change the messages given out by its policies and the way it communicated with employees in order to support the values of the business more effectively. The consultant, using processes to get feedback from employees, showed that the company's approaches to recruitment and selection, appraisals, reward and recognition and management development were not consistent with its stated values. Using feedback mechanisms, the consultant helped the client to identify actions which employees perceived would bring the policies in line. The way these policies were communicated was also aligned so that it too reinforced the stated values, particularly those of openness and responsiveness to customer needs.

GUIDELINES FOR APPLICATION OF THEORY AND/OR METHOD

Consultants developing their expertise in the area of communication may find the following advice useful when carrying out this type of consulting.

Many situations that are presented as a communication problem do in fact have more deeply rooted causes. Frequently 'poor communication' is used as code for poor relationships between different groups in an organisation. By helping those groups to identify common ground and to work towards new communication styles, the consultant can enable groups to generate a consensus about what needs to happen for them to work most productively together in support of organisation objectives.

The culture of the organisation provides important clues to the type and style of communication that will be most effective in helping to achieve organisation goals. By using communication processes to help people in the organisation to articulate and understand the prevailing culture, the consultant can open up discussion about how communication can be improved.

Behaviour speaks louder than words. While it is obviously important that the words are appropriate and that they are used to communicate consistent messages across and through the organisation, it is the observable behaviour of leaders and the messages from the silent communicators, that communicate most powerfully. And yet it is these to which least attention is paid in most organisations. The consultant who uses communication to open the organisation's eyes to these factors and enables them to confront and tackle them constructively, can lead the way in transforming communication so that it becomes a truly strategic management tool.

There needs to be a clear business case for investment in communication if it is to achieve the recognition it deserves and the commitment it needs inside the organisation. Only when an explicit link can be made between communication strategy and the organisation's ability to achieve its objectives, will communication find its way onto the agenda of those who will influence the status it has in the organisation in terms of human and financial resources required for it to be undertaken effectively.

Without the buy-in, commitment and ownership of managers at all levels in the organisation, the consultant will be restrained in terms of how far up the hierarchy they can operate. By involving managers at the outset in defining desired outcomes for communication and making the business case for communication, the consultant will most likely only be able to operate in the area of the traditional information channels. Once managers can see the personal and organisational benefits of improved communication, it is easier for the consultant to work with them in improving communication behaviours.

Measures of success linked to organisation objectives and accountability for delivering these, reinforced by open measurement and evaluation processes, provide a necessary structured framework that will ensure that the communication strategy and plan is delivered appropriately. The organisation has a responsibility to its members not only to be clear about what is expected of them in communication terms, but also to enable them to deliver against these requirements. Failure to build the right type and level of capability will make victims of managers and drive them further away from the best practice models desired.

THE FUTURE FOR COMMUNICATION CONSULTING

The developing skills of communication management consultants will be applied to business, management and organisational problems in much the same way that traditional management consultants working from other disciplines now apply their skills. Within a few years, we believe that the central role of communication in management and organisational life will be recognised and given focused attention, rather than disregarded and overlooked. There are, we believe, too many current examples of organisations finding themselves in difficulty because they have failed to communicate adequately internally or externally.

For communication management consultancy, questions will arise regarding the role of consultants in this area. Will they continue to be regarded as specialists, outside the mainstream of management consultancy, or will they be drawn realistically into multi-disciplinary teams of consultants? Will they, as a group, have the resources to develop the research base that will inform their practice? Finally, will they have a contribution to make to the development of improved organisational forms to meet the aspirations of an increasingly complex world?

REFERENCES AND FURTHER READING

CBI/KPMG, (1990) *Employee Involvement: Shaping the Future for Business*, London.

Coulson-Thomas, C. (1992) 'Communicating for change', *Internal Communication Focus*, February–March.

Department of Employment (1993), *Investing in People: the Benefits of Being an Investor in People*, London: Department of Employment.

Department of Trade and Industry, Innovation Advisory Board, (1993) *Getting the Message Across: Improving Communication between Companies and Investors*, London: Department of Trade and Industry.

Foehrenbach, J. and Goldfarb, S. (1990) 'Employee communications in the 90s: greater expectations', *IABC Communications*, World, May–June.

Hedron (1993) *Communication: Why Managers Need To Do More*, London: Hedron.

Marchington, M., Goodman, J., Wilkinson A., and Ackers, P. (1992) *New Directions in Employee Involvement*, Manchester School of Management, UMIST and Department of Employment.

Royal Society for the Encouragement of Arts, Manufactures and Commerce (1995) *Tomorrow's Company: the Role of Business in a Changing World*, London: Royal Society for the Encouragement of Arts, Manufactures and Commerce.

White, J. and Mazur L. (1995) *Strategic Communications Management: Making Public Relations Work*, London: Addison-Wesley.

Index